BEER
SAFARI

*To Shawn, my beer muse, and to Kai, who gives
me something to talk about other than ale.*

LUCY CORNE

CHEERS

This book has been a real labour of love (no really, travelling around the country tasting beer involved plenty of labour...) and I'd like to thank all of the brewers for their support. There were some who went way above and beyond, inviting me to stay in their homes, treating me to dinners out or braais with their families – I hope I don't leave anyone out. Massive thanks to Travis and Caroline Boast, the entire Standeaven family, Theo and Sarie de Beer, Sean and Morné Barradas, Gert and Wilna Jacobs, Lance and Linky Kabot, Andy Turner and Natalie Danks, Brendan and Tracy Watcham, Jo Barton, Melanie and Tania Nieuwoudt and Peter Dean.

I've gleaned a lot of help, knowledge and insight from the increasing army of beer aficionados in South Africa. Thanks to all of those who helped out with ideas, contacts and snippets of wisdom, especially Kevin Ryan, Jason Cederwall, Chris McLeod, Stuart Lamb, Jaco Hamilton-Atwell, Holger Meier, Dion van Huyssteen, Megan Gemmell, the members of the Wort Hogs and East Coast Brewers who helped out on Facebook and, of course, to all the boys in the SSBSS – you know who you are!

Thanks also to the team at Toscana Enologica Mori for the support and to everyone at Penguin Random House, particularly Bev, Joy, Jessie and my latest beer convert, Linda.

Lucy

TOSCANA ENOLOGICA MORI SA (PTY)LTD
OLIVE | WINE | BEER EQUIPMENT
www.tem-sa.co.za

Published in 2015 by Struik Lifestyle
(an imprint of Penguin Random House (Pty) Ltd)
Company Reg. No. 1953/000441/07
The Estuaries, 4 Oxbow Crescent, Century Avenue,
Century City, 7441
P O Box 1144, Cape Town 8000, South Africa

Publisher: Linda de Villiers
Managing editor: Cecilia Barfield
Editor and indexer: Joy Clack
Designer: Beverley Dodd
Design assistant: Randall Watson
Photographer: Lucy Corne
Product photographer: Matthys van Lill
Illustrator: Pinewood Studios – Jessica Pearson
Proofreader: Laetitia Sullivan

Reproduction by Hirt & Carter Cape (Pty) Ltd
Printed and bound in China
by Leo Paper Products Ltd

MIX
Paper from responsible sources
FSC
www.fsc.org   FSC® C020056

This book is printed on FSC®-certified paper. Forest Stewardship Council® (FSC®) is an independent, international, non-governmental organization. Its aim is to support environmentally sustainable, socially and economically responsible global forest management.

ISBN 978 1 43230 486 7

All contact details correct at time of going to print.

CONTENTS

ABOUT THE BOOK

When people bought *African Brew*, I kept hearing tales of how they planned trips using the book. They plotted beery weekends away, they booked family vacations that were conveniently close to some South African microbreweries and at least one person took a road trip from Cape Town to Durban, stopping at every brewery along the way. With this book I wanted to tap into that, to help people take a 'vacaletion'. It was for me the perfect marriage, combining my two passions and indeed my two professions – writing about beer and writing about travel.

The book is set out geographically and within each province the breweries are laid out to represent a provincial ale trail. Of course, you can tackle the breweries however you wish, but the idea is that if you're in a certain spot, or you're planning a visit to a particular place, you can easily dip into the book to find any other breweries in the vicinity.

This time around I opted not to include tasting notes for every beer. This was largely because there are just so many beers now that if every pint had a description there wouldn't be much room left for the stories, and these journeys from homebrewing or beer appreciation into microbrewing are just as important as the journey you'll follow as you attempt to taste every beer featured here. You will find tasting notes, but just for a few select beers. I've called them 'Big 5 Pints' – the ones that you'll really want to tick off along your journey. They're the beers that are true to style or that are generally flawless. They're never disappointing, always drinkable and they're worth seeking out. Fortunately, like unmissable animals in Africa, there are more than five of them, but I kind of liked the name.

The rest of the beers are listed in each brewery's beer menu, with just their ABV (alcohol by volume) percentage alongside. In some cases, where the beer has an unfathomable name, the style has been included in brackets. Rather than list the beers from light to dark or light-bodied to full-bodied, I opted to list each brewery's beers in order of my preference. If you agree with my choices, that's awesome. If you don't, even better, for beer is a very personal thing and I love a good discussion, especially when it involves beer...

At the start of each brewery write-up, you'll also find a selection of icons indicating what facilities you might find at the brewery – here's what they mean:

accommodation

food

tastings

accommodation within walking distance

merchandise

tours

family-friendly

off-sales

tours by appointment

> May your beer safari be filled with amazing ales and affable brewers. And if you don't have a designated driver along for the ride, please stick around a while, sleeping over after you've tackled a taster tray or worked your way through the brewery's beer menu.
> **CHEERS!**

THE RENAISSANCE OF SOUTH AFRICAN BEER

Mitchell's Brewery was ahead of its time. It launched in a small town far from major urban centres in a country of staunch lager lovers. So when Lex Mitchell opened his microbrewery – South Africa's oldest – in 1983, he did what any smart brewer would do. He launched with a lager. It wasn't quite the lager that people were used to – a little hazier, a little less fizzy – but he gave South African beer drinkers something familiar, garnering trust in his pint-sized Garden Route brewery.

But companions on the small-scale brewing scene were slow to emerge and for almost a decade, Mitchell's flew the flag solo, gradually trying to add a little ale to all that lager. When microbrewed beer would finally take off, almost three decades later, the new wave of brewers would follow the same strategy, wooing long-time lager drinkers with something familiar before weaning them on to ales that were darker, fruitier, hoppier or heavier.

Other breweries came and went – KwaZulu-Natal (KZN) had a flourishing beer scene for a while, but many of its early ale houses – Wartburger Brauhaus, Farmers' Brewery, the Luyt Brewery – have long since closed. It wasn't until the mid-nineties that a few longstanding names emerged – names that could well be familiar to you today. In Pretoria, Moritz Kallmeyer founded Drayman's. In the KZN Midlands, Nottingham Road opened its doors. Birkenhead quietly launched in the pretty Overberg village of Stanford, while a little later Cape Town got its first new brewery in centuries in the form of Boston. Each stayed afloat serving those in the immediate catchment area, but most people had no idea there were microbreweries in their midst – or even what a microbrewery was.

Fast-forward a decade or so and suddenly they were everywhere. Breweries began to pop up in the unlikeliest locations – from far-flung farms to industrial districts, wedged in between steel manufacturers and machinery merchants. The latest braai accessory became a six-pack of microbrewed beer and whether they were cooking with it, brewing it, serving it or just drinking it, everyone wanted a piece of what has become known as 'the craft beer revolution'. Craft beer – that is, beer produced on a much smaller scale than South Africa was used to –

SOUTH AFRICAN BEER HISTORY AT A GLANCE

Circa 1st century AD – The Khoisan stumble upon !karri, an early version of mead (a fermented honey beverage). Later, Nguni tribes migrating from central and East Africa begin to brew sorghum beer.

1657 – After ordering brewing supplies from the Netherlands, Jan van Riebeeck brews South Africa's first 'clear beer' in Cape Town.

1820 – Jacob Letterstedt sets up Mariendahl Brewery, named for his wife, in Newlands, Cape Town.

1854 – A Cape Town census shows 13 breweries in the city. Thanks to its water, Newlands is the epicentre of the South African beer scene.

1881 – Norwegian-born Anders Ohlsson builds his first brewery in Newlands, later taking over three other breweries in the area, including Mariendahl.

1884 – Charles and George Chandler begin brewing in the diamond rush town of Kimberley, later moving their setup to modern-day Gauteng.

1888 – Charles Glass launches the Castle Brewery along with his wife, Lisa. Meanwhile, ambitious teenager Frederick Mead lays the groundwork for the Natal Brewery Syndicate in Pietermaritzburg.

has certainly arrived. The question is, where did it come from?

Varying theories circulate as to what sparked this beer renaissance. Was it an imported trend, inevitably reaching our borders at last? Was it the work of a few forward-thinking business brains? Or part of a larger trend towards getting back to basics where consumables were concerned?

It was all of these. By the time craft beer really began to take off around 2010 or 2011, a similar scene had existed in the United States of America for more than two decades. This hankering for hops had bubbled over and spread to the United Kingdom, to Australia, to New Zealand and Italy, South Korea and Scandinavia, Germany and Japan, so it was really just a matter of time before it would wash up on South African shores as well. But a rebirth of beer was never going to happen by itself. There needed to be a catalyst, and indeed there were several.

Ross McCulloch played no small role in the renaissance. If he didn't actually give birth to the vibrant beer scene himself, he was surely there in the labour room, urging it on. Along with Megan

Jack Black co-founder Ross McCulloch was a key player in the craft beer revolution

1895 – After buying the Castle Brewery, Frederick Mead merges the two and re-christens his brewing conglomerate South African Breweries (SAB). Soon afterwards, Africa's first lager beer is brewed in Johannesburg; its name: Castle Lager.

1928 – The Liquor Act is passed, banning black South Africans from legally buying beer. Illegal drinking dens, known as shebeens, start to pop up.

1935 – Commercial hop farming commences in the foothills of the Outeniqua Mountains, near George.

1956 – SAB buy out rival brewers Ohlsson's – brewers of the popular Lion Lager – and Union, which grew out of the Chandler's Brewery.

1962 – The Liquor Act is finally repealed, opening up clear beer to a vast new market.

1972 – Louis Luyt sets up a brewery in KwaZulu-Natal, but it is later bought by SAB.

1983 – Lex Mitchell opens Mitchell's, South Africa's longest-running microbrewery.

MacCallum, he launched Jack Black back in 2007 and while it took a little time to get off the ground, their lager soon became the beer to be seen with. Soon afterwards an imported beer arrived on the scene, though back then many drinkers thought that Brewers & Union was a local brand. The German brews included a hazy weissbier and a dark lager – brave additions to a scene that until then had been almost exclusively made up of clear, golden beer. The marketing gurus behind the brand also did something crucial – they put beer into the hands of the hipsters. They took this drink, which had long been unfairly considered inferior to wine; which was thought to be something you swill without thinking at a braai; which was generally associated with bulging-bellied men, and they made it cool. Even hipster-haters have to admit that this was one of the keys to craft beer's success.

Suddenly people wanted to be seen swigging beer, and people were demanding the beer list from their local bar or restaurant, a request that was more often than not met with a look of utter bewilderment.

But imported brews and business acumen can only go so far. You can brew the stuff, but people have to have a real interest if you expect them to pay a little more and try it out. Luckily this interest already existed, albeit in a slightly different form. South Africa's market culture had already begun to gain momentum. In was a real back-to-basics movement that saw people shopping the way their grandparents had. People wanted to know where their sandwich had come from: they wanted to see where the bread was baked, to meet the guy who had cured the salami, to chat to the team behind the pickles and shake the hand that had produced the cheese. So it made perfect sense that they would also want to know more about the beer they bought to go with that sandwich – to ask the brewer how it was made and to support a small, local business just getting off the ground.

Craft beer started to gain a firm foothold, initially in Cape Town where the markets were most abundant. Soon afterwards came the festivals – the Cape Town Festival of Beer launched in November 2010 with just enough craft beer to fill a single stand. In its fifth edition, craft was most definitely king, with beers from the larger brands serving as supporting acts rather than the main event. Just months after that first Cape Town event, another fledgling festival emerged, with the Clarens Craft Beer Festival now being one of the hottest tickets on the annual beer calendar.

Since then the breweries have sprouted up thick and fast – from just over 40 in mid-2012 to triple that number three years later. Imports have risen, from warming Belgian ales to barrel-aged beers from Scotland, from American brews infused with hazelnut to in-your-face hop bombs from maverick British breweries. Local brewers too have become more adventurous in what they add to the kettle, moving from the light lagers with which they initially enticed drinkers to ales laced with fynbos herbs or naartjie peel, beers infused with rooibos or blended with pinotage. In fact, the interest in alternative beer has become so great that, in 2014, SAB launched their own 'small batch brewery', Fransen Street, which produces a range of beer styles with nary a pale lager in sight.

TAKE A TOUR THROUGH HISTORY

Mitchell's might be the oldest microbrewery in the country, but in Cape Town there's a larger brewery that goes way, way back.

It was 1820 when Swedish businessman Jacob Letterstedt decided to build a brewery in the shadow of Table Mountain. It was clear that the man knew what he was doing, since an important brewery still stands on that same site – undoubtedly SAB's prettiest premises, Newlands Brewery.

Jacob's reason for building his brewery here is the same reason a spate of 19th-century breweries popped up in the area; the same reason SAB still brews here today – its proximity to a pristine source of what many brewers consider to be beer's most important ingredient – water. The Newlands Spring and the lesser-known Kommetjie Spring both feed the brewery, which has owned the rights to the water for more than 150 years. Anders Ohlsson later bought the brewery and it remained a part of Ohlsson's Cape Brewing until 1956, when South African Breweries took over the historic site. Although Newlands is not SAB's largest brewery, it quickly expanded and today the historic brewing buildings have been retired in favour of a larger, more modern plant.

The malt house, oast house (where hops and barley were once dried) and 19th-century tower brewery still stand, though, and form an essential part of the highly recommended Newlands Brewery tour, showcasing the Cape's brewing history and giving insight into how beer-making practices have changed throughout the ages. One practice that has been revived is that of delivering beer by dray – the traditional horse-drawn way to transport beer. On the first Friday of each month, fresh kegs of Castle Lager are taken to three nearby pubs and tapped for patrons to drain.

Brewery tours (R80 per person) take place Monday–Friday at 10am, 12pm and 2pm, and Saturdays at 10am and 12pm. There are also evening tours on Tuesdays and Wednesdays. Bookings are essential.

3 Main Road, Newlands, Cape Town; newlandsbrewery.co.za; 021 658 7440

So where is this all heading? Is the rapid growth sustainable or can we soon expect to find Gumtree awash with used breweries up for sale? The USA certainly had a few lean years, where brewpubs closed in droves and increasingly discerning drinkers turned their backs on those making inferior brews. In South Africa, another factor is likely to place a ceiling on the sector's growth – cost. With imported ingredients and smaller batches driving the cost up, and an increasing trend towards slapping a premium price label on the brews, craft beer is an unaffordable luxury for many.

But it's fair to say that South Africa's love affair with beer isn't going to disappear. A few short years ago, beer lovers would jump with joy if they found a solitary ale on a restaurant menu. Nowadays, an absence of interesting ales is reason for many diners to move on to the next eatery. Food magazines are featuring beer, even wine writers are penning pieces about the amber nectar, and an expanding army is quietly brewing in their houses, ensuring that this revolution doesn't end anytime soon. The homebrewers are growing in number, practising their recipes on 20-litre stove-top setups and fermenting in bathrooms, kitchens and garages. With their thirst for brewing knowledge matched only by their thirst for beer, many will move on to become the next wave of microbrewers, making sure that South Africa's beer renaissance stays very much alive.

WHAT IS BEER?

Although herbs and spices, fruit, flowers and all manner of other grains can be added to a brew, beer is basically made up of four ingredients:

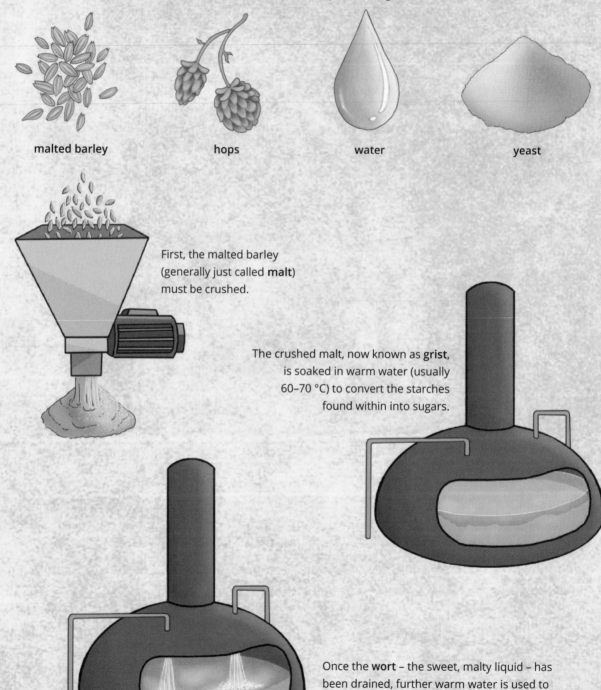

malted barley

hops

water

yeast

First, the malted barley (generally just called **malt**) must be crushed.

The crushed malt, now known as **grist**, is soaked in warm water (usually 60–70 °C) to convert the starches found within into sugars.

Once the **wort** – the sweet, malty liquid – has been drained, further warm water is used to rinse the grains and extract as much sugar as possible. This step is called '**sparging**'.

The wort is then boiled for at least an hour. Hops are added to give bitterness, flavour and aroma to the brew.

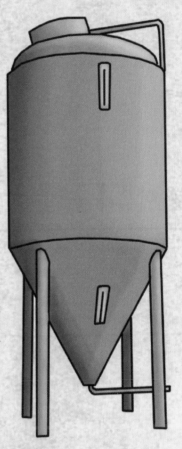

The wort is quickly cooled and transferred to a fermenter, where yeast is added. Lagers ferment at cooler temperatures (6–13 °C) for two to three weeks; ales ferment slightly warmer (18–24 °C) for around seven to 10 days.

Once the beer has had time to 'condition' (basically to sit until the beer's desired flavour profile is achieved), it is sometimes filtered before being used to fill kegs, bottles and, later on, glasses, mouths and tummies.

PEACH, PEPPER AND PINE –
THE MANY, MANY FLAVOURS OF BEER

'It smells like beer' is the apologetic summation often heard at beer tastings. But there's no need to apologise – beer smelling like beer is better than it smelling like wine. Or cider. Or, heaven forbid, vinegar. But what are the components that make up that beery smell? And do all beers smell and taste the same?

Beer is a complex beverage. From the four base ingredients, you have almost infinite possibilities – you can use one type of malt or seven types of malt, a single hop variety or a veritable hop salad. Even a degree or two can totally alter the flavour profile when you're talking about fermentation temperatures. Because of the sheer variety and the fact that beer begins with a quartet of ingredients, it can be a much more complex beverage than its often more highly thought-of cousin, wine.

The malt, hops and yeast all contribute to the aroma and flavour of the brew. Water, of course, plays its part, with certain water profiles better suited to a certain style of beer, but you'd have to have a serious nose to be able to pick out which water a brewer had used from a quick sniff or sip. The other ingredients, though, lend a very particular stamp to the finished pint.

Malt tends to lend hearty, almost warming flavours – if you're smelling or tasting toffee, coffee, caramel or chocolate, toast, biscuit or just plain grain, these characteristics are courtesy of the malted barley. Yeast can offer anything from bubble gum to spice, from freshly baked bread to overripe bananas. Hops, aside from lending the all-important bitterness to the beer, deliver a cornucopia of aromas and flavours depending on the hop strain and from where it hails. American hops are ballsy and in-your-face – think lychee, granadilla, peach and pine, gooseberries, mango and citrus fruits of all kinds. English hops have a tendency to be a little more subtle – lots of pepper and wood and earthy spice. The Noble Hops of Germany and the Czech Republic lend a refined, herbal spiciness to a beer, while New Zealand and Australia are experimenting with bold hops pungent in lime, berries, grass and flowers. And what about the local version? Grown only along the Garden Route, South African hops have typically been used mainly to give a smooth bitterness to lagers, but new hops have been bred to mimic American strains, such as the rather unimaginatively named 'J17' with its granadilla and grapefruit aromas.

And then, of course, you have all the extras – brewers have been known to use anything from coriander and citrus peel to cocoa nibs and rose petals to flavour their brews. The beer might be barrel aged or injected with *Brettanomyces*, and the style guidelines for beer, laid out by the American Beer Judge Certification Program (BJCP), have to evolve to keep up with brewers constantly experimenting and inventing new styles.

So, with all of this in mind, can beer really taste of absolutely anything? Well no, not quite. There are

Hop pellets, pale malt and roasted malt, all waiting to fulfil their destiny as ingredients in beer

SNIFF, SIP, REPEAT

Like wine, beer can be appreciated, admired, sniffed and savoured. Here's a basic guide to tasting beer, for those occasions when you want to give your pint a little extra love:

LOOK

First check out the colour, something that's created by the malts used. Is your beer topped with a frothy or foamy head? Although some styles sport less than others, all beer should have some foam. Look for carbonation (but remember that some styles areless bubbly than others) and for clarity. Don't worry about a little haze – many craft beers are unfiltered.

SNIFF

Swirling the glass vigorously is not ideal as it can affect the carbonation and head retention. A slight swirl, however, isn't going to hurt anyone. Look for malt, hop and yeast characteristics when you inhale.

SIP

Swishing beer around your mouth, as you might with wine, is not the done thing as you'll kill the carbonation. If you want the full-on tasting experience, though, try to let the beer cover your entire tongue. Look for both flavour – is it sweet, dry, bitter, sour? – and mouthfeel, which could be light and fizzy, velvety, heavy or creamy.

SAVOUR

Beer tasters do not spit, since the aftertaste, or finish, is an important part of beer tasting – at least, that's the excuse given! Hops tend to impart a palate-cleansing, bitter finish. A sweet finish could be from malt or from added sugars, as with Belgian beers.

REPEAT

'A fine beer may be judged with only one sip, but it's better to be thoroughly sure.' So goes the oft- quoted Czech proverb. Enjoy your beer, hopefully noticing new aromas and flavours with every sip – just remember to drink responsibly!

certain things a beer should never taste of – aromas and flavours that suggest something has gone wrong with the brew, whether it's equipment that didn't quite get cleaned, water from an unsuitable source, fermentation temperatures that rose too high or a batch of infected yeast that needs to be disposed of and replaced. Some off-aromas are easy to discern – no-one wants the butyric brew (smells like baby vomit), the chlorophenol-filled pint (it will smell like the inside of a first-aid kit) or the beer with a hint of ethyl acetate (aromas of paint thinner or nail polish remover). Other inappropriate characteristics are easier to forgive, but if you're getting notes of cider or green apples, tinned vegetables, sherry, pear drops or vinegar, then the beer in your hand should be replaced with another, more palatable version.

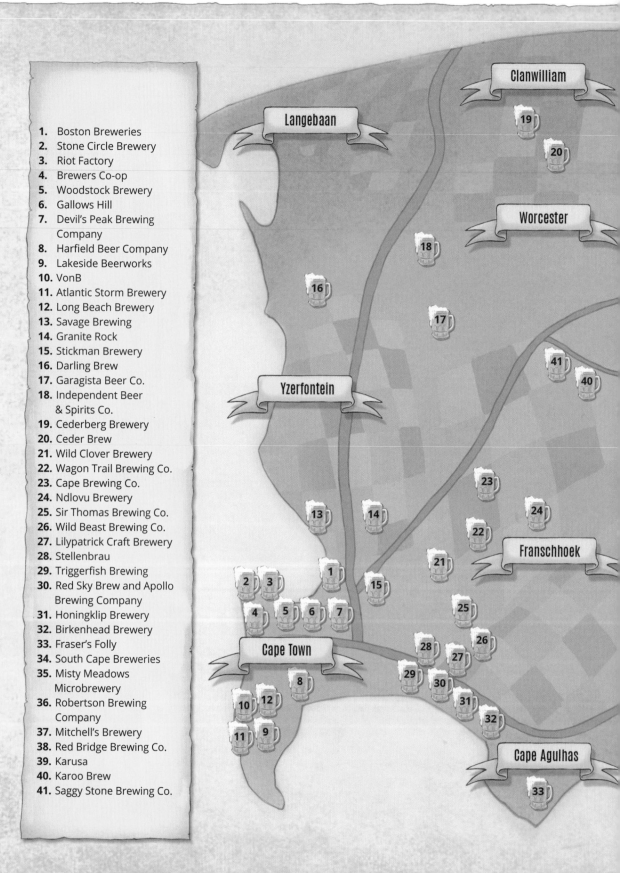

1. Boston Breweries
2. Stone Circle Brewery
3. Riot Factory
4. Brewers Co-op
5. Woodstock Brewery
6. Gallows Hill
7. Devil's Peak Brewing Company
8. Harfield Beer Company
9. Lakeside Beerworks
10. VonB
11. Atlantic Storm Brewery
12. Long Beach Brewery
13. Savage Brewing
14. Granite Rock
15. Stickman Brewery
16. Darling Brew
17. Garagista Beer Co.
18. Independent Beer & Spirits Co.
19. Cederberg Brewery
20. Ceder Brew
21. Wild Clover Brewery
22. Wagon Trail Brewing Co.
23. Cape Brewing Co.
24. Ndlovu Brewery
25. Sir Thomas Brewing Co.
26. Wild Beast Brewing Co.
27. Lilypatrick Craft Brewery
28. Stellenbrau
29. Triggerfish Brewing
30. Red Sky Brew and Apollo Brewing Company
31. Honingklip Brewery
32. Birkenhead Brewery
33. Fraser's Folly
34. South Cape Breweries
35. Misty Meadows Microbrewery
36. Robertson Brewing Company
37. Mitchell's Brewery
38. Red Bridge Brewing Co.
39. Karusa
40. Karoo Brew
41. Saggy Stone Brewing Co.

Clanwilliam

Langebaan

Worcester

Yzerfontein

Franschhoek

Cape Town

Cape Agulhas

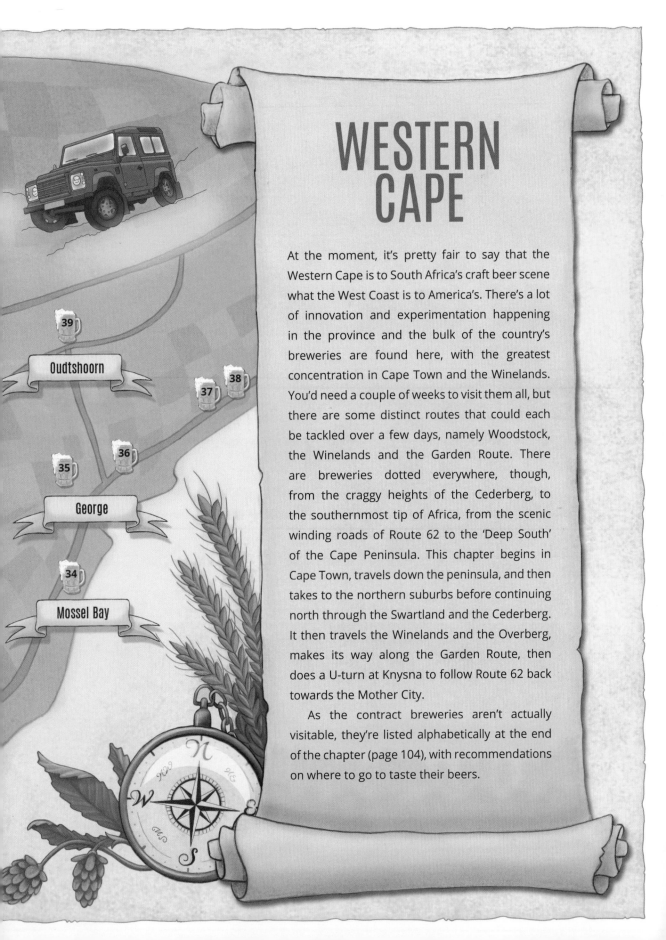

WESTERN CAPE

At the moment, it's pretty fair to say that the Western Cape is to South Africa's craft beer scene what the West Coast is to America's. There's a lot of innovation and experimentation happening in the province and the bulk of the country's breweries are found here, with the greatest concentration in Cape Town and the Winelands. You'd need a couple of weeks to visit them all, but there are some distinct routes that could each be tackled over a few days, namely Woodstock, the Winelands and the Garden Route. There are breweries dotted everywhere, though, from the craggy heights of the Cederberg, to the southernmost tip of Africa, from the scenic winding roads of Route 62 to the 'Deep South' of the Cape Peninsula. This chapter begins in Cape Town, travels down the peninsula, and then takes to the northern suburbs before continuing north through the Swartland and the Cederberg. It then travels the Winelands and the Overberg, makes its way along the Garden Route, then does a U-turn at Knysna to follow Route 62 back towards the Mother City.

As the contract breweries aren't actually visitable, they're listed alphabetically at the end of the chapter (page 104), with recommendations on where to go to taste their beers.

39

Oudtshoorn

38

37

36

35

George

34

Mossel Bay

BOSTON
BREWERIES

48 Carlisle St, Paarden Eiland, Cape Town; bostonbreweries.co.za; 021 300 0625
Tasting room: La Bottega, 160 Sir Lowry Rd, Woodstock, Cape Town

★ **BREWERY CLOSED TO THE PUBLIC.**
TASTING ROOM OPEN MON–FRI 8AM–7PM, SAT 11AM–8PM ★

Chris Barnard is the owner of Cape Town's longest-running craft brewery

Chris Barnard's son, Matthew, is proud of the fact that if it wasn't for him, Boston Breweries might never have been launched. Not that Matthew had any hand in the brewing process of course – he wasn't yet in pre-school when Boston sold its first pint. But if Matthew's nappies hadn't overtaken Chris's humble plastic fermenters, he might never have made the leap from home- to craft brewer.

It all started years before when Chris and now-wife Babette took an extended trip to Europe. 'We were in this tiny village in Germany and we wanted a beer, so we went to the local bottle store, which was basically a cellar underneath a woman's house. Back in the eighties, we didn't have much to choose from in South Africa, and here we saw all these different beers, so we said "give us two of every beer you've got".' Chris perhaps underestimated the sheer range of beers available, for when the delivery arrived, he got a little more than he bargained for. 'In came this guy with a crate of beer. As he was bringing it through there was another knock and in came another person with a crate. In the end we got about four crates of beer. It was an absolute eye-opener – we'd come from having about four brands to having in excess of 40 different brands in this one tiny village!'

LAGER OR ALE - WHAT'S THE DIFFERENCE?

Essentially, there are just two branches of the world's beer family – lager and ale. The difference comes down to one main ingredient – the yeast.

Ale yeast – *Saccharomyces cerevisiae* – does its work at the top of the fermentation vessel and works best between temperatures of 18 and 24 °C. Too cold and the yeast won't work; too warm and the beer will potentially become prone to off-flavours. Ales are not usually as highly carbonated as lagers and as a general rule are not served as cold. Ales are often favoured by homebrewers and craft brewers partly for the less complicated procedure and equipment required to produce them, and partly because there is a greater range of styles, giving a brewery's beer menu a greater array of flavours.

While ale has a longer history, lager has also been made throughout the ages, though by chance rather than design. It wasn't until the 1800s that brewers began to understand the lagering process and to opt for these clearer, crisper beers. Lager yeast – *Saccharomyces pastorianus* – sinks to the bottom of the yet-to-ferment beer and likes temperatures of between 6 and 13 °C. Because of the cold temperatures, lager takes longer to ferment than ale and is often subject to cold maturation after fermentation. This maturation period – where the beer is kept on the yeast at very cold temperatures – is known as lagering, from the German verb meaning 'to store'.

While most lagers are golden and relatively low in alcohol, there are a number of lager sub-types, such as Marzen, Dunkel and Bock, which can be anything from golden to dark brown, and might have ABV percentages up to a whopping 14.

On returning to Cape Town, Chris decided that the only way he could get his beer fix was to brew it himself. Saturday mornings were spent at the only shop selling brewing supplies, the kitchen was commandeered and the bathroom became overrun with fermenters. Once Chris and Babette got married and Matthew came along, Chris felt he could no longer take over the kitchen all weekend – and when he started finding baby gear in his fermenters, he decided it was time to find a new home for his brewery. It was then that he upgraded to a 100-litre system and set it up in the family factory in Paarden Eiland. He soon found himself with a problem that many people would be keen to suffer with – even with an increasing amount of friends to assist, Chris just couldn't get through all the beer he was brewing. Some of the factory workers started taking beer home and it was then that the foundations for a brewery were laid. 'A shebeen owner phoned me and asked me where my rep was, saying that he needed stock. I didn't know what was going on! Then I found out that the guys from the factory were reselling it to shebeens to make some money and that they'd taken the company name – Boston Bag – and just written

Boston Breweries on the beer labels.' Thanks to their entrepreneurism, Chris suddenly found himself with a functioning brewery – and a name for it too.

Boston Breweries proper was launched in 2000 with the flagship beer, Boston Lager. For the next six years, the brewery's success waxed and waned with just two beers in the range – the lager and Whale Tale Ale. Chris began to import malt, allowing him to introduce new styles including the surprise hit, Van Hunks Pumpkin Ale, brewed as a one-off after a friend challenged him to create a spiced ale. The beer, which has added cinnamon and nutmeg, gained an instant following and became a part of the staple Boston range, which today features three lagers and six ales.

These days Chris spends more time behind his desk than he does at the brew kettle, but he has two assistant brewers to keep things ticking over. He does, however, take the helm when a new beer is added to the catalogue and still prides himself on his hands-on quality control. 'I test every batch we brew,' he says – no mean feat for a brewery that operates 24 hours a day, five days a week.

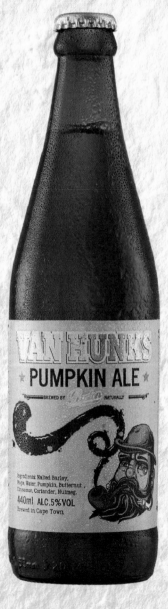

Boston Breweries survived for a decade through South Africa's lean beer years, but since the country's beer scene began to boom, Boston has flourished, with their ever-expanding range now found on tap and in bottles countrywide. The brewery itself is not open to visitors, but the full beer menu can be sampled at their taproom at La Bottega, an Italian trattoria. The taproom sits at the start of the rapidly developing Woodstock brew route – an appropriate spot for a brewery that has been there since the start of Cape Town's love affair with microbrewed beer.

BEER MENU

★

VAN HUNKS PUMPKIN ALE (6%)

BOSTON PREMIUM
LAGER (4%)

LOADED CANNON ALE (10%)

JOHNNY GOLD
WEISS (5%)

BOSTON IPA (5%)

WHALE TALE ALE (3.5%)

NAKED MEXICAN
LAGER (4.5%)

BLACK RIVER
COFFEE STOUT (6%)

'GIVE US TWO OF EVERY BEER YOU'VE GOT!'

STONE CIRCLE
BREWERY

Solan Rd, Wembley Square, Cape Town; stonecirclebrewery.co.za

★ OPEN MON–FRI 10AM–5.30PM ★

'I'd rather be brewing than doing what I'm doing.' This was the sentence that had been echoing around Nick Worsley's head for some seven years before he finally took the leap and launched Stone Circle Brewery in early 2015, along with good friend and long-term brew buddy Nick Shaw.

Nick Worsley's beer awakening came, as so many South African brewers' did, when he was living overseas – in the United Kingdom to be precise. After returning to Cape Town following a six-year stint in England, he quickly launched himself into homebrewing. It was 2005 and supplies were very difficult to get hold of – Nick couldn't even get his hands on a kit beer – so the main ingredient for that first batch was molasses. 'It tasted good,' says Nick, 'but it wouldn't ferment, so I couldn't call it beer.' Eventually he tracked down The Beer Keg in Johannesburg (page 150) and started brewing on a more serious level, along with Nick Shaw.

Soon after, the two Nicks decided that brewing was something

BEER
MENU
★
HALLELUJAH
BLONDE ALE
(8%)

GREEN LOTUS
PALE ALE
(5%)

Located in Wembley Square, Stone Circle is ideal for a quick post-work pint

they longed to turn into a business, but it took several years to put the plan into action. One of the things that took a while was the brewery, an idiosyncratic setup that the Stone Circle team built from scratch, using old juice vats to convert into a mash tun, hot liquor tank and brew kettle. The brewery sits behind tinted glass in the up-and-coming Wembley Square district of Cape Town, and if you peep through the windows on a brew day, you'll be able to watch Nick and Nick at work, brewing their next batch of Hallelujah Blonde or Green Lotus Pale Ale.

Stone Circle's beer names have somewhat spiritual connotations and as Nick Worsley says about the moniker of his pale ale, 'the lotus is a symbol of natural simplicity and peace, exactly what we want to express with these beers.' The ethos of the brewery is perhaps best summed up by the tagline on the particularly striking labels: 'As in life, best when chilled'.

The third beer in Stone Circle's line-up is a weissbier

RIOT
FACTORY

The Palms, 145 Sir Lowry Rd, Woodstock, Cape Town; riotfactory.co.za; 076 657 1745

★ OPEN THU–FRI 12PM–LATE, SAT 10AM–2PM ★

David Coleman and Marc Fourie are clearly having a lot of fun. The two childhood friends are the driving force behind Riot Factory, a funky addition to the Cape Town brewing scene based in the equally funky suburb of Woodstock.

Everything about the brand is hip, from the slightly scary mural dominating the brew bar to the 'chandebeer' light fitting hanging over the bar; from the simple wooden tap handles to the striking bottle art designed by Stellenbosch studio Fanakalo.

Riot launched in late 2014 with a couple of events at their bar followed by a full-scale hello to the South African beer-loving public at the Cape Town Festival of Beer. But the brewery has been a long time coming. Marc started working behind bars in London in the late nineties and quickly developed a penchant for hops. After a decade and a half in the UK, he returned to South Africa, bringing his homebrewing hobby with him and the idea that became Riot Factory started to form.

David's background is brewing of a different sort and the original idea was to also have a coffee

WOODSTOCK BREW ROUTE

The gentrified neighbourhood of Woodstock has become Cape Town's unofficial capital of craft beer, with a walkable route that visits some seven breweries and taprooms. Start at La Bottega, the taproom for Boston Breweries, then drop in for tasters at Riot Factory and the Brewers Co-op before stopping for a tour at Woodstock Brewery, perhaps sticking around for sustenance at the upstairs steakhouse, the Local Grill. Gallows Hill were planning a taproom near the Old Biscuit Mill when this book was being researched and from there it's just a short walk to the taproom at Devil's Peak, where a food and beer pairing platter is highly recommended. The whole route is about 3 km and is best tackled on a Saturday, when all of the various stops are open.

BEER MENU

★

SESSION
GOLDEN ALE
(4.5%)

VALVE IPA
(5.9%)

roastery under the same roof as the brewery. 'We were originally going to call it "The Portland Project",' explains David, referring to the Oregon city's renowned foodie culture. 'We were going to have a range of craft drinks under one roof, but the licensing procedure eventually pushed us to a brew bar.' He acknowledges now that it was probably for the best, at least for the moment. They want to keep the team small and, as David admits, 'this is as much as two people can manage.'

They're managing pretty well, though, experimenting with unusual ales to possibly feature as seasonal offerings alongside the two staples and working on beer snacks to offer alongside the brews. Marc sums up the Riot ethos by explaining how the name came about. 'It just kind of happened,' he says, 'and we loved it. The name reflects that beer should have flavour, that beer should have character and that beer should have personality.' Having spent a couple of hours at the Factory, I can confirm that not only the beers, but also the brewers and their bar easily meet all three requirements.

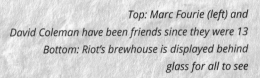

Top: Marc Fourie (left) and David Coleman have been friends since they were 13
Bottom: Riot's brewhouse is displayed behind glass for all to see

BREWERS
CO-OP

135 Albert Rd, Woodstock, Cape Town; brewersco-op.co.za

★ OPEN THU 5PM–9PM, FRI 5PM–10PM, SAT 12PM–4PM ★

The Brewers Co-op is quite unlike anything else on the South African brewing scene, but for one of the brewer-members it seemed like such an obvious idea. 'For me it was a no-brainer,' says the man behind the concept, Richard Andrew. 'Lots of people would like to set up a brewery, to sell their beers and see the public tasting them, but they'd like to do it without giving up their day job.' Richard's idea has allowed 16 Cape Town beer enthusiasts to do just that.

It's a fairly simple concept. Starting up a brewery is expensive, especially if you want to do it properly and on any sort of scale – and as Richard says, not all brewers want to abandon their careers for beer. So the Brewers Co-op is the perfect solution. After advertising with local homebrew supply shops and clubs, Richard found 15 like-minded beer lovers who have put in an equal amount of funds to buy brewing equipment. The 120-litre, automated system has been imported from the USA and, following a year of talks between the brewers, it saw its maiden brew in January 2015.

The Co-op team is an eclectic bunch whose day jobs bring various levels of expertise to the table – there are accountants and software engineers, business-minded members and those with an art and design background. There are three BJCP-qualified judges, several dedicated members of the SouthYeasters homebrewing club, a dentist, a DJ and a former professional brewer. Many members have, of course, worked in a bar or restaurant at some point and between them they have more than 50 years of brewing experience. Not all 16 members are brewers, though – two will be focusing on the design and marketing aspects of the business, which leaves a nice tidy timetable for the others to brew to – 14 brewers, seven days in a week, two potential brewing slots per day.

That will be the long-term plan, but in the short term, the brewhouse probably won't see quite as much action. A priority in the early days is getting the Co-op's 'house beers' ready. Recipes are still being tweaked, but there will be four beers permanently available on tap at the Co-op's mountain-facing bar. The rest will be up to the individuals and the range will reflect the beer tastes and brewing preferences of the members. Eventually you can expect up to 18 beers on tap and while the bar itself won't be serving food, you'll be able to order from the adjoining Italian restaurant.

There's a great sense of camaraderie here, and while everyone in the team obviously would like to make a few bucks from their beers, profit is not the only goal. 'It's about taking a hobby and turning it into something self-sustaining,' says Ralph Borland, whose arty background is going to be a huge asset in turning the former fruit and veg store into a funky Woodstock bar. 'It's about homebrewers being able to meet up with the public and share their passion. Of course, we need to make a profit, but we would like to make the beers accessible to all and to avoid the hiked-up prices that seem to come with the craft beer territory. Ultimately I would love for it to be transparent – we could show the public exactly how much a beer costs, how much goes to ingredients, how much goes to SARS and how much the brewer makes.'

This notion of accessibility is one that runs through the whole ethos of the co-operative. 'As far as possible, the house beers will focus on local ingredients,' says Richard, 'in order to keep costs down. We want beers that are accessible and approachable both from a price point of view and from a taste point of view. Many places describe themselves as "exclusive". We very much want to be inclusive.' This is the very nature of the Co-op and, who knows, in the future there might even be opportunities for other aspiring brewers to be included in the Co-op's brewing ranks.

Richard Andrew checks on the Co-op's inaugural brew

BREWER
Spotted on
_____
Date
_____
Signature

BEER
MENU
★

AMBER
ALE (5.5%)

PALE
ALE (4.5%)

WOODSTOCK
BREWERY

252 Albert Rd, Woodstock, Cape Town; woodstockbrewery.co.za; 021 447 0953

★ OPEN MON–FRI 9AM–5PM ★

'Beer is a beautiful combination of business, art and science,' says Woodstock Brewery's owner André Viljoen

It's fair to say that the Woodstock Brewery has been a long time coming. Owner André Viljoen has been working on the idea for over five years – and that was after some extensive research took place to even come up with the brewery concept. 'I looked at 20 different business models in four countries I was eager to live in,' says André. 'I wanted to do something that really interested me, something I was passionate about and with beer being a relatively new thing in South Africa then, it was obvious which business plan I was going to go with.'

Where to position the brewery was an easy decision – Woodstock is close to the city and the suburbs and has easy access to Cape Town's two major highways. André couldn't have known back then when he bought the building that this would become 'beer central' in Cape Town, but the brewery now sits right at the heart of a 3 km ale trail that cuts through the industrial-turned-arty neighbourhood. André had a slightly unorthodox way of finding the building that now houses the 20-hectolitre brewery – he used Google Earth to pick out what looked to be an appropriately sized building, then drove by to serendipitously discover a for sale sign on the building's exterior. It certainly wasn't much to look

CALIFORNICATOR IPA

There's mostly pine on the aroma of this American-style IPA, though it's slightly more balanced than some, with background hints of toffee-like malt. It's pleasantly bitter, and while you pick up a touch of caramel, it's mostly about the hops when you sip – piney and with hints of stone fruit.

at back then, but after four years of painstaking refurbishments, the Woodstock Brewery's interior – and exterior – are befitting of a boutique brewery and restaurant. 'I had a *Field of Dreams* philosophy,' says André. 'If you build it, they will come and drink in it!'

André would happily admit that he's more at home tasting beer than brewing it, but he quickly sought out expert advice when it came to designing the beer range. The recipes and styles have been put together by American homebrewer-turned-craft brewer Greg Crum, Dutch brewing consultant Carel Heister and later, Dewald Goosen, who was at the helm when the brewery launched.

An avid homebrewer, Dewald met André through a mutual friend and instantly knew he wanted to work at the Woodstock Brewery. He approached André, offering to 'sweep the floors, carry grain, anything' and quickly learnt the ropes of the brewery. Moving from the typical pot-on-a-stove homebrew setup to a partially automated system with a brew length of 2 000 litres was certainly daunting. 'The first time I brewed on this system I was sweating bullets and sh*tting my pants all at the same time!' Dewald laughs with the honesty and humility you find in many of the country's microbrewers. Dewald has since moved on to Cape Brewing Company in Paarl, but his brewing assistant – also a one-time homebrewer – was set to take the reins at Woodstock.

Considering the time, money and massive amounts of work that have gone into the brewery, it launched with little fanfare in 2014, the long-awaited beers just kind of trickling onto the market. They're found at a few select venues around the city, but the best place to taste them is, of course, at the brewery itself. Upstairs there's a branch of the popular Johannesburg steakhouse The Local Grill, whose vast balcony is perfect for pint-sipping and people-watching. Plans were also underway to open a beer garden serving light snacks and, of course, plenty of beer. A bottle store was also in the wings, which will sell beers from surrounding breweries as well as Woodstock's range. True to his *Field of Dreams* philosophy, over the course of almost five years André has indeed 'built it' – and I'm fairly sure that the beer lovers will fill their end of the bargain as well.

BEER MENU

★

CALIFORNICATOR
IPA (6.8%)

POT BELGE BELGIAN
AMBER ALE (5.8%)

HAZY DAZE
WITBIER (5%)

HAPPY PILLS GERMAN
PILSNER (5.2%)

RHYTHM STICK ENGLISH
PALE ALE (5.4%)

BREW TALK...
HOPHEAD
A person who enjoys heavily hopped, bitter beers, such as IPAs and imperial IPAs.

GALLOWS HILL

gallowshillbrewing.com

★ OPEN BY APPOINTMENT ONLY ★

If you've been a follower of the Cape's craft beer scene for a while, then the name Gallows Hill might be familiar to you. The brewery, run by brothers Christoff and Schalk Marais, made its first appearance at the 2011 SouthYeasters homebrewing festival and, with the professional branding on display, it looked likely that the brothers would go pro sooner rather than later.

But while they kept on brewing, it took Christoff and Schalk another three years before their beers would be found on liquor store shelves. 'We weren't that proactive in looking for a venue,' explains Christoff, 'and when we did, it took 10 months for the licence to come through.' What with that and their full-time jobs being pretty demanding – Christoff is a doctor and Schalk an engineer – things ticked along rather slowly.

The journey actually started in 2008 when Christoff began brewing in his kitchen while living overseas. 'I was studying for my medical exams and I found a homebrewing book, which seemed more interesting!' he says. He brought the newfound passion for beer back to South Africa with him, where he recruited his brother to join in the brewing. The two brewed at Schalk's home, but it was a chance meeting with a well-known face on Cape Town's beer scene that convinced them to turn their hobby into something bigger.

'We have friends in the wine industry and they have an annual wine event at their home,' Schalk tells. 'We rocked up with a case of our beer and there we met Martin Tucker.' Martin, among other beery things, is the founder and organiser of the Cape Town Festival of Beer. After tasting their brews, he encouraged the Marais brothers to go commercial and they began to take gradual strides towards doing just that.

Today, even though the brewery is finally up and running, the Gallows Hill beers are hard to find, brewed in small batches and only available in a smattering of Cape Town locations. Perhaps what they're best known for is the ever-rotating hops they use in their IPAs and, of course, the quirky labelling. Each Gallows Hill brew comes with a toe tag detailing the hops used and the IBUs of the beer, part of the slightly macabre branding that comes with the brewery's name. 'Lots of breweries overseas run somewhat dark themes,' says Schalk, adding that they were looking for a local name to use for their beers. Gallows Hill was the area now known as De Waterkant, where a sand dune visible from Cape Town's historical harbour entrance was the spot where early dissenters were hanged. The brewery name is joined on the label with the tagline 'Craft beer to die for'.

Although production is still on a small scale, there are plans to upscale the brewhouse and launch a small taproom that will likely be open only on Saturdays to coincide with the very nearby Old Biscuit Mill's popular market. A time frame wasn't in place when this book was being researched, but for those who are as crazy about hops as the Marais brothers are, it will certainly be worth waiting for.

Schalk (left) and Christoff Marais showcase their beers with fellow hopheads at the Cape Town Festival of Beer

BEER MENU
★
PALE ALE (5%)
IPA (6.5%)

FIVE BEST BREWERIES FOR HOPHEADS

1. Devil's Peak Brewing Company (Western Cape)
2. Gallows Hill (Western Cape)
3. Mad Giant (Gauteng)
4. The Cockpit Brewhouse (Gauteng)
5. Triggerfish Brewing (Western Cape)

DEVIL'S PEAK
BREWING COMPANY

95 Durham Ave, Salt River, Cape Town; devilspeakbrewing.co.za; 021 200 5818

★ OPEN MON 11AM–4PM, TUE–SAT 11AM–11PM ★

While other breweries have tiptoed towards the bold styles that they really want to make, conscious of keeping the consumer happy, Devil's Peak has basically punched South Africa in the face with a bag of hops. Launching to a fanfare of praise in 2011, the brewery seemed to emerge from nowhere with its brazen American beers. But of course this brewery did not come from nowhere – it is the product of years of planning, passion and hard work.

It began in 2008 when Russell Boltman began to sneak beer into his wine tasting group. Having lived in San Francisco and travelled extensively in the US, Russell had got hooked on hops and was intent on convincing the others in his tasting group that beer, too, could be sipped and savoured. One member of the group was Dan Badenhorst, Russell's varsity friend and now partner in Devil's Peak. Together they started to formulate plans for a brewery, recruiting an American homebrewer to the team. After furiously brewing on a 90-litre system to stockpile enough beer, they debuted their now famous King's Blockhouse IPA at the 2011 Cape Town Festival of Beer. Although most people attending the festival had never tasted anything quite like Devil's Peak's in-your-face flavours, the beer was an instant hit.

Grab a taster tray at the taproom so you can pick out what you like best before ordering a pint

Peak has been showered with praise – the décor is admired, the food has won a staunch local following and the beer that launched the brewery has become one of the most raved-about in the country. The IPA in question gets glowing reviews from drinkers, has won 'best micro ale' at three outings to the Cape Town Festival of Beer and took the top spot in the 2014 National Craft Brewers Championship.

Winemaker-turned-head brewer JC Steyn is rightly proud of his flagship beer, which has gained a kind of cult following in South Africa. 'I credit a lot of its success to timing and its distinctiveness at the time of release,' JC says. 'When we released it in 2012 there was very little, if anything, that could compare with its explosive aromas and flavours.'

Some would say that there's still very little like it on the South African market, but there's certainly more to the beer's success than mere timing. 'We have never compromised on the quality of the key ingredients that define King's Blockhouse,' JC continues. 'I do believe it is a really fantastic and unique beer – if it wasn't, it wouldn't be as popular. You can't fool the consumer. Making a bad beer and "selling" it through active marketing will only get you so far.'

Since then, the brewery has expanded and become a must-visit destination for beer enthusiasts visiting South Africa. From humble beginnings in a garage in Somerset West, the Devil's Peak team has moved into smarter premises more befitting of their image – and their name. The glass-fronted taproom and restaurant offer prime views of the landmark mountain that gives the brewery its moniker. Since the taproom opened in September 2013, Devil's

BIG 5 PINT

THE KING'S BLOCKHOUSE IPA

'The first bite is taken with the eye' they often say about food, but this is just as true when it comes to a pint of beer. And where Blockhouse is concerned, that visual sip is almost as good as the first literal one. Golden, clear and topped with a creamy white head, it's a textbook example of an American IPA. You have to hold off on the first actual sip for just a moment longer, for this is a real sniffer's beer. There's a massive whiff of pine with plenty of tropical fruit and some citrus for good measure. Flavour-wise, no-one would call this a balanced beer – it's hops, hops, hops all the way, though with enough body to back up all the *Humulus*. Expect a lingering, bitter finish that cleanses the palate, ready for the next sip.

BEER
101

IPA

The origins of India Pale Ale are the subject of much debate among beer fans, but the style essentially grew out of the English Pale Ale and gets its name from the country it was shipped to in order to cater for thirsty Colonial Brits. Since hops could help preserve the beer on the long journey to India, more hops were added to the standard pale ales, with the style later becoming known as India Pale Ale. An American adaptation takes the British version to a new extreme and is one of the most popular styles among beer fans today. The main difference between an English IPA and an American one is the hop profile, the former having earthy characteristics while the latter gives a dominant smack of

tropical fruit, citrus and/or pine. The English IPA is a more balanced beer, with toasty, toffee malt notes, while the American IPA is really all about the hops. Many South African brewers bitter their IPAs with local hops, which I suppose would put them in the category of 'South African IPA'. Wherever it's from, it should be around 5–7.5% ABV, and always a bitter brew.

It's not all about the Blockhouse, though. As well as the IPA, the core range features an amber ale, golden ale and saison. At the taproom you'll find four more beers in the 'Explorer Series', plus some truly innovative brews appearing on the specials board. Since the taproom opened, beer fans have flocked to taste barrel-aged saisons, beer-wine hybrids, sour ales and spiced ales. Co-founder Dan credits the brewery's success to a range of factors – sticking to their principles when it comes to quality, the talent of the passionate team behind the beers and, of course, to the open-minded public always keen to try something new. 'Hopefully our "fans" have come to know that they can be guaranteed of a quality product when they choose Devil's Peak,' says Dan, modest in his reluctance to admit that Devil's Peak has a loyal bunch of devotees, 'and that their journey in beer will never be dull if they stick with us.'

BEER MENU

★

THE KING'S BLOCKHOUSE
IPA (6%)

BLACK IPA (6%)

WOODHEAD AMBER
ALE (5%)

AMERICAN PALE
ALE (3.5%)

IMPERIAL IPA (7.5%)

FIRST LIGHT GOLDEN
ALE (4.5%)

ENGLISH ALE (4.5%)

SILVERTREE SAISON
(5%)

HARFIELD
BEER COMPANY

30 River Park, 77 De Waal Dr, Diep River, Cape Town; harfieldbeer.com; 021 705 0656

★ OPEN BY APPOINTMENT ONLY ★

BEER MENU
★

1831 AMBER ALE (5.5%)

TRED GOLD (5.5%)

BUCHANAN ROAD ENGLISH IPA (5.5%)

HARVEY BROWN (4.5%)

DURHAM SWIFT (5%)

'SOON ENOUGH, MATES STARTED ASKING IF THEY COULD BUY ANY OF THE BEER FROM ME AND THE IDEA STARTED THERE.'

Fraser and assistant brewer James Aupiais mash in

It's no wonder that the residents of Harfield Village, a small area with proud and passionate residents in the southern suburbs of Cape Town, are lapping up this beer. Not only do the bottles bear the name of the suburb, each one in the range focuses on an important place, person or event from the area.

'The idea was to create a real sense of place behind the brand,' explains Fraser Dodge, Harfield's brewer and co-owner. Alas, residents will be disappointed if they're hoping to visit the brewery in their midst, for Harfield's brewhouse is actually in a small industrial park a little further south in Diep River. But the beers are easily found in a number of the restaurants that line Harfield's Second Avenue. The reason for the branding is a simple one – both Fraser and his partner Tafadzwa Mushonga are long-time Harfield residents who conceived the idea right in the suburb where they live and work.

Fraser first got a taste for ales while living overseas and decided to take a shot at making his own when he returned to South Africa. 'I did one "beer cordial",' says Fraser, referring to the kit beers that most brewers start out with, 'and then tried a few "brew in the bag" beers before I moved to brewing all-grain. Soon enough, mates started asking if they could buy any of the beer from me and the idea started there.'

Tafadzwa, who had previously worked as the in-house legal counsel for Brandhouse, was keen to jump in and with financial assistance from a third, silent partner, Harfield Beer Company was formed. Suitable premises in Harfield were unlikely to materialise, so the team looked a little further south and with a sizable unit secured, tackled the licensing red tape – something that was doubtless eased by Tafadzwa's legal background.

With a solid local following already established, the Harfield team are hoping to expand their fan base and plans are underway for a major upgrade to their equipment. As Fraser gears up to turn brewing into a full-time profession, it seems rather ironic that the brewery he named after Harfield Village is going to end up keeping him away from the beloved suburb.

Fraser Dodge has already upscaled Harfield's brewhouse once, but is planning a further upgrade soon

LAKESIDE
BEERWORKS

20 Fish Eagle Park, Kommetjie, Cape Town; lsbw.co.za; 021 783 0169

★ OPEN BY APPOINTMENT ONLY ★

Morné Uys mashes in a batch of American Pale Ale

Many South African microbrewers run their beer business alongside another enterprise: they brew in the evenings or on weekends, or they hire someone to handle the brewhouse while they keep slogging it out at their day job. Morné Uys and Pierre-Charl du Preez (better known as PC) hadn't even sold their first pint when they packed up their desks and turned brewing into a full-time career. 'We had to jump right in,' says Morné, 'otherwise it might have never happened. We needed the incentive – if we had jobs to fall back on, we would have had an excuse not to make a go of it.'

It was February 2013 when Morné left his job as a financial advisor and PC resigned as spokesperson for Western Cape Premier Helen Zille. They had only been brewing together for a matter of months and hadn't even found premises for their brewery. But they were convinced that they could sell their beer and it turns out they were right, with Lakeside's ales gracing many bar menus and liquor store fridges around Cape Town and the Winelands.

PC and Morné actually met over a beer – one of Morné's homebrews in fact. He'd come to a braai equipped with a case of his weiss and, after a few sips, PC wanted to know how to make his own beer.

At the time Morné's brew kettle – a converted urn – was out of action, so he told PC they'd need some sort of pot to brew in. 'He said "no problem – I can sort that", then he rocked up with this giant 450-litre pot!' Morné laughs. They began brewing together shortly afterwards in the garage of PC's Lakeside home. That first brew didn't go entirely to plan. 'The pot was enormous and we brewed about 200 litres of beer,' recalls Morné, 'but we didn't have enough space to ferment it, so we had to clean out the mash tun and ferment it there. It was not ideal!' But soon they had fine-tuned their beers – and their brewing process – and started to look into how to make some money from it.

Around the time they left their jobs, PC and Morné started to brew at Honingklip Brewery (page 84). Under Honingklip's licence they could brew beer to sell and they started to stockpile for Lakeside's launch in April 2013. Actually, the first time Lakeside's brews were available to the general public, they weren't for sale – it was at that year's SouthYeasters summer festival (which generally takes place in autumn) that people first got to taste what PC and Morné could brew. It was a roaring success, with their weissbier coming out on top in the people's choice competition. With this high praise from Cape Town's beer geeks under their belts, they were ready to start selling beers, with their first paid-for pint being poured at Wild Clover's Hops Harvest Festival in May. 'The festival was great,' says Morné. 'We got good feedback and thanks to the beers we sold, we were able to buy some labels for our bottles!'

The next stage was to get their own brewery and it was around this time that the Lakeside team met Glenn Adams of Valley Brewery. He had been toying with the idea of closing his brewery for a while and, after some negotiation, Morné and PC took over the brewhouse in July. Despite the fact that their brewery is in Kommetjie, the original name remains, testament to the first beer the duo brewed together.

Since moving into their new brewing home, much has changed. New brews have been added, capacity has increased and further equipment

BEER MENU

★

LONDON ALE (4.5%)

AMERICAN PALE ALE (4.5%)

IPA (6.6%)

RED OCHRE ALE (4.5%)

HEFEWEIZEN (4.5%)

upgrades are on the cards. The kettles are constantly bubbling, with brews happening five days a week and while Morné and PC ended up giving up their full-time jobs only to take on careers that have even more demanding schedules, there's not a moment of regret. 'Making something with your own hands and selling it for a profit is far more rewarding,' says Morné. Before he gets back to hopping the batch of APA currently in the kettle, he adds a final thought and one that has been echoed many times. 'The people in the craft beer industry are pretty darn awesome too,' he says. I couldn't agree more.

BREWER
Spotted on
_____
Date
_____
Signature

BEER
MENU

★

SOUTHERN –
A COPPER ALE (5%)

LIGHT –
A MILD ALE (3%)

VONB

32c Fish Eagle Park, Kommetjie, Cape Town; vonbcraftbeer.com; 072 800 4633

★ OPEN BY APPOINTMENT ONLY ★

When I visited VonB (pronounced 'von bee'), in January 2015, their beers had only been on sale for a month. The brand, named for its brewer-owner Rainer von Brandis, was just starting to trickle onto the South African beer scene from the brewery's Kommetjie home less than 100 m from Lakeside Beerworks' HQ.

Rainer had been brewing at home for three years, but by popular demand he decided to transform a hobby into what will hopefully become a full-time job. His current profession – marine biologist – keeps him working on a small Seychelles island for up to a month at a time and while it might sound idyllic, Rainer is hoping to one day make the switch from biologist to brewer. 'I really want to be at home for my kids,' he says, his second child born just a couple of weeks after the brewery launched.

Of course, being away for such long periods isn't entirely conducive to keeping the brewery ticking over, so Rainer relies heavily on his wife, Kim, for help. 'She has a marketing background and takes care of that side of things with the brewery, but she also brews when I'm away,' Rainer adds. When he's back in Cape Town, Rainer is at the mash tun almost every day, brewing up the next batch on the 180-litre system he engineered himself.

The VonB beers, which bear the family crest on the label, are designed to be 'sessionable', with both of the brews in the initial line-up designed to be easy-drinking ales. A third beer is planned, but the style and recipe were still to be decided. With a brewery so new, there are obviously lots of plans for the future and it's going to be fun to watch VonB grow up alongside Rainer's brand-new son.

Like its lighter counterpart, the Copper Ale is designed to be a session beer

ATLANTIC STORM
BREWERY

27b Heron Park, Wildevoëlvlei Rd, Kommetjie, Cape Town; atlanticstorm.co.za

★ OPEN BY APPOINTMENT ONLY ★

Cameron and Barry check that the wort is transferring from mash tun to kettle on their brand-new system

It's fair to say that the SouthYeasters, Cape Town's homebrewing club, has been a training ground for many microbrewers and its monthly meetings a huge help to those looking to improve their brews. For Atlantic Storm, a team of three beer-mad friends, it was the club's annual festival that made them take the leap from being homebrewers to putting their beers out on the market.

'We had the idea before, but it was kind of a pipe dream,' says Cameron Doubell, 'but then we won an award for our spiced ale at the 2013 SouthYeasters festival and that, coupled with the great feedback, really inspired us. People kept asking "where can we buy your beers?" and we thought, wow, there might just be something in this.' The following year another beer, the pale ale that would become the base for their flagship Cape Doctor, also won acclaim, placing in the top three in the people's choice competition. The decision was made and Cameron, along with Barry O'Donoghue and Nick Engelbrecht, started taking steps to turn their homebrewery into a commercial craft brewery.

It really started back at university, where funds are typically tight and the need for beer is great. 'We were all broke students,' says Cameron, 'so four of

us clubbed together to buy a beer kit.' Two of the four – Cameron and Nick – continued brewing together, later joined by Barry. Today, the three manage the duties between them, with Nick, a qualified chartered accountant, focusing on the brewery's financials and Barry taking charge of social media while Cameron mans the brewhouse.

In late 2014, Atlantic Storm moved into premises in a Kommetjie industrial park and brewed the first batch of pale ale on their new 500-litre system. The vibe there is exuberant – the three friends clearly have a lot of fun together and jovial ribbing is the order of the day. Surfing flicks play non-stop on a massive TV screen and it's easy to see that the brewery is heavily influenced by their other passion. 'Nick and I were on the way to the beach one day,' recalls Cameron, 'and the brewery name just kind of happened. Our brewery is on the Atlantic side, we surf on the Atlantic side and we're in the Cape of Storms. It just made sense.'

The beer that basically launched the brewery – the spiced ale that was so well received at Atlantic Storm's first festival – is set to become a seasonal addition to the beer menu, brewed at Easter and Christmas, and there will be plenty of other occasional and experimental beers on offer throughout the year. Cameron's first goal is to give up his job in IT and become a full-time brewer. Well, more or less full-time. If you happen to rock up at Atlantic Storm's brewery and you find the place all locked up, you can pretty much guarantee that you'll find the team surfing the ocean whose name is emblazoned on their beers.

(L-R) Nick Engelbrecht, Cameron Doubell and Barry O'Donoghue are having a ball with their new brewery

LONG BEACH
BREWERY

Unit 6e, Hou Moed Ave, Sun Valley Industria, Noordhoek, Cape Town;
longbeachbrewery.co.za; 021 785 1010

★ OPEN BY APPOINTMENT ONLY ★

BEER MENU

★

DEEP WATER PORTER (5%)

GREEN ROOM INDIA PALE ALE (5.5%)

BOMB SHELL BLONDE ALE (4.5%)

'If you ask me my drink of choice, I am more comfortable with a beer in hand,' says Roger Burton, half of the brewing team at Long Beach. It might seem like an obvious comment for a brewer to make, but Roger hasn't always been in the business of beer – he has worked as a winemaker for more than a decade, at wine farms in Constantia and Piekenierskloof. In fact, it was wine than got Roger more interested in beer – he participated in harvests in Australia, Germany and California, all countries with solid beer cultures, and started to taste a vast range of different styles.

The brush with beer might have remained a passing interest, but for a meeting with Jaco de Beer, now the other half of the Long Beach team. The two met through a mutual acquaintance and started the evening talking wine, but the chat soon turned to the beverage they were both drinking: beer. 'About a year after we first met, he phoned me with the idea of starting our own brewery,' says Roger, and the Long Beach wheels were set in motion.

Jaco was already an avid brewer and, in 2013, Roger started brewing on a small scale at home. 'I've got British heritage,' he says, 'so it's not too much of a leap from wine to beer!' Like many winemaker-brewers, he considers brewing more difficult. 'I feel that I'm a natural farmer, and wine is really made in the vineyard. On a brew day, you have to be so aware of everything that's going on. The winemaking background certainly helps, but I've had to unlearn a lot of things to become a brewer!'

Roger likes to nip out the brewery for a quick surf or a stroll along the beach when he can

But the unlearning – and relearning – are starting to pay off. Long Beach's porter was ranked in the top 10 beers at the 2014 Cape Town Festival of Beer, just nine months after the brewery first opened. The porter is certainly their most talked-about beer, though it is not their biggest seller. With the beach that gives the brewery its name just a few kilometres away, it's no surprise that a beer better suited to warm weather is what locals most want to sip – the blonde ale. In fact, once the brewery has undergone some revamping, Jaco and Roger plan to add a lager to their range as it's what the customers are asking for.

Roger and Jaco have big plans to upgrade and upscale the brewery, and hopefully put in a tasting room – you can't see the beach, but this is certainly the best view you get from any of the breweries found in South Africa's small industrial parks. Long Beach is making great strides and it's clear that Roger is thrilled with his choice to switch from grape to grain. 'It's so great to come into such a free-flowing industry. You can really put your personality into the beer and pretty much do whatever you want,' he says, before grabbing a surfboard and heading to the beach, perfectly proving his point.

BEYOND THE BREWERY:
FIVE PLACES TO FIND GREAT BEER IN CAPE TOWN

1. Banana Jam Café
157 2nd Ave, Kenilworth, Cape Town; bananajamcafe.co.za; 021 674 0186
Cape Town's original craft beer hangout is still one of its finest, with 30 constantly-rotating beers on tap plus many more in the bottle, including limited-availability brews shipped from America.

2. Beerhouse on Long
223 Long St, Cape Town; beerhouse.co.za; 021 424 3370
With kegs and tap handles for bathroom sinks, an interior decked out in shades of lager, 20 beers on tap and a menu featuring a whopping 99 bottles of beer from around the world, this is a real homage to beer located in the city centre.

3. Den Anker
V&A Waterfront, Cape Town; denanker.co.za; 021 419 0249
The Belgians were producing exquisite ales centuries before the term 'craft' was ever applied to beer and Den Anker was serving them in Cape Town long before the beer boom hit. The Waterfront restaurant serves mussels and frites, has six Belgian brews on tap and stocks five of the six Belgian Trappist ales. The only thing that can match the beers is the postcard view of Table Mountain that you get to drink them in front of.

4. The House of Machines
84 Shortmarket St, Cape Town; thehouseofmachines.com; 021 426 1400
The local selection here is fairly standard, but it's the range of canned American craft beers that you really come for, including brews from Samuel Adams and Sierra Nevada.

5. Saints Burger Joint
Eden on the Bay, Cnr Big Bay Boulevard, Blouberg; saintsburgerjoint.co.za; 021 554 9709
Grab a pint of one of the 30-plus draught beers on offer, design your own burger and enjoy wonderful views of Table Mountain from the terrace.

SAVAGE
BREWING

Unit 1, 62 Killarney Ave, Killarney Gardens, Cape Town; savagebrewing.co.za

★ OPEN BY APPOINTMENT ONLY ★

When David Savage describes the path to opening his own brewery as a 'very rapid journey', he's not exaggerating. In the space of three years, he has made the leap from non-brewer to homebrewer and from homebrewer to commercial microbrewer. Not only that, he has become an integral part of the South-Yeasters homebrewing club as well as a familiar and well-respected face on the Cape craft beer scene.

You could tell from the start that he was going to be serious about brewing. It all began when an old school friend got a beer kit for his birthday. 'If I think back now, that beer was...shocking!' David laughs. 'But it was alcoholic and it was drinkable – just about.' Soon afterwards, David was gifted a kit of his own and admits that after making one batch he was hooked. While many homebrewers try out one or two kits and then move straight on to all-grain beers, David completed no fewer than eight kit beers. 'After the first one I thought, "I'm sure it's not supposed to taste like this" and I set myself a challenge to make a kit beer that tasted like actual beer!' he says, explaining how he ignored instructions and went about adding a range of hops to the brews.

But kit beers were never going to taste like the real thing and, after about six months, David knew he needed to start upping the ante if he hoped to recreate the beer that had really inspired him – Brewdog's Punk IPA. 'I tasted it and I thought – "all beer should taste like this".' This first encounter with serious hops would inspire many of David's beers

Assistant brewer Clemence Hunda mans the mash tun

BEER MENU

★

IPA (6%)

PALE ALE (4.8%)

AMBER ALE (5%)

UN-LAGER (5.1%)

WEISS (5%)

David Savage (right) is the brewery's founder, but Michael Woolley takes care of the day-to-day brewing

and if it was up to him, I think he might brew nothing other than IPAs.

Around the same time he started brewing all-grain beers, David also started attending South-Yeasters meetings, quickly becoming a part of the club's committee. And it was these meetings that would have a large impact on David's choice to start up a microbrewery. From the very first time he entered a beer at the bi-monthly competition meet-ups, David came out on top in a people's choice vote. In fact, he won so many times that the results announcements started to get a touch tedious. 'Everybody was asking me where they could buy the beers,' he says, 'so I started to think very seriously about opening a brewery. I've always been an entrepreneur and gone for what feels right, and this certainly felt very right.'

It was only 18 months from his very first kit beer to the day when David decided to go pro. The next 18 months would see him sourcing equipment (a rather unorthodox system that spent its former life producing Wella hair products), changing the name of the brewery from 'Bad Dog' to 'Savage', securing premises in Killarney Gardens and eventually launching the Savage range of beers at the 2014 Cape Town Festival of Beer.

David is very much involved with new recipe development, but his primary business in IT keeps his days occupied, so it's good friend Michael Woolley who does the day-to-day brewing. Michael was converted to homebrewing after tasting one of David's beers and left a decade-long career in restaurant management in 2014 to start brewing full-time. Asked if he made the right decision in changing his line of work, he is quick to respond: 'It's not work if you love it,' he says.

There's certainly a lot of passion at the Savage brewery and also a lot for the true beer enthusiast. While the brewery itself isn't that well set up for visitors (though David does welcome fellow beer geeks by appointment), the Savage brews, including the extreme, experimental beers that David plans to brew once a month, are available at the core craft beer establishments in Cape Town – Banana Jam Café, Beerhouse on Long, Roeland Liquors and the like – as well as through League of Beers. David is no longer eligible to enter homebrewing contests, but watch this space – you might just see his ales picking up a few microbrewing prizes before long...

GRANITE ROCK

Hillcrest Estate, Tygerberg Valley Rd, Durbanville; 021 970 5800

'I was supposed to retire at 65,' says Graeme Read, who was a month shy of his 69th birthday when we met, 'but I thought – "what am I going to do then?" I don't play golf, I'm no good with my hands and there's only a certain number of books you can read in a month. So I thought I could learn to brew.'

It's not the first time Graeme has taught himself to make booze. The winemaker at Hillcrest Estate has spent 14 years at the Durbanville cellar, but his background was in biology, not in oenology or viticulture. 'I'd never made a bottle of wine in my life when they decided to give me a try,' he says of the wine farm's owners, then only producing grapes to sell to surrounding cellars. So it kind of made sense that they would also give Graeme the chance to prove himself at brewing when he went to the winery with the idea.

'I know it's getting big,' Graeme says, referring to the country's beer industry. 'It's growing exponentially and you want to get in early – not at the top of the curve.' Graeme started brewing in early 2014 and has avidly been reading up and researching the local beer market. Things have started on a very small scale at Hillcrest, with a 40-litre system fashioned from old kegs, but Graeme is hoping that brewing will become a big part of the wine farm's offering in the foreseeable future. He'd love to see a

Graeme siphons off a little of the still-conditioning and yet-to-be carbonated Red Ale

beer garden built in the restaurant's pretty grounds and was planning to add to the beer line-up just as soon as the harvest – which he claims might be his final one – was over. There have already been a couple of beer festivals held at the quarry adjoining the winery, and with a bit of luck the amiable wine-maker-brewer will see his own beers sold alongside those of other Western Cape breweries the next time the estate hosts an event.

Granite Rock's equipment has started out in a rudimentary way, with milk churns used as fermenters

'IT'S GROWING EXPONENTIALLY AND YOU WANT TO GET IN EARLY – NOT AT THE TOP OF THE CURVE.'

STICKMAN
BREWERY

23 Rivers Edge Business Park, Winelands Cl, Stikland; stickmanbrewery.co.za; 021 945 1133

'I'd been in IT for 24 years,' says Stickman's owner and head brewer Johan Burger. 'I think you get to a space in your life when either you carry on, you do the same thing all over, or you have a big change. This is the start of the second part of my life.'

Johan hasn't done things by halves. Rather than starting on a pots and pans type brewhouse that will gradually be upgraded as the beer money trickles in, Johan has launched his brewery in style – with a 1 000-litre system imported from China on which he hopes to produce up to 12 000 litres per month. His market is a largely untapped one, with only a couple of small-scale breweries existing in Cape Town's northern suburbs, so there are certainly plenty of potential customers.

Alas, they'll have to seek out the beers at a local bar or liquor store, or settle for a tasting at the brewery, for Johan's initial brewpub plan hasn't yet come to pass. He explains the two-year journey he took in order to find a location, a journey that ended in a modern, tidy industrial park close to the N1. Every avenue leading to a possible brewpub turned out to be a dead end and, keen to get his beers out

SAB INTERVARSITY BEER BREWING CHALLENGE

Each year, brewing teams from universities across the country come together at SAB's Training Institute in Johannesburg to showcase their beers and taste those of their competitors. A team of BJCP-qualified judges gets together to select the winning beers, which are brewed throughout the year on each university's 50-litre system, funded by SAB.

BREWERS
Spotted on

_____
Date
_____
Signature

BEER MENU

★

G-MAN AMBER ALE (5.4%)

Johan Burger (left) and Olaf Morgenroth plan to have four beers in the final Stickman range, plus one-off brews available only at the brewery

on the market, Johan has put the pub plan on the back burner for the moment.

But there's still plenty on the cards. The maiden brew was yet to take place when I visited, and only one Stickman beer had been finalised, but there were various others in the pipeline, including an IPA, a California Common and a Vienna lager. Johan has been working on his recipes for a couple of years and now has extra input from his assistant brewer Olaf Morgenroth. Olaf was studying for his Master's degree in Wine Biotechnology when he joined the Stellenbosch intervarsity brewing team and changed boozy career path.

The two are planning to mainly keg their beers and hope to see them on tap at outlets throughout the city, as well as in the taproom overlooking the brewery. It might not have been the pretty location Johan had envisaged for a brewpub, but for many who drop into Stickman for a tour and a tasting, looking out over the steaming mash tun and bubbling kettle will be the most inspiring view they can imagine.

The Stickman team was just preparing to ferment their first brew when Beer Safari *was being researched*

DARLING
BREW

48 Caledon St, Darling; darlingbrew.co.za; 022 492 3798

(The new premises were not open at the time of researching this book so opening times are subject to change.)

When Kevin and Philippa Wood set off on a nine-month trip through Africa, there was one goal in mind – to seek out spots for the new safari company they were planning to launch. They were three days into the trip when the entire plan changed.

'We stopped in Nieu-Bethesda because I'd always wanted to see the Owl House,' explains Kevin. 'A friend had also told me to go to the brewery there to taste the kudu salami, so we dropped in. I wasn't a big beer drinker at all and when I got to this brewery and said I was there for the kudu salami and cheese platter, the guy looked at me like I was mad – I mean, who comes to a brewery and doesn't order a beer?' Although hesitant to sample 'home-made beer', the brewer – André Cilliers of Sneeuberg Brewery (page 118) – convinced Kevin to taste, telling him that if he didn't enjoy it, he wouldn't have to pay. 'I tasted the beer and it was really nice and that's basically where it started,' says Kevin.

Kevin could instantly see the Nieu-Bethesda concept working in his adopted home town of Darling and before they left the little Karoo dorp, Kevin had made a deal to buy equipment and recipes from André. 'We quickly forgot about the safari idea,' he admits. 'Suddenly it was all focused on how many beers there were available in the countries we went to. We started to notice lots of new things – from the flavour of the beer to the size of the bottle and during the trip we talked a lot about opening a microbrewery.'

BEER MENU
★

BONE CRUSHER WITBIER
(6%)

SLOW BEER (4%)

NATIVE ALE (4%)

BLACK MIST (5%)

SILVER BACK 'BLACK WIT'
(4%)

Nine months later they returned home and began to put all the theories and plans into action. André arrived from Nieu-Bethesda with the equipment – a bakkie full of plastic vats, some hops and malt extract – leaving Kevin wondering how on earth he'd ever make any money from his new brewing venture. As problems rained down, Kevin kept brewing, fastidiously churning out 100 litres of beer every day in a bid to build up considerable stock before launching his brand. Luckily he took to the whole process, falling instantly in love with the aromas emerging from the boil. 'I thought the smell of brewing was the most amazing smell from the first batch we did,' he recalls.

Today, Darling is a successful company and you'd struggle to find anyone with the vaguest interest in beer who has never tried a Slow Beer or a Bone Crusher. The brand was crucial in helping launch a craft beer culture in South Africa, but being a pioneer isn't all plain sailing. Frustrations ran high in those early days and Kevin openly admits that he was in way over his head. 'You're almost embarrassed because people think that you don't know what you're doing – and they're quite right!' he says, thinking back to those early days when he had close to 6 000 litres of beer that he couldn't sell. Capital was running low and the project was starting to look doomed when someone recommended that he chat to Chris Barnard of Boston Breweries (page 16).

'I went to meet Chris, not to see if he would brew my beer for me, but to see if he could bottle and keg it,' says Kevin. 'Imagine the situation – I've got 6 000 litres and only five kegs!' Kevin poured out his story to Chris and, by the end of the meeting, Kevin was so impressed with Boston that he decided he would like Chris to brew the beer for him after all. Kevin brought his recipes and Chris soon started to produce the beer that Kevin had been so desperately trying to create and sell.

The first pint of Darling Brew as we know it today was poured at a Stellenbosch market in May 2010. With production fully up and running, the next issue was how and where to sell it all. But when he looks back you can quickly tell that Kevin doesn't regret a moment. 'Craft brewing is everything one wants. There's adventure, innovation. People say I'm living the dream and in a way that's exactly what I'm doing. I'm able to take my corporate knowledge and my biggest passion, which is wildlife, and put it all together.' The wildlife side can be seen in the labels, which feature a South African animal hand-picked to represent each beer.

Darling continued to be contract brewed at Boston until 2015, when the initial idea of opening a brewery in Darling itself finally began to take shape. When I visited for this book, premises had been secured and a state-of-the-art, 20-hectolitre brewery was on its way. By the time you read this, you'll be able to visit Darling's taproom and sample a range of new brews alongside the classics that have become a familiar sight in South African restaurants and bars.

BREWERS
Spotted on

Date

Signature

Darling's taproom, the Slow Quarter, has become a popular watering hole in the arty Swartland town

GARAGISTA
BEER CO.

Short St, Main Rd, Riebeek Kasteel; garagista.co.za; 022 448 1125

★ OPEN MON–SAT 10AM–6PM ★

BEER MENU

★

TEARS OF THE HIPSTER APA (5%)

PALE ALE (3.7%)

Some breweries quietly open their doors and you only learn about them several months down the line, when a friend invites you over for a beer and opens a bottle whose label is unfamiliar to you. Garagista was not one of these breweries.

The advertising campaign that preceded the brewery's launch was legendary. It was even discussed on a couple of international advertising blogs. Everyone was retweeting the YouTube clip of a bunch of hipsters hijacking a craft beer truck, stopping to take selfies or tune their harmonicas as they swiped cases of the 'limited edition' brew. Some loved the campaign, others hated it. 'Making fun of hipsters is so hipster', they said. But whether they loved it or loathed it, people were talking about it and by the time Garagista opened its doors in July 2014, there was a swarm of thirsty beer fans waiting on the other side.

'We thought we'd brewed enough,' says Steve Miller, the man behind the Garagista brand, 'but we had a media launch and they pretty much wiped us

out before we'd even had the proper public launch!' Steve is not new to the beer industry, working for five years as SABMiller's Global Innovations Director. He went, as he puts it, 'from Goliath to not even David' when he 'totally fell in love with craft beer' on a trip to California in 2013. Soon afterwards, the Garagista wheels started turning, with the YouTube clip and a series of hipster-mocking ads appearing in the early months of 2014.

BREWER
Spotted on

Date

Signature

Garagista's new tasting room in Riebeek Kasteel exudes character and class

'You have to take beer seriously while you're brewing,' says Steve, 'but once it's in the bottle it's all about fun.' Local ad agency FoxP2 was chosen to put together a campaign, their brief being 'to be a bit cheeky and to get Garagista noticed'. They certainly succeeded on both points and Garagista has continued to run with the theme, releasing their 'Tears of the Hipster' American Pale Ale at the 2014 Cape Town Festival of Beer.

Steve admits that there's a heavy dose of irony in the brewery's ad campaign. 'We started off being a craft brewery based in a Woodstock art gallery. You don't really get much more hipster than that!' Since then, Garagista has moved to the equally hip country town of Riebeek Kasteel. 'Having been chased out of Woodstock by irate hipsters, we've moved to what used to be Mullineux Family Wines' cellar,' says Steve, who lives in the Riebeek Valley and was getting tired of the long commute. A brewery makes a fine addition to the boutique wineries and family olive farms for which the town is known.

The new premises are wonderful – a 240 square-metre space with wooden beams and raw brick walls. The art gallery remains, but has expanded, and the brewhouse is also exhibited for all to see. Production is up and after a short hiatus, Steve has returned to the kettles. 'I have taken back the brewing and am loving it,' he smiles, going on to discuss the experimental chocolate stout, ginger beer, and Bohemian pilsner that could soon become a part of the Garagista collection alongside the staple APA, pale ale and the apple and pomegranate ciders.

There are some other interesting things happening at Garagista, notably Steve's attempts to use UV photo purification on the beer to extend the shelf life. After leaving SABMiller, Steve worked with a company that produced the machines as an alternative to pasteurising milk and admits that thus far using the equipment with beer has been challenging. 'When it comes to beer, UV light is the evil of all evils,' he says, 'so it's certainly an interesting ride to get it right.'

Book in advance to join Steve for an entertaining 30-minute tutored tasting of the various beers and ciders on offer, and to admire the latest art hanging on the Garagista walls.

GARAGISTA BEER CO.

INDEPENDENT
BEER & SPIRITS CO.

Off the R44, Porterville; ibsco.co.za

★ OPEN BY APPOINTMENT ONLY ★

The Krugers have transformed the family citrus farm outside Porterville into a destination brewery

Although Bernard and Susan Kruger are now more focused on the beer part of their company's name, it hasn't always been that way. They joined legendary 'Stillman' Roger Jorgensen for a couple of distilling courses at his Wellington farm and were bitten by the spirits bug. At the time, Susan was studying for her MBA and was so inspired by the idea of setting up a boutique distillery that she decided to undertake a thesis looking at South Africa's craft distilling industry. 'We were looking at perhaps producing a gin or a vodka and flavouring it with oranges from the farm,' says Bernard, talking about the citrus groves on the family property.

Funnily enough, it was this interest in distilling that led them along the path towards brewing. 'After doing the course with Roger we wanted to practise our distilling,' says Susan, 'so Bernard went to the Porterville Cellar to get some distilling wine for us to practise on.' It was at the cellar that they crossed paths with Johnny King, a winemaker and hobbyist distiller-brewer. 'One thing led to another and soon we were going over to Johnny's place to watch him brew. This made us want to try it ourselves and we soon found out that we had a knack for it,' Susan continues.

This was in 2010 and a year after their first 20-litre brew Susan and Bernard started to look into the licensing process. On discovering that the micro-manufacturer's licence covered both beer and spirits, they decided to marry the two hobbies and quickly settled on the name of the company. That was the easy part – following over three years of applications, rezoning of the farm, reapplications and neighbourly disputes, the Independent Beer & Spirits Co. at last sold its first beer.

With the red tape finally manoeuvred, Bernard can now focus on perfecting his recipes and on preparing the adorable pub, The Mash Tun, for visitors. The Mash Tun is probably one of the most appealing in the country, with a quaint wood-panelled bar, a wood-fired pizza oven outside, and walls decked out with striking murals painted by artists Care & Isya from the well-respected One Love Studio, based in Muizenberg. Outdoor tables offer views over citrus groves and, further afield, the Olifant's River Mountains.

Although the focus is on the beer for now, Bernard and Susan haven't forgotten the process that inspired them to become artisanal drinks producers and intend to live up to their company's name with gin, vodka and possibly a brandy. For now, though, there are three beers featuring staunchly South African ingredients like rooibos leaves and fynbos honey. The striking labels – also designed by Care & Isya – claim a little added ingredient in each brew: the red ale lists 'adventure', the porter contains 'character' and perhaps most apt in this often sweltering part of the province, the blonde counts on a little 'summer magic'.

BEER MENU ★

PORTERVILLE PORTER (6%)

24 RIVER BLONDE SPECIALITY ALE (4.5%)

COCHOQUA RED ALE (6%)

Bernard Kruger gets ready to serve in the adorable Mash Tun pub

CEDERBERG
BREWERY

Cederberg Private Cellar, Dwarsrivier Farm; cederbergbrewery.com; 027 482 2827

★ OPEN MON–SAT 8AM–12.30PM & 2PM–5PM, SUN 9AM–12PM & 4PM–6PM ★

They say it takes a lot of beer to make a good wine and Alex Nel, one of the winemakers at the Cederberg Winery, could certainly verify this. It was while working on a Californian wine harvest in 2010 that he and his wife, fellow winemaker Tammy, really started to appreciate the nuances of beer. 'We were there for three months and we basically ended up drinking beer all of the time,' says Alex, adding that they got hooked on hops while in the USA. Having done plenty of 'research' into IPAs, Alex knew that the bold style was going to be the first he would attempt when he started homebrewing on his return to South Africa. They came back well equipped as Alex explains: 'I left most my clothes there and brought back a whole load of hops!'

Alex and Tammy moved to the Cederberg in 2011, joining resident winemaker David Nieuwoudt on the acclaimed wine farm. Gradually he convinced David that beer is just as fine as wine and the two started brewing together in David's kitchen shortly afterwards. The first major outing for the beers was at Alex and Tammy's wedding on the Cederberg farm in 2013. Then, in late 2014, with little fanfare, Cederberg Brewery launched their first two ales –

Tasters of the Boggom Blonde Ale

BEER
MENU

★

BOGGOM
BLONDE ALE (4.5%)

VOERTSEK INDIA
PALE ALE (6%)

BREWER
Spotted on

Date

Signature

Boggom, a blonde ale, and Voertsek, an IPA. The beers are named for two characters, generally presumed to be baboons, that live, play and eventually die together in a poem by local poet C. Louis Leipoldt. Like the baboons, the beers are designed to be inseparable and Alex says that the idea is to always buy the beer in pairs.

Much has gone into the *Boggom en Voertsek* connection. The poem was later turned into a song by South African folk singer David Kramer, who positioned the two baboon buddies in an old Pontiac. Alex and David successfully got their hands on a delightful old car in Durban and schlepped it along the winding dirt roads to one of South Africa's highest brewery (at 1 036 m above sea level). It will become a fixture at beer festivals and the plan is to use the Pontiac for keg deliveries. If you see it out and about, approach the owners and you might just get a sample beer. Either that or a baboon might leap out and steal your sandwiches.

Back at the brewery, a taproom was in progress to ensure that you're guaranteed spectacular views with your quirkily named brews. When David's grandfather, Oom Pollie, first started producing wine high in the Cederberg, the critics were sceptical. Today, the winery is revered for its crisp sauvignon blancs and many of its bottles are adorned with gold medals. With a bit of luck – and a bit of mountain water to use as brewing liquor – the beer will enjoy a similar level of notoriety.

Alex Nel is enjoying the new challenge of brewing after many years producing wine

CEDER
BREW

Kromrivier, Cederberg; cederbrew.co.za; 027 482 2807

★ OPEN MON-SAT 8AM-6PM, SUN 8AM-12PM & 2PM-6PM ★

BREWERS
Spotted on

Date

Signature

*'We calm each other down when we're stressed' say
Melanie (left) and Tania Nieuwoudt*

'It seems that you learn to drink beer in Europe,' says Tania Nieuwoudt, smiling. She's referring to the fact that she only really started enjoying beer while studying for her Master's degree in Sweden, and that older sister, Melanie, was also converted to beer overseas. 'I never really drank beer while I was studying for my undergrad,' admits Melanie, 'but then I went to the Netherlands for part of my Master's and there I really had no choice as to what to drink!'

Melanie might have learnt to drink in Europe, but it was back in South Africa that she learnt to brew. And when she learnt, it was not the leisurely, gradual process that most beginner brewers enjoy. It was a seriously intensive learning curve that formed the basis of her PhD. 'I was studying cereal science,' she explains. 'I was looking at how the raw material, barley, affects the end product, particularly with regard to shelf life and foam stability.' For the research to be statistically viable, Melanie had to brew a lot of beer – and quickly. Fetching gallons of water from the Newlands Spring in Cape Town, she brewed her first dozen batches of beer within seven days on the engineering department's brewhouse – a system funded by SAB for the Intervarsity Beer Brewing Challenge (page 48).

Tania had actually started brewing just before Melanie's research began, albeit on a slightly more relaxed timetable, so adding a microbrewery to the guest farm that their family has lived on for the past seven generations seemed to make perfect sense. By May 2014, the brewery that Melanie had designed was ready, constructed by a Stellenbosch steel company.

BEER MENU

★

THE CHUBBYHEAD
DRY STOUT (4%)

THE CATFISH ALE (5%)

THE SANDFISH WEISS (5%)

JAN PAMPOEN SPICY
PUMPKIN ALE (4%)

THE YELLOWFISH LAGER
(5%)

The first beer they brewed was the Catfish Ale, based on the recipe that Melanie had brewed and brewed and brewed again for her research. Together they worked on recipes for the other beers, counting on support from American homebrewing forums and from each other.

Ceder Brew had a quiet, largely unannounced launch, with the first beers being sold to guests staying on the farm. A following soon started to develop and the girls could see a clear favourite among their beers. 'The stout was selling well, so we decided to enter it in the 2014 National Craft Brewers Championship,' says Melanie. Entering the beer was easier said than done, thanks to the farm's remote location. 'Our beers ended up in Newtown, Calvinia, rather than Newtown, Johannesburg!' laughs Tania. 'It was two days before the deadline when we had the case rerouted. The organisers said that they'd call when the beer arrived and we never got a phone call, so we thought it had never arrived.' Imagine their surprise then, a couple of weeks later, when a call came that told them their beer had not only arrived, but during judging it had been voted in the top 10 beers nationwide. Quite the accolade for a brewery that had only been open for a matter of months.

The remoteness of the farm is also what gives the brewery extra appeal. Nestled alongside the Krom River, far from any towns, villages or paved roads, it's a very peaceful place for a pint. The river supplies the beer names – or at least the endemic fish within it do – as well as swimming opportunities for guests. With accommodation on-site and views that can only properly be described with clichés like 'breathtaking' and 'awe-inspiring', this really is one of the prettiest places to drink a beer in the country.

WILD CLOVER
BREWERY

R304, Stellenbosch; wildcloverbrewery.co.za; 021 865 2248

★ OPEN SAT-SUN 11AM-5PM ★

Beer before wine makes you feel fine, they say, but for Ampie Kruger, opting for wine first has also worked out pretty well – making it that is. An accomplished garagiste winemaker, Ampie's Notre Rêve winery put out its first vintage in 2007 – the year he was also introduced to the hobby of homebrewing. It had been a long time coming for Ampie, who experimented with kit beers while at university. 'I was drinking beer like hell as a student,' he says, 'but after a while I just couldn't drink it anymore. Then whenever I went to England, the beer was fantastic.'

In 2007, Ampie hosted a braai to which a friend brought a batch of homebrew. 'I tasted it and said, "yes, this is the beer that I remember from the UK; this is what I can drink" and I asked how to make it.' Ampie soon fell in love with the process and introduced his friend Karel Coetzee to the hobby, sealing Ampie's fate. 'I had my reservations about homebrewing,' admits Karel, who became a discerning beer drinker during a six-year stint living in Chicago, 'but I realised that this was good stuff and in 2009 I told him the beer was good enough to put onto

FIVE FAMILY-FRIENDLY BREWERIES

1. Wild Clover Brewery (Western Cape)
2. Emerald Vale Brewing Company (Eastern Cape)
3. Oakes Brewhouse (Gauteng)
4. Saggy Stone Brewing Co. (Western Cape)
5. Honingklip Brewery (Western Cape)

Ampie plans to move the brewery to a larger building soon

Ampie Kruger pours tasters in the Wild Clover pub

The English Brown Ale is one of Wild Clover's most popular brews

the market.' The two decided to embark on a commercial microbrewery together. Ampie was already looking for a spot for his winery, feeling the time was right to move out of his garage. That's when he happened upon Wild Clover Farm in the northern reaches of Stellenbosch.

Plans to upgrade from the 30-litre homebrew system were put into place, though all did not run smoothly with the first 300-litre brew. 'It was farcical,' Karel laughs, going on to describe the gas accident that nearly saw them burning the brewery's newfound home to the ground and the hole in Karel's hand – the 'blood all over the place'. And then there was the issue of a 300-litre batch of undrinkable beer. 'You think it will be easy to scale things up 10 times,' says Ampie. 'Wow, what a wake-up call that was!' Fluctuating mash temperatures meant the starch converted to the wrong type of sugar so although it fermented, Ampie admits he didn't finish a single glass.

Luckily, things picked up quickly and since Wild Clover launched in 2012, it has become a popular stop on the Western Cape brew route, particularly for families. For kids there are mini bikes to play on, farm animals to admire and, if they're not exciting enough, wildlife drives to see zebra, giraffe and antelope are on offer in the adjoining game camp. For grown-ups there's clay pigeon shooting and archery, there are brewing courses offered once a month and the annual Hops Harvest Festival held each

May. There are also some very exciting expansion plans for the brewery, which will likely be in operation by the time you read this. 'At the moment we don't have a problem selling our beer,' says Ampie, 'but we do have a problem producing enough to meet demand. In time, that might change and that's going to be a whole new interesting challenge...'

WAGON TRAIL
BREWING CO.

Off Simondium Rd, Klapmuts; anura.co.za; 021 875 5360

★ OPEN TUE-SUN 9AM-4.30PM, WED & SAT 6.30PM-9.30PM ★

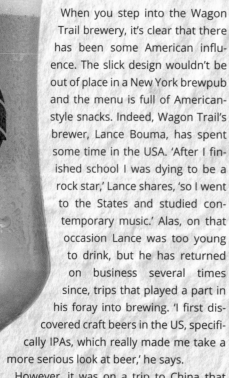

When you step into the Wagon Trail brewery, it's clear that there has been some American influence. The slick design wouldn't be out of place in a New York brewpub and the menu is full of American-style snacks. Indeed, Wagon Trail's brewer, Lance Bouma, has spent some time in the USA. 'After I finished school I was dying to be a rock star,' Lance shares, 'so I went to the States and studied contemporary music.' Alas, on that occasion Lance was too young to drink, but he has returned on business several times since, trips that played a part in his foray into brewing. 'I first discovered craft beers in the US, specifically IPAs, which really made me take a more serious look at beer,' he says.

However, it was on a trip to China that Lance really got interested in the idea of brewing. He had been making wine on the family-owned farm, Anura, since 2006,

a role that often took him overseas. In 2012 he was attending a wine exhibition in Shanghai when he stumbled across a stand showcasing not wine equipment, but mash tuns, kettles, lauter tuns and conical fermenters. A year later the brewhouse had been ordered and Lance suddenly realised they needed somewhere to put it. 'We started renovating the function hall, but it was a big job and the equipment arrived in the interim. For my first few brews it was basically still a building site!'

Lance really launched himself into the deep end with beer, his first ever brew being on the imported 500-litre system. And unlike most first-time brewers, who tackle something like a blonde or a pale ale, Lance started with what can be a very difficult style to brew – a light lager. Lots of reading followed and, over the next few months, Lance gradually developed the recipes for Wagon Trail's core range.

The brewery name has historical roots and the family still has the farm's old title deeds stating that ox wagons must be allowed access through what is now Anura as they made their way from Cape Town's harbour to present-day Franschhoek. These days, you're more likely to want to stop for a while than drive right by. The atmospheric brewpub serves not

BEER MENU

★

BAVARIAN WEISS (4%)

OXBLOOD AMBER ALE (5%)

WAGON TRAIL
PALE ALE (4.5%)

LONG ROAD LAGER (4%)

'I just kind of fell into brewing,' says Lance Bouma

only beer-perfect dishes like chicken wings and ribs, there are also platters piled with cheese, bread and charcuterie, all made on the premises.

The brewery launched in late October and over the Christmas season the Wagon Trail team almost failed to organise the proverbial piss-up. 'We very nearly ran out of beer,' Lance says sheepishly. 'I had no idea just how big the demand would be.' Lance plans to keep his beer approachable and 'not too left field' and it seems he made the right call – the Long Road Lager is their biggest selling beer. That said, Lance does want to branch out into bolder beers and he knows exactly what he wants to brew – a West Coast-style IPA to complete the American offering.

The brewpub hosts regular live music – a perfect partner for the beers and snack platters

CAPE BREWING CO.

Suid-Agter Paarl Rd, Paarl; capebrewing.co.za; 021 863 2270

★ OPEN DAILY 10AM–5PM ★

'I'm a strong believer that beer isn't made by a brewer,' says Wolfgang Koedel, 'it's made by a team.' This emphasis on teamwork, on every cog being as important as the next, is clearly a crucial part of the Cape Brewing Co. (CBC) philosophy. That said, of course, the brewing team does have an outstanding leader. Originally hailing from Bavaria, Wolfgang has 30 years of brewing experience under his belt; he's opened breweries on three continents and is one of very few qualified master brewers on the South African microbrewing scene. He's also utterly humble about the whole thing and prides himself on the fact that anyone coming to him for help will find the advice they seek.

For Wolfgang it all started in southern Germany. 'I wanted to study chemistry, but my father sent me off to get a job in a brewery,' he tells, a twinkle in his eye as he pauses for a sip of his acclaimed German pilsner. 'Each worker at the brewery, regardless of their position, got to take home 140 litres of beer a month, so my father had his

reasons! I come from a long chain of beer lovers, so it was decided that someone in the family had to actually produce beer.' It turned out not to be such a hardship – 'you obviously fall in love with it,' Wolfgang declares. Three decades later, he is still in love with the process and he shares that love and passion with the CBC team – and anyone who wanders in to taste a beer or ask a question about protein rests or mashing temperatures.

Friendly tutored tastings take place in CBC's 'tasting pods'

Michael Smith is CBC's chief keg operator

Today, CBC is one of South Africa's largest and most successful breweries, but getting this far didn't come easily – or quickly. 'You could say that the project took a long time in the secondary fermentation stage,' says Andy Kung, the chief operations officer at Spice Route, the farm that CBC shares with a host of other artisanal enterprises. Andy first thought up the idea to add a brewery several years ago, along with Charles Back, wine guru and owner of Spice Route and neighbouring Fairview. 'The question was, "what else can you do with yeast?" – we already had bread, wine and cheese, so beer was a natural addition,' says Andy. From the get-go, Andy and Charles knew exactly who they wanted as their brewmaster, but at the time Wolfgang was running the brew kettles at the Paulaner brewpub at the V&A Waterfront. Meanwhile, things were starting to take shape for what would become the Cape Brewing Co. Charles

was spending time with old friend Hendrik Dunge, managing director at Swedish brewery Åbro, when the subject of a collaboration came up. 'Hendrik had the visionary foresight to say yes,' Andy continues. 'This is what really sparked off the whole project. Without Åbro there would be no brewery.'

The timing was exquisite. No sooner had Hendrik agreed to come to the table than word got out – Paulaner had decided to close their Cape Town branch. 'They phoned me two days after Paulaner closed,' remembers Wolfgang. 'I'm a very loyal person and I never would have gone with them otherwise. I considered moving back to Asia to continue with Paulaner, but I was not done with South Africa yet.' Yet it wasn't simple to persuade Wolfgang to join the CBC team. 'They asked me if I was interested and I said no. Then Hendrik asked, "can I meet you for a beer?", so I told him sure – if you're buying. Looking back I think I was quite cocky!' Cocky is not a word many would use to describe Wolfgang, who quickly came around to the idea, impressed with Hendrik's style.

Wolfgang and Andy are effusive about the Swedish brewery that owns a stake in CBC. 'Their commitment and passion for CBC – I've never seen anything like it,' Andy admits. 'I was always looking for the catch, but for them it was a once-in-a-lifetime chance to build a brewery from scratch.' Wolfgang has likewise been humbled not only by Åbro's support, but also by the

BIG 5 PINT

CBC PILSNER

It's tough to choose just one beer from the CBC range, since they're all pretty much flawless, but the pilsner is outstanding and certainly the best example brewed in South Africa. On first entry, this medium-bodied lager has a hint of grainy sweetness, not unlike chewing on a handful of yet-to-be-mashed malt. But on sipping, the noble hops shine through, leaving a refreshing, bitter finish that just keeps you coming back for more.

FIVE SOUTH AFRICAN WEISSBIERS TO TRACK DOWN AND TASTE

1. CBC Amber Weiss (Western Cape)
2. Brauhaus am Damm Weizen (North West)
3. That Brewing Co. Good AdWeiss (KwaZulu-Natal)
4. Robertson Classic Weissbier (Western Cape)
5. Zebonkey Weiss (Coming soon..., Western Cape)

Wolfgang Koedel is fastidious about checking the beer at every stage of the process

level of autonomy they've afforded the South African team. 'There is so much trust,' he says. 'It's like they parked this Ferrari, gave us the key and didn't even check if we had a driver's licence! So we, of course, are making sure we don't disappoint!'

They haven't. Since opening, the brewery has expanded rapidly, their range of beers being distributed around the country and receiving high praise pretty much wherever they are sipped. The core range speaks of Wolfgang's German roots, but the local hankering for hops has encouraged the team to add an IPA and an imperial IPA to the permanent line-up. There will be plenty of brewer's edition beers coming in the future, with recipes and ideas being very much a group effort.

The sense of community at CBC is something that echoes around Spice Route, where you'll find handmade chocolate and charcuterie, wine tasting and tea tasting, a distillery, two restaurants and a farm shop selling homemade preserves. 'I hear a lot of people say, "you can feel the craft here", which is just the best compliment you can get,' beams Wolfgang, adding that there is a 'glass approach' to everything that happens on the farm, intended to make every visitor feel like a member of the craft family.

When you visit Spice Route, think of it as the extended family you wish you had. Instead of clock-watching and wondering when you can politely head home, you can happily spend a whole day sampling salami, sipping grappa, learning how chocolate is made, stopping for tea and, of course, enjoying a pint or two of CBC's flawlessly made brews.

BEER MENU
★

PILSNER (5.2%)

CAPE OF GOOD HOPS
IMPERIAL IPA (7.5%)

MANDARINA BAVARIA IPA
(6.5%)

AMBER WEISS (5.4%)

LAGER (5.1%)

KRYSTAL WEISS (5%)

NDLOVU
BREWERY

3 Excelsior Rd, Franschhoek; ndlovubrewery.com; 021 876 4000

★ OPEN BY APPOINTMENT ONLY ★

Rob Armstrong's explanation for just how Ndlovu Brewery came to be is as simple as it is logical: 'I met Wayne over a beer at the Elephant and Barrel in Franschhoek about a decade ago. We've been talking about setting up a brewery ever since.' But it wasn't until 2013 that Rob and brewing partner Wayne Lister-James finally got around to brewing their first batch. They launched later that same year at the Cape Town Festival of Beer with an experimental witbier and a lager that would become their signature brew.

It wasn't a bog-standard lager, though. In fact, very few of Ndlovu's beers are run-of-the-mill. The lager they launched with had been fermented – not aged, actually fermented – in a wine barrel, giving it a unique and, for most, acquired taste. The idea comes from Rob's main profession as winemaker at Haut Espoir, the Franschhoek vineyard owned by his mother. Unusual and experimental brews have become something of a regular happening at Ndlovu. In their first year of business, they also produced a

Brewed in the Franschhoek winelands, Ndlovu shares its space with the Haut Espoir winery

Ndlovu's lager is, unusually, fermented in a wine barrel

beer-wine hybrid made up of 50 per cent lager wort and 50 per cent chardonnay must, fermented with a concoction of beer and wine yeasts. They also teamed up with Chris Erasmus, chef and owner at new Franschhoek restaurant Foliage, to produce three slightly wacky brews – a rooibos lager, a weiss featuring suikerbossie flowers picked on Rob's family farm and, most bizarrely of all, a chocolaty stout fermented with fresh mushrooms.

The brewery is a simple system only a little larger than the average homebrewer's setup. It sits in Rob's wine cellar, though there are plans to expand and move the brewhouse to its own building with views of the Franschhoek Mountains. Rob talks about the deck they'd like to construct where visitors could enjoy the brews, and his eyes light up almost as much as they do when he talks about the experimental beers he likes to try out. And it is indeed a wonderful view, which, in part, is the reason for the brewery's name. Franschhoek was originally known as Olifantshoek, so named for the elephants that crossed the mountains to calve in the valley. Ndlovu – Zulu for elephant – sits opposite the mountain where the Franschhoek

Pass – once one of the elephant trails – snakes between the verdant mountains. And if you ask one of the brewers, they'll also point out the mountain that's even slightly shaped like a pachyderm.

And, of course, the name might, in part, have something to do with the pub where the whole idea was born. Alas, Ndlovu's beers are not found behind the bar there today, but if you hop from restaurant to restaurant on Franschhoek's main road, you certainly will find a lager that's been fermented in wood, a weissbier brewed with flowers, or even a dark beer infused with something you might never have expected to find in a fermenter – mushrooms.

SIR THOMAS
BREWING CO.

Summerhill Wine Farm, R44, Stellenbosch; sirthomasbrew.com; 021 200 2522

★ OPEN BY APPOINTMENT ONLY ★

Sometimes we sail through life without questioning some of the most commonplace things around us. So one day, while they were out surfing, floating around waiting for a wave, Braam Rademeyer and Marius Malan got to talking. 'Hey, do you know how to make beer?' Braam asked. Marius conceded that he did not and so the two set out to find the answer.

It started as most homebrew setups do – a cooler box mash tun, a pot and a couple of plastic buckets in the shed. But Braam and Marius quickly started talking about selling their beer and looked into applying for a licence in their home town, Pringle Bay. Their shared passion for the seaside village is evident, but, alas, their fellow residents did not share their dream of setting up a microbrewery and the licence application was blocked. Unperturbed, Marius and Braam moved their operation to the Winelands, but they did manage to take a little of Pringle Bay along with them.

'We still wanted to do something for the town,' says Braam. 'We love Pringle Bay, so our brewery, as well as some of the beers, have names taken from the town.' The brewery was named for Thomas Pringle, the royal navy officer for whom the town was named. The logo also features a stylised baboon, for the marauding primates are a common sight in Pringle Bay.

The brewery is now positioned on the Summerhill Wine Farm just north of Stellenbosch and the Sir Thomas team hope to get a restaurant and tasting room up and running alongside the brewhouse. The

Labels ready to affix to Fokofpolisiekar's bottles

beer range was likewise being tweaked and expanded, with plans to try some seasonal brews, including a barrel-aged stout. They're also brewing a beer for Afrikaans alternative rock band Fokofpolisiekar, a blonde ale they call Dag Dronk, and there are plans to do three more bespoke brews for the band.

The brewery didn't end up being quite where Braam and Marius wanted it to be, but they're both happy with how things turned out. 'It worked out better this way,' says Marius, referring to the fact that their spot on a major road in the Winelands means they'll get a lot more passing traffic. 'The commute sucks, but we really don't want to move away from Pringle Bay.'

BEER MENU ★

ROOI BAARD AFRICAN TEA-INFUSED AMBER ALE (5%)

BREWERS' BLONDE (4%)

HANGKLIP ALE (5%)

BEYOND THE BREWERY:
FIVE PLACES TO FIND CRAFT BEER IN THE WESTERN CAPE

1. Craft Wheat and Hops
Andringa St, Stellenbosch; 021 882 8069
Right in the heart of Stellenbosch, Craft largely offers beers from the Winelands and Cape Town – 16 on tap and a similar number in bottles. There's a light menu featuring open sandwiches and tapas.

2. The Thirsty Scarecrow
Cnr R44 & Annandale Rd, Stellenbosch; 021 881 3444
There's a good range of local and international beers on tap at this farmstall, plus Red Crow, a strawberry-flavoured beverage that can be sipped overlooking the strawberry fields.

3. Zucchini
Timberlake Organic Village, N2 between Wilderness & Sedgefield; zucchini.co.za; 044 882 1240
With an emphasis on local and organic produce, Zucchini seems the perfect place to serve a range of craft beers. Between Wilderness and Sedgefield, it's an extremely family-friendly spot with a focus on beers from the Garden Route and Klein Karoo.

4. Franschhoek Station Pub & Grill
4 Main Rd, Franschhoek; franschhoekstationpub.co.za; 021 876 3938
Situated in the old station building, there are more than a dozen local and imported beers on tap, plus pizzas and classic pub grub on the menu.

5. Reuben's
19 Huguenot Rd, Franschhoek; reubens.co.za; 021 876 3772
The flagship restaurant for celebrity chef Reuben Riffel has an excellent range of craft beer from home and abroad. Try your hand at pairing the beers with some of the upmarket bistro dishes on offer.

WILD BEAST
BREWING CO.

Remhoogte Wine Estate, R44, Stellenbosch; wildbeastbeer.com; 082 858 8399

★ OPEN MON–FRI 9AM–4.30PM, SAT 10AM–3.30PM ★

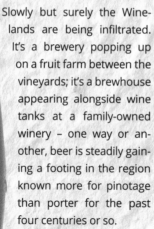

Slowly but surely the Winelands are being infiltrated. It's a brewery popping up on a fruit farm between the vineyards; it's a brewhouse appearing alongside wine tanks at a family-owned winery – one way or another, beer is steadily gaining a footing in the region known more for pinotage than porter for the past four centuries or so.

But this coming together of grape and grain is not a new thing, nor is it unique to South Africa. There are many regions where pockets of microbreweries appear on the map amid wineries, and it's really not a surprise. Winemaking is thirsty work and beer just hits the spot better on a hot harvest day than a glass of wooded cabernet. And where there is wine, there is generally a cuisine scene; where there is fine cuisine, there are foodies – and where there are foodies, there is a desire to drink quality, full-flavoured beer.

Chris Boustred has found this out for himself. After studying oenology and viticulture at Stellenbosch University, Chris spent time in Australia and discovered that while Margaret River is best known for wine, there is a solid craft beer scene popping up between the vines. He also joined a harvest in California – a hub for hopheads that is becoming as famous for its IPAs as for its zinfandels. Chris is the winemaker at Remhoogte, the 19th-century farm that his family bought in 1993. He is also the brewer at the farm's latest addition, Wild Beast Brewing Co.

Chris runs the brewery with his brother, whose introduction to the beer world was a little different. With a background in marketing, Rob worked on the sales team for foreign lager giants Carlsberg and Corona, and later as an account manager for SAB. He had an early introduction to the Cape's craft beer scene, meeting Ross McCulloch from Jack Black (page 110) in the days when Ross had just started bottling his beer.

Chris began brewing in 2010 and soon afterwards the brothers decided to open their own brewery on the farm. The 550-litre brewhouse sits in the

BEER MENU

★

AMBER ALE (5%)

BLONDE ALE (5%)

There is room for a third Wild Beast beer at the tasting room – watch this space

farm's oldest building, a former stable. Upgrades are ongoing and seasonal brews are in the pipeline, but for the moment Chris and Rob produce just two ales under the Wild Beast banner. The name comes from the farm's wildebeest, named Mumsy and Beth for Chris and Rob's grandmother and her friend. 'They're two oldish ladies and we see a lot of similarities,' says Chris with a glint in his eye. Mumsy and Beth graze in a small game camp overlooked by the tasting room, where you can sit and sip beer – or wine if you're so inclined – and watch zebra, springbok and even a quagga-cross, with the backdrop of the Simonsberg, Jonkershoek, Stellenbosch and Helderberg Mountains completing the picture.

Traditionally, wineries seem to have always occupied the prettiest parts of their province or state, and Remhoogte is no exception. Luckily for aficionados of ale, breweries are muscling their way in, ensuring that cerevisaphiles, too, can enjoy a pretty panorama with their chosen tipple.

BREWERS
Spotted on
_____
Date
_____
Signature

Chris (left) and Rob Boustred brew together on the family's wine farm near Stellenbosch

WILD BEAST BREWING CO.

LILYPATRICK
CRAFT BREWERY

Packham Farm, Klapmuts Rd, Stellenbosch; 079 136 1458

★ OPEN WED, FRI & SAT 11AM–7PM ★

Lilypatrick's quartet of beers are all malt-forward ales

BEER MENU

★

MILK CHOCOLATE STOUT (6%)

TRACTOR SHED
BROWN ALE (4%)

HOOLIE'S IRISH RED ALE (4.5%)

DOG FREE PALE ALE (4%)

There is an Irish influence behind the Lilypatrick Craft Brewery, though not quite in the way you might think. 'It was an Irish guy who got me into brewing about five or six years back,' says Frank Geraghty, though he goes on to explain that the brewery's name is not taken from some Irish borough known for its stout, or from his favourite brewery on the Emerald Isle. The name actually has its roots far closer to home, named for the first daughter of Frank's brewing partner 'Boeta' de Koker and Frank's first son.

The two friends had literally just started their venture when I visited. In fact, they were actually putting up the sign at the farm's entrance just as I pulled off the road. The 20-hectare property belongs to Frank's in-laws and until recently was a functioning plum farm, but the fruit is no longer financially viable, so Frank was looking for ways to breathe new life into the place.

The idea began as many beer-related ones do, over a few homebrews at a braai. Then, in 2013, Frank's brown ale took the top spot at a local homebrewing competition. The brew he refers to as 'the beer that made me give up teaching' joins three more in the core Lilypatrick range, including a chocolaty stout that is another nod towards his

Irish influences, and the oddly named Dog Free Pale Ale. The name refers to a batch that soured in the fermenter when an errant dog hair found its way in. This led to the brewery becoming a strictly 'dog-free' zone. And Frank is quick to add, grinning, that 'it doesn't mean that the other beers do contain anything dog-related!'

With financial backing from his brother, Justin, Frank took a rather large leap of faith and in August 2014, before the brewery was anywhere close to functioning, he left his job as a high school history teacher to focus full-time on getting the beer in order. The idea is not just to serve beer, but to turn the old plum packing sheds into a permanent artisanal food market. With a local baker already on board, Frank and Boeta would like to see a coffee roaster, a cheesery and a charcuterie fill up the remaining spots on the farm. With both partners having young children, there's sure to be an emphasis on this being a family-friendly way to spend a day.

The Lilypatrick team are oozing with enthusiasm for their new venture and the instantly likable Frank is well known in the area for his zeal for beer, described by a neighbouring brewer as 'one of the most passionate beer guys I know'.

STELLENBRAU

The Woodmill, Vredenburg Rd, Stellenbosch; stellenbrau.co.za; 021 883 3622

★ OPEN MON-FRI 10AM-6PM, SAT 11AM-3PM ★

It's no exaggeration to say that when Deon Engelbrecht first tasted Luyt Lager, he enjoyed it so much he bought the brewery. The brewery wasn't even for sale at the time, yet just 18 months after his first sip, the equipment and recipes were enjoying a new home in Stellenbosch.

The initial plan was to brew under licence from the long-established Ballito-based brewery, but within months the plans changed and Deon was offered the chance to buy the brewery outright. He snapped it up and began the preparations to move both the extensive brewing equipment – and his entire life – to the Cape Winelands. By February 2012 the brewery was installed, along with assistant brewer Nosh Cingo, who was so passionate about his job that he uprooted to continue brewing in the Cape.

Those joining a Stellenbrau tour can sample the beers in the stylish tasting room afterwards

The entire Stellenbrau brewery was transplanted from KwaZulu-Natal

The head brewer, though, is a new addition to the team. After interviewing a number of established commercial brewers, Deon and his interview panel met Stephen de Jager. Stephen had been homebrewing for 15 years, but it wasn't just his obvious passion for beer that wowed his prospective employer – there wasn't a single technical question that they threw at him that Stephen couldn't answer. 'I was basically waiting 12 years for this job,' says Stephen, who first started brewing at university. 'The whole thing actually started way back when I was in standard six,' he remembers, his eyes lighting up at the chance to discuss his passion. 'I walked past a chemist and saw a "make your own beer" kit. I told my dad I wanted it and he said, "there is no chance in hell, your mother would kill me!"' But at the first opportunity Stephen started to brew, shunning commercial kits in favour of a 200-litre stainless-steel setup that he made himself. From the first brew, he knew it was what he wanted to be doing with his life.

Stellenbrau completed its first brew in June 2012 and, since then, three more beers have been added to the menu. But it is the Craven Craft Lager that remains Stellenbrau's biggest seller, a beer based heavily upon the recipe that caused Deon to change his whole life.

BEER MENU
★

JONKER'S WEISS (4.5%)

CRAVEN CRAFT LAGER
(4.5%)

ALUMNI ALE
(4.5%)

GOVERNOR'S RED
LAGER (4.5%)

TRIGGERFISH

BREWING

Paardevlei, De Beers Ave, Somerset West; triggerfishbrewing.co.za; 021 851 5861

★ OPEN MON–THU 12PM–7PM, FRI 12PM–9PM, SAT 12PM–5PM ★

BEER MENU

★

HAMMERHEAD IPA (6.2%)

TITAN IMPERIAL IPA (8%)

BONITO BUCHU BLONDE (4.2%)

EMPOWERED STOUT (5.2%)

OCEAN POTION APA (5%)

SOUTHERN RIGHT SOUTH AFRICAN ALE (5.2%)

ROMAN RED (5.2%)

SWEETLIPS BLONDE ALE (4.2%)

PICASSO PILS (5%)

BLACK MARLIN RUSSIAN IMPERIAL STOUT (10%)

There was definitely something in the water in Eric van Heerden's year at varsity. No fewer than four of South Africa's craft breweries were set up by graduates of the same year at the University of Pretoria – one of which is Triggerfish in Somerset West. In fact, it was a couple of Eric's university pals who introduced him to the idea of homebrewing – André de Beer of The Cockpit Brewhouse (page 166) and Stephan Meyer of Clarens Brewery (page 210). '

After a few months of lengthy phone calls with his brewing buddies up north, Eric brewed his first batch in 2007, but it was a move to the USA a year later that would see Eric's homebrewing take off. He regularly entered his beers for critique at meetings of the local homebrew club, learning from the club's highly knowledgeable and very experienced members.

When Eric returned to the Western Cape in July 2010, he had a year of intensive brewing behind him and the decision to start up a microbrewery didn't take long to reach, thanks in part to a nudge from his old friend Stephan. 'He is the ultimate optimist and remembers only the good,' Eric smiles. 'He was the one who convinced me to go into it commercially.' The decision was sealed when Eric took some of his American-brewed beers for tasting at

The old dynamite factory has turned out to make a great base for a brewery

the local homebrewers' club, the SouthYeasters, and they met with instant approval.

Equipment was upgraded and, in late 2010, Eric launched his beers at a Stellenbosch market to instant acclaim. Premises were sought, though costs prohibited Eric from finding what he considered the perfect location, instead setting up the brewery at an old dynamite factory outside Somerset West. 'I was still actively looking for premises for a taproom,' says Eric, 'because I was behind a security gate in the middle of nowhere and nobody knew where it was!' These days, though, this seemingly bizarre location has become a bustling beer garden on weekends, with a devout local following filling the outside tables to sip Eric's latest experimental brew with a view of the Hottentots-Holland Mountains.

Eric has become well known for his innovative beers and the sizable beer menu, which includes barrel-aged stouts, experimental sour ales, seriously high IBU beers and collaborations with both local winemakers and other craft brewers. The core range bears the oceanic names with which Eric launched his brand – names that come from his passion for scuba diving. Eric always knew that his brewery would be named for some form of ocean life, but pinning down a specific sea creature ended up being a very last-minute decision. 'I'd been trying to think of a name for six months,' he recollects, 'but in the end we came up with it the night before I handed in my licensing application! They needed a name on the form so we had to make the decision.' It was, in part, homage to Eric's brewing hero, Sam Calagione of Dogfish Head Brewery in the USA, but the final choice came from something that Eric's wife, scuba instructor Wilna, commented on. 'She said that when she took students on a dive, the one fish they always asked about was the clown triggerfish,' says Eric, and so the striking and instantly memorable fish became the name of the brewery and its gold-and-black markings the company logo.

Today, Eric concentrates on recipe development and organising the many collaborative brews – including one with the Global Association of Craft Beer Brewers, which saw breweries in seven countries following the same recipe. The day-to-day brewing is now overseen by James Beyile, who has been a part of the Triggerfish family since 2011. Along with Kuda Kuwanda, he keeps Triggerfish ticking over while Eric works out how to squeeze in a few extra IBUs, infuse another South African herb, or source a barrel in which to age his latest experimental ale.

Triggerfish has one of the longest beer menus of any brewpub in the country

BREWER
Spotted on

Date

Signature

RED SKY
BREW

Unit 2, 9 Industria Rd, Gordon's Bay; redskybrew.co.za; 079 502 1531

★ OPEN BY APPOINTMENT ONLY ★

BREWER
Spotted on
_____
Date
_____
Signature

'It's more of a lifestyle choice than anything else,' says Mark Goldsworthy of his decision to leave the nine-to-five grind and set up his own business. Mark is a member of the increasing army of wine-maker defectors choosing to swap grapevines for hopvines. In 2013, he ditched a Stellenbosch cellar in favour of a garage in Gordon's Bay, where he and his wife Kelly opened a small-scale brewery.

Red Sky kegs wait to be filled with Amber Ale and the particularly popular Robust Porter

There was no great epiphany, no life-changing moment that led Mark to start brewing. His introduction to homebrewing was simple and perfectly logical – he spotted a beer kit at a local wine equipment store and was instantly intrigued. As is generally the case, the kit morphed into an all-grain setup and when Mark's maiden all-grain brew – interestingly a pilsner – won one of the monthly people's choice awards at a Cape Town homebrew club meeting, Mark started to consider the possibility of opening his own brewery.

While away on holiday, no doubt mourning the impending and inevitable return to work, the decision was made. The Goldsworthys would launch their own microbrewery and call it Red Sky Brew. The branding harks back to an earlier era in Mark and Kelly's relationship, when they resided at opposite ends of the country. Planes obviously played a big part in keeping them together and they wanted to honour that in their first business together. The name came to them as they sipped one of Mark's earlier brews, while watching the setting sun gradually turn the sky several shades of crimson.

While awaiting their licence, Mark and Kelly started selling homebrewing supplies and offering

brewing courses, and while the latter have largely fallen away save for the occasional group booking, the Goldsworthys still supply local homebrewers with hops, grain and equipment. The company – brewing, teaching, supplying – sits under the banner of The Winemakers Club, a nod to the fact that those who produce wine tend to drink a lot of beer.

Red Sky's range of beers has gradually expanded and includes a couple of innovative offerings. Goshawk is South Africa's first gluten-free beer, brewed with a combination of malted maize and sorghum in lieu of barley. With the appearance of a witbier and a slightly sour taste from the sorghum, it's something of an acquired taste, though it has gained a loyal following. In 2014, Mark teamed up with winemaker Beyers Truter, renowned for his pinotage vintages, to create Pinotale, a beer-wine hybrid using must from that most South African of grapes, added to the Warhawk Red Ale at the final stage of fermentation.

Since Red Sky took off, business has boomed, with sales in December multiplying ten-fold from 2013 to 2014. Mark says he's loved the journey so far, but he's also planning a diversion. A spot of distilling is on the cards and now that the beers are established, The Winemakers Club will also be getting back to its roots, with a maiden wine vintage expected soon.

FIVE SOUTH AFRICAN STOUTS AND PORTERS TO TRACK DOWN AND TASTE

1. Dog and Fig Stewige Stout (Free State)
2. Apollo Stout (Western Cape)
3. Red Sky Vampire Robust Porter (Western Cape)
4. Doctrine Brewing Darker Vision Russian Imperial Stout (KwaZulu-Natal)
5. Ceder Brew Chubbyhead Dry Stout (Western Cape)

APOLLO
BREWING COMPANY

Unit 2, 9 Industria Rd, Gordon's Bay; apollobeer.com; 081 725 0812

★ OPEN BY APPOINTMENT ONLY ★

You could say that Chris Spurdens has a natural interest in making booze. After studying viticulture and oenology at the University of Brighton, he worked at wineries in France, California and, perhaps most interestingly, a year-long stint producing sparkling wine in the south of England.

Following eight years overseas, Chris returned to South Africa and continued his wine career, starting as a harvest hand and moving on to assistant winemaker positions at a range of Cape wineries. But a desire to work for himself, to start his own business, was lingering in the background, and for that Chris decided to turn to another type of beverage.

'In the wine industry you could never hope to start a small business like this,' says Chris, looking around the small garage-style setup where he brews the Apollo beers. 'It's just not sustainable.' Chris had his first brush with brewing a decade earlier while still living in the UK, but the kit beer he tried failed to impress him and he admits he lost interest. The interest was rekindled in 2012, though

Chris Spurdens shares brewing space with Mark Goldsworthy of Red Sky Brew

the plan wasn't to make a business out of it. 'It was just supposed to be a hobby,' says Chris, 'but after getting compliments from some well-respected people in the industry, I considered taking it further. The wine industry was in a bit of a slump at the time, and the craft industry sounded exciting!' After exploring a number of possibilities for setting up his brewery, including installing a brewhouse on the wine farm where he lives, Chris was introduced to Mark Goldsworthy of Red Sky Brew (page 80). The two struck up a deal whereby Chris would share Red Sky's brewhouse and premises and, in 2014, Apollo sold its first beer.

That maiden pint was poured at the Constantia Craft Beer Project in March, and Apollo quickly gained a following, particularly for the dry stout. The stout took second place in the BJCP-sanctioned competition at that year's Cape Town Festival of Beer and has become the flagship beer. Chris is rightly proud of the brewery's success in its first year, but he's quick to add that the plan is to keep things manageable. 'We produce enough to pay a salary to the directors – myself and my wife, Nix,' says Chris, 'and to grow the company, and that's enough for us.'

BEER MENU

★

STOUT (4%)

AMBER ALE (5%)

IPA (5.3%)

BLONDE ALE (4.5%)

Assistant brewer Clayton Chigudu gets to grips with the wine barrel mash tun

APOLLO BREWING COMPANY

HONINGKLIP
BREWERY

R43, Botrivier; honingklip.co.za; 082 735 9868

BREWERS
Spotted on

Date

Signature

★ **OPEN TUE–SUN 10AM–6PM** ★

'I couldn't afford to go to Den Anker every Friday,' jokes Mark ter Morshuizen, attempting to explain how Honingklip Brewery began. He refers to the Belgian bar at Cape Town's V&A Waterfront and his particular penchant for Belgian-style beers.

For those who have been involved in the Cape's beer scene for a while, Mark is a familiar face. And if you don't recognise Mark, any long-running homebrewer would certainly recognise Analize. The husband-and-wife team were key players in the SouthYeasters Homebrew Club for several years, chairing meetings and running the summer festival.

Their interest in beer dates back much further, though, to the early nineties, when they spent almost eight years working and travelling in Europe. Stints in the Netherlands got them hooked on Belgian ales and on returning to South Africa for the millennium New Year celebrations, they realised that beer was a

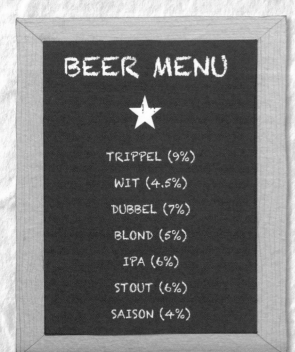

BEER MENU
★

TRIPPEL (9%)

WIT (4.5%)

DUBBEL (7%)

BLOND (5%)

IPA (6%)

STOUT (6%)

SAISON (4%)

Mark and Analize ter Morshuizen have long been involved in the Cape beer scene

bit behind in their homeland. It would take a while before they would start brewing their own beer, though, and it was an encounter with the homebrewing club they would later run that set the ball rolling.

'I happened to walk past A. White Chemist,' says Analize, referring to the city centre pharmacy that was at one time pretty much the only place to buy brewing supplies. 'I saw a beer kit and bought it for Mark for Christmas. It sat in the cupboard for months and eventually I told him – either you do it now or I'm going to chuck it away!' Mark completed his first kit brew and shortly afterwards Analize spotted a sign for the SouthYeasters, also at the Plein Street chemist's shop. Mark's earliest brews had mixed results – the first one he describes as 'fine'; the second time around he recalls spraying stout all over the ceiling of their bachelor apartment.

Mark and Analize hadn't been brewing for long when a couple of local businesses – beer companies before their time – closed down and Mark swooped in to buy equipment at auction. With kegs galore from former Somerset West brewery Helderbrau and draught tap systems from Stellenbosch beer bar Forum, Mark had only one choice of what to do next. 'We really had to start a brewery then,' he says, 'as I needed something to do with all those taps!'

The Ter Morshuizens already had an idea of the type of brewery model they wanted – 'somewhere nice, with a view and a tasting room on-site', so they moved out to Mark's family farm in Botrivier, brewing regularly to decide on styles and to perfect reci-

The Honingklip taproom certainly fills Mark's main requirement – 'somewhere with a view'

pes. Meanwhile, Analize had essentially taken over the reins at the SouthYeasters, which was then a fairly small group of beer enthusiasts.

Eventually, after extensive building work and countless brews on a 50-litre system, Honingklip Brewery, named for the farm it resides upon, opened its doors in late 2012. What began as a part-time business, open to the public only on Friday, Saturday and Sunday, has now become a family-friendly brewpub open six days a week. The couple's early dealings with Belgian brews are still evident, with even their IPA having a Belgian twist. With tasty, well-thought-out beer food on the menu and superb views from the deck, the Ter Morshuizens certainly got the brewing venue they wanted. So has it all turned out as they had initially thought? 'The original plan was "let's brew some beer",' admits Mark. So I guess that's a resounding 'yes!'.

THE SOUTHYEASTERS HOMEBREW CLUB
southyeasters.co.za

The SouthYeasters meet once a month in a Cape Town craft beer bar to talk and taste beer. Guest speakers cover a range of technical topics and there are regular homebrewing contests with prizes donated by local breweries and homebrewing supply stores. The club also holds an annual festival in April, when members get together to share their brews with the beer-loving public.

BIRKENHEAD
BREWERY

R320, Stanford; walkerbayestate.com; 028 341 0183

★ OPEN DAILY 10AM-5PM ★

The Klein River Mountains provide a marvellous backdrop to the Birkenhead Brewery

Breweries are sometimes seen as being aesthetically inferior to wineries – as places that are more industrial than attractive. There are, of course, breweries that are designed more for takeaways than for a lingering pint, but Birkenhead Brewery is not one of those places. Perched just outside the picture-perfect town of Stanford, the brewery – and the estate that it sits upon – boasts comfy couches, roaring fires in winter and picnic tables in summer offering majestic views of the Klein River Mountains beyond. This is definitely a place that you come to sit and savour a pint of their long-established beer.

The brewery was founded in 1998 and named for the ship that sank in nearby waters 146 years earlier. The survivors sought refuge on a Stanford farm and, in launching the Western Cape's second microbrewery, the original owners hoped to provide refuge for beer drinkers seeking something different to the mainstream beers then available.

The brewery has changed hands since that time, but some staples remain. The beer catalogue is largely unchanged, the grounds are still as picturesque as ever, and Benson Mocuphe is still a solid member of the Birkenhead staff. Benson joined Birkenhead when it first opened its doors, originally working in

Birkenhead's brewhouse is on show to the public

Bottles get unpacked and washed before being filled with Birkenhead beer

the storage area of the brewery. It took only a few weeks for his work ethic to be noticed, and he was soon promoted to working in the fermentation room. From there Benson became the protégé of Andy Mitchell, Birkenhead's initial brewmaster, who learnt the trade through a career with SAB.

Today, Andy has moved to Australia, but Benson remains and is now the head brewer at Birkenhead. 'I love my job,' he beams, his enthusiasm instantly contagious. 'I love to brew, though I'm not a big drinker.'

Like the general public, Benson's favourite in the range is the premium lager, though he insists that since his 2007 marriage he is a taster, not a drinker.

Birkenhead has stuck to its tried-and-tested recipes, adding only the Laughing Croc in recent years – a blend of two existing beers. But attempts have been made to keep up with the hordes of breweries that have popped up – labels have been updated and shaded tables in the garden make it a more pleasant place than ever to sip a Honey Blonde on a hot day.

BEER MENU

★

PILSNER (3.5%)

PREMIUM LAGER (4%)

HONEY BLONDE (4.5%)

PRIDE (3.5%)

CHOCOLATE STOUT (4%)

BREWER
Spotted on
_____
Date
_____
Signature

BEER
MENU
★
STOUT (4%)
PALE ALE (3.7%)

Frasers Folly

FRASER'S FOLLY

Struisbaai Industrial Area, Struisbaai; 076 305 7974

★ OPEN BY APPOINTMENT ONLY ★

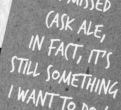

'I MISSED CASK ALE, IN FACT, IT'S STILL SOMETHING I WANT TO DO.'

'I take my cues from the UK,' says Fraser Crighton, his English accent a dead giveaway as to why. He is referring to the style of beer that he makes – easy-drinking ales that are fairly low in alcohol and not too highly carbonated. 'I think English beers offer a drinkability that a lot of beers don't,' he adds. And drinkability is an important thing for a beer to have, for as passionate as any brewer is, the moment he or she transforms from homebrewer to commercial craft brewer, the hope is, of course, to make some money from the process.

Fraser seems to have got that part down. Unlike many brewers who man their kettles part time while juggling another career, Fraser has turned his 'Folly' into a day job. He moved to South Africa in 2010, having met his wife, Marile, in the UK. His studies in winemaking and background as a sommelier were a good basis for a career in brewing, but it was actually a lack of ale that made Fraser begin to brew his own beer in South Africa. 'I missed cask ale,' he says. 'In fact, it's still something I want to do.'

Two years after starting to brew, he began to think that it might actually make a viable business and eventually he moved away from his wife's family business, a bar-restaurant in Struisbaai's harbour, to open his microbrewery in the town's industrial area. Originally named Bulldog Brewery, he changed the brand's name at the suggestion of a friend who told him to 'put your name on it'.

His ales have since gained a loyal local following and in 2014 he expanded, purchasing the equipment from the defunct Napier Brewery. Having said that, Fraser says he doesn't want to get 'too big' and has no plans to open a brewpub in the area. He is planning to add new beers to the range, though, including an annual barrel-aged English Special Bitter. His beers are found on tap at select spots throughout the Overberg and in bottle stores slightly further afield – look out for the unique, fish 'n' chips-style paper wrapping emblazoned, as he was recommended to do, with the name of the brewer himself.

Fraser Crighton was in the process of upgrading his brewhouse, having bought the equipment from the defunct Napier Brewery

SOUTH CAPE
BREWERIES

Mossdustria, Mossel Bay; southcapebreweries.co.za; 083 215 2827

★ OPEN BY APPOINTMENT ONLY ★

Johann Baker has been brewing since the early eighties

'We're a training centre, not a brewery!' jokes Johann Baker, one of the partners in South Cape Breweries. His students are not wannabe brewers keen to learn how to make beer, though, they are thirsty drinkers who were initially sceptical of a microbrewery in their midst. 'We are busy educating people about what a craft brewery is,' he adds. And when you're the first in your region, it's a particularly important task.

Sometimes, people hear 'craft brewery' or 'microbrewery' and they think 'homebrew'. Not that this is necessarily a bad thing – there are undoubtedly some homebrewers out there producing world-class beers. But some people remember the sour cidery mess they produced on their sole attempt at brewing their own, or the tale of the exploding bottles in the bath that their friend has told them. So first, a microbrewer has to convince them that small breweries can make great beer – and perhaps the best way to do that is to start with something people are familiar with.

South Cape opened in late 2012 in Mossel Bay. The fact that the town didn't yet have much of a craft beer culture, coupled with the beachy climate, led Johann and his business partner Jan van der Walt to launch with a lager. Some would question the decision, asking why bother with a style that is already available in abundance, but it's a move that has worked again and again in the South African beer scene and one that does make a lot of sense – first you convince the public that you can make a good beer; then you can start introducing new flavours and styles. It has worked well for Johann and Jan – business is booming and they can hardly keep up. 'First we wanted to get the brand settled,' says Johann. 'Now, everyone knows the brand and people are fighting for taps – we don't have to beg for counter space anymore!'

In fact, South Cape was just about to double its capacity when I visited, and a bottling line was on the cards. Big investment is not something that Johann and Jan have been afraid of. Nothing at South Cape has been done by halves, starting with research into the market. Johann started homebrewing in the early eighties, though he jokes that his beer career began at the age of four, when, on being asked by his father what he'd like to drink, he requested not a cool drink but a beer! His destiny was clearly already written, but it wasn't until 2010 that he really started looking into the nitty-gritty of brewing for a living. Over the next two years, a huge amount of research took place, which culminated in Johann and Jan teaming up to import a brewery from the Czech Republic – the first of its kind to be installed in South Africa. Along with the brewery came a Czech brewmaster to spend three months training the team – including school-leaver Marius Schonken – how to use the equipment.

Marius must be the envy of his friends, scoring what many would agree is one of life's coolest jobs straight after completing matric. Each day he brews Glenhoff lager on the impressive brewhouse, a setup in one of the most spotless breweries you'll ever see. Next door, a sizable reverse osmosis plant purifies the municipal water ready for brewing. 'You need perfect water,' asserts Johann. 'We clean it up and basically have a blank slate. We can then add what we need to get the profile right for the style we want to brew.'

Visits to the industrial area east of Mossel Bay are strictly by appointment, but Johann is hoping to open a brewpub in the town at some point. Until then, the beer is found on tap along the Garden Route, with rustic Kaai 4 in Mossel Bay's harbour being a particularly atmospheric spot to sip. The South Cape team is ready to start adding new brews to the line-up, with a light lager, a red Irish ale and a stout now in the pipeline. And with locals firmly converted to the craft beer camp, you can be sure that the new brews will soon be infiltrating Mossel Bay's restaurants and bars.

BEER MENU

★

GLENHOFF DRAUGHT (4.4%)

BIG 5 PINT

GLENHOFF DRAUGHT

A lager is a lager is a lager, right? Not at all, and Glenhoff is a particularly fine example. Closest to a Dortmunder Export in style, the beer has some definite grainy sweetness, but delivers the crisp, dry finish you expect when sipping a lager. Best of all is the carbonation level – lively enough to refresh, but not so fizzy that you can't manage a second pint.

MISTY MEADOWS
MICROBREWERY

R102, George; 044 876 0464

BREWER

Spotted on

_____

Date

_____

Signature

★ OPEN BY APPOINTMENT ONLY ★

Situated on a former dairy farm just outside George, Misty Meadows is a tranquil place where both the weather and landscape often live up to the brewery's name. Established in 2008, it is the brainchild of Joburg-based property developer Howard Rawlings. 'I looked all over the country for a spot to set up,' Howard explains. 'One day I was driving from Groot-Brakrivier and suddenly I was hit by all this

Misty Meadows sits in the foothills of the Outeniqua Mountains, close to the country's hop-growing region

The cavernous tasting area can be booked for private functions

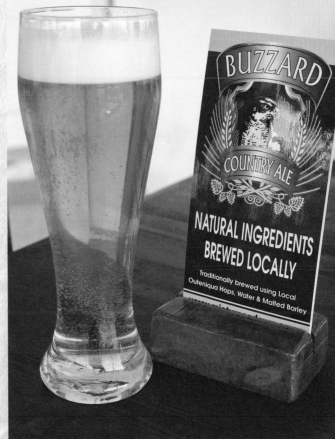

green. It was amazing and I knew immediately I'd found the right spot.'

It turned out to be the right spot for more than just its view. Close to the country's hop-growing region, Howard was sourcing ingredients when one of the hop farmers mentioned a retired SAB brewer living in George. Howard now had property, a recipe designed by Moritz Kallmeyer of Drayman's in Pretoria (page 164), a brewery and the missing piece of the puzzle – a brewer, Johann Steenberg. 'I didn't say yes straightaway,' says Johann, who had retired in 2005 after 34 years with SAB. 'But it, of course, raised some interest. Once a brewer, always a brewer!' It didn't take too long for Johann to relent and the first batch of Buzzard Country Ale was brewed at the end of 2009, a process that for Johann was like going back to his early brewing years. 'The equipment here is, of course, totally different to what I was used to at SAB,' he says. 'You're doing things manually and nowadays in large breweries it's all computerised – I refer to them as TV-screen brewers. But when I started, it was very much a manual process and this is like stepping back to my roots. It's much more hands-on.'

Howard had plans to create a self-sustaining village filled with hands-on artisanal foodies here, but for the moment, at least, those plans are on hold. The brewing courses that once took place here have also ceased, but interested parties can visit by arrangement and sip a pint of South African ale with a pretty view of the Outeniqua Mountains. Whenever demand dictates, Johann brews an 800-litre batch along with Artsheal Oktober, who lives and works on the farm. The bulk of the beer now gets shipped to Picolino's, a bar in the Joburg suburb of Fourways – not quite as picturesque as Misty Meadows, but an area that's become quite the Joburg beer hub.

ROBERTSON
BREWING COMPANY

1 Memoriam St, George; robertsonbrewery.com; 082 659 2650

★ OPEN MON–SAT 10AM–7PM ★

BEER MENU

★

CLASSIC WEISSBIER (4.5%)

JAZZ APA (4.5%)

CELTIC SCOTTISH ALE (4.5%)

GAELIC IRISH STOUT (4.8%)

RHYTHM & BLUES
BLONDE ALE (4.5%)

COUNTRY LIGHT
BLONDE ALE (2.5%)

REGGAE IPA (6%)

Time and time again in the South African microbrewing industry, you hear unlikely tales of generosity and openness. Stories of established brewers who willingly assist newcomers to source equipment and build systems, who offer help and advice, and even share recipes with people who are potentially going to become direct competitors. Kevin Robertson can attest to this, for the help he received from a fellow South African brewer was instrumental in helping his brewery get off the ground.

Kevin engineered the snazzy eight-line bottle filler

The journey started in the USA in 2012, where Kevin's son and co-brewer Courtney decided 'on a whim' to spend time working on yachts. While there, he started sampling from the vast range of beers available and came back with an idea for a father-son project. Kevin, no stranger to setting up a small business, was hooked on the idea and delved into researching the market, equipment, raw ingredients – and, of course, the process, since the two were completely new to brewing. 'People said I was crazy to try and set up a brewery here,' Kevin recalls. 'They tried to deter me.' Unswayed, Kevin called around and was directed to Stephan Meyer of Clarens Brewery (page 210), a long-term brewer well known for his willingness to assist anyone interested in the art.

Kevin and Courtney spent three days with Stephan in Clarens, learning about the local industry, how to build a brewery and gleaning useful tips on the ins and outs of brewing. 'He even gave me a recipe!' says Kevin, talking about the blonde ale that is now a part of the beer line-up. By March 2013, the Robertsons were ready to brew their first batch – a task that didn't entirely go to plan, as Kevin admits:

'Somehow we added 100 litres too little water!' Along the ride they threw at least a half-dozen batches down the drain, but gradually got it right and, in September 2013, the Robertson Brewing Company officially opened near the train station in George. Since then, the brewery has expanded and moved to larger home premises. Here, a quirky mural taking up one wall explains the brewing process, simple food is served and Kevin and Courtney can be seen brewing their ever-growing range of ales, each named for a musical style. 'We thought long and hard about a theme for our brand,' says Courtney, 'and since our family is quite musical, we decided that was the way to go. We all listen to music after all!' As with musical styles, the Robertsons realise that everyone's beer tastes are different and they hope to offer something for everyone. And for budding brewers, Kevin is more than willing to take Stephan's kindness and, in the spirit of the craft beer industry, to pay it forward.

BREWERS
Spotted on

Date

Signature

The brewery was Courtney Robertson's idea – something he wanted to work on with dad Kevin

MITCHELL'S
BREWERY

10 New St, Knysna, mitchellsbrewing.com; 044 382 4685

★ OPEN MON-SAT 10AM-6PM ★

You know a beer is good when it stops someone in their tracks and alters their entire life plan. This is just what happened to Dave McRae in 1985. Fresh from university and with the smell of Cape Town in

Dave McRae has been a part of Mitchell's for the past 30 years

his nostrils, Dave left his native Port Elizabeth, travelling the coast en route to a Mother City job hunt. On the way, he stopped off in Knysna to host his 21st birthday bash at his parents' holiday home on the lagoon. When he popped into the newly opened Mitchell's Brewery, he couldn't have known that opting to put on draft beer for his party guests would have changed the course of his whole life, for Dave never quite made it to Cape Town. Dave walked into Mitchell's to buy a birthday keg and essentially never left.

'The brewery had just started and I went in to get a keg of Forester's,' says Dave. 'I remember helping Lex carry it up the 39 steps to my parents' place. Jokingly I said: "If you ever need anyone to sell your product, I'm your man."' A month down the line, the brewery's founder and then owner, Lex Mitchell, offered Dave a sales position and Dave has never looked back.

You could say that Lex Mitchell is the godfather of craft brewing in South Africa. University dabblings with pineapple beer escalated into a career with SAB in 1977. 'They put you through all departments very thoroughly, so you get an incredibly good grounding,' says Lex, though four years later the urge to brew his own way took hold. 'When I joined SAB, it was the first time I'd been exposed to a brewing magazine and in

BEER MENU

★

BOSUN'S BITTER (3.6%)

FORESTER'S LAGER (3.6%)

MILK & HONEY (5.5%)

RAVEN STOUT (5%)

90 SHILLING SPICED ALE (5%)

OLD WOBBLY STRONG
LAGER (7%)

the very first magazine I looked in there was an article about small breweries in Britain.' A year later Lex and his beer-loving wife, Sue, toured British breweries for six weeks 'stealing with their eyes' on a fact-finding mission that would result in the opening of South Africa's first and longest-standing microbrewery.

Mitchell's was established in 1983, originally at Thesen House in Knysna's town centre, moving to the industrial area two years later. The brewery has changed hands a few times over the years, and for a time had branches in Johannesburg and Cape Town. But today, all of the beer is once more brewed in Knysna and Mitchell's is again a locally owned company, with Dave McRae as a director and shareholder. In 2014, the brewery, which had long since outgrown its premises, moved to a fabulous spot on the waterfront, with the outdoor beer garden offering views over Thesen Island. The brewhouse has expanded, with capacity almost doubling to meet the demand that South Africa's recent love affair with microbrewed beer has created. And for the moment, at least, Dave – who has long been kept in his office by administrative tasks – is back at the brew kettles.

The beers have remained largely unchanged since the eighties and nineties. The original beer, Forester's Lager, is still the most popular, with the more-ish and very drinkable Bosun's Bitter coming a close

second. 'Bosun's was launched in the mid-eighties and it shot to 80 per cent of our sales immediately,' says Dave. 'People were crying out for something different – we'd had lager, lager, lager until then.' Next up were Raven Stout and 90 Shilling Ale, the latter designed as a carbo-loader for the Knysna Forest Marathon, but whose unusual cinnamon notes made it a perennial favourite. Milk & Honey Ale and Old Wobbly Lager completed the family in the early nineties.

Lex no longer has a stake in Mitchell's, but in 2012 made a welcome and long-awaited return to the craft in his Port Elizabeth brewpub, Bridge Street (page 124). He fondly recalls his early encounters with Dave. 'In 1985 I realised I needed somebody else at the brewery,' says Lex. 'I'm not very happy being the frontman and I decided that I needed a buffer and that David was going to be it.' But demand outstripped supply and Dave quickly moved from sales to brewing. 'I cleaned tanks and scrubbed floors and learnt the ropes from Lex,' Dave laughs. 'It's the last thing I thought I'd end up doing.' Yet, more than 30 years down the line, Mitchell's is as much a part of Dave's life as Dave is a part of the Mitchell's story.

RED BRIDGE
BREWING CO.

10 Jonker St, Knysna Industria; redbridgebrewing.co.za; 083 671 9399

★ OPEN BY APPOINTMENT ONLY ★

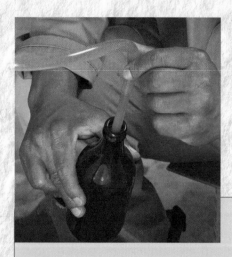

Of all the brewery launches in South Africa, Red Bridge's has to be the most innovative – and probably the most dangerous. Darren Berry, owner-brewer of the Knysna-based nanobrewery, decided he wanted to deliver his first keg in style and so rolled it onto a boat and rowed it from Buffels Bay, in through the infamous Knysna Heads – a notoriously dangerous stretch of water. 'The idea was to deliver beer the way it would have been delivered 100 years ago,' says Darren, adding that as a

MICRO, MACRO, NANO OR CRAFT?

If there's one question that gets asked more than any other in the worldwide beer scene, it is this: 'What is the definition of craft beer?' In South Africa at the moment, there is no official definition and for many it is more of an ethos – a hand-crafted product, made locally in smallish batches and, dare I say, made with love, each batch of beer nurtured as though it were the brewer's own child.

Perhaps more useful, and certainly easier to define, are the terms nanobrewery, microbrewery and macrobrewery. These terms all refer to the size of the brewery or, more correctly, the amount of beer a brewery produces. Again, there are not yet official definitions for each category in South Africa, but as a general guide, a macrobrewery churns out vast quantities of beer – hundreds of millions of litres per year. A microbrewery produces on a much smaller scale – an average monthly output in South Africa is around 5 000 –10 000 litres per month. A nanobrewery is a tiny setup, often producing batches only slightly larger than those of the average homebrewer.

BEER MENU

★

NO. 17 GOLDEN ALE (4.5%)

PRIVATEER IPA (6%)

WOODCUTTER SAISON ALE (4%)

member of the local sea rescue station, he is familiar with the intricacies of the Heads.

The keg in question, filled with Red Bridge's No. 17 Golden Ale, was delivered to the East Head Café just before Easter 2013 and today his first customer still stocks bottles of Red Bridge's brews. Since then, Darren has stuck to bottling his brews, though he does plan to get back into kegs in the future.

Red Bridge's name comes from a historic bridge over the Knysna River which, according to Darren, 'anyone who has grown up here has jumped off'. The beer names also have their origins in Knysna – No. 17 refers to the weight of a gold nugget found here in 1876, the saison's moniker comes from Knysna's ties with the timber industry and the Privateer IPA honours Knysna's naval links. Labels each come with a story focusing on local history and Darren supports local projects through his brand, using crates crafted by disabled artisans at a local charity and donating a portion of each bottle sold to the National Sea Rescue Institute.

It was a simple love of beer that got Darren homebrewing in 2010, a love that was garnered somewhat by overseas travel. Two years on, he decided to scale back his other business in waste water treatment and instead focus on turning water into liquid gold. He brews double batches on a self-built 120-litre system, counting on 12-hour brew days

to meet the local demand for his beer. In 2014, he launched to a wider public at the Cape Town Festival of Beer and Red Bridge's brews are now available at select spots in the Mother City as well.

But for the most part, Darren is keen to keep it local and while he doesn't intend to revive his beer-by-boat scheme, Darren does have other ideas, including a plan to deliver by donkey...

BREWER
Spotted on
_____
Date
_____
Signature

Darren Berry's 120-litre system is one of the smallest commercial breweries in the country

KARUSA

Schoemanshoek, near Oudtshoorn; karusa.co.za; 044 272 8717

★ OPEN MON–FRI 9.30AM–4PM, SAT 10AM–2.30PM ★

BEER MENU
★

LONG NECK BLONDE (4%)

CAVEMAN'S DRY STOUT (4%)

ZWARTBERGER KAROO DRAUGHT (4%)

Brewing was a natural leap for Jacques Conradie. Having already produced wine, port and MCC, it was only a matter of time before he added beer to his repertoire. A trained winemaker with years of experience working at Graham Beck and Boplaas, among others, he eventually took the reins at his family vineyard just outside Oudtshoorn. 'We pretty much reached our maximum wine volume, so the beer just seems to make sense,' says Jacques, himself a keen beer drinker.

Indeed it makes sense in more ways than one. Karusa sits just off the road to the Cango Caves, giving Jacques a steady stream of thirsty tourists passing by. Add to that the Klein Karoo summer heat – perfect beer-drinking weather – and it seems he's onto a winner. In fact, the biggest problem has been keeping up with local demand – well, that and mastering the finer points that set brewing aside from winemaking.

'I've struggled with my mash temperatures and fermentation temperatures,' says Jacques, whose first foray into brewing was in 2011. 'But it's coming together now. I understand winemaking holistically and it's important that I do the same with brewing, so I've been doing a lot of reading and a lot of practising.'

Self-taught from brewing books, his background in booze production has surely been a help, though Jacques is well aware of the differences between wine and beer – not least the resilience of the former and the absence of preservatives in the latter, something that Jacques admits he finds challenging, especially with Oudtshoorn's high summer temperatures.

Jacques's trio of ales are on tap at Karusa and a couple of venues in Oudtshoorn, as well as in bottles to sip at home. It's a gorgeous place to drink a beer, nibble on a plate of tapas and if you fancy something stronger, to taste the wines, port and bubbles also produced here.

Winemaker Jacques Conradie has turned his hand to brewing

KAROO BREW

38 Bath St, Montagu; themystictin.co.za; 074 886 3521

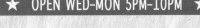

★ OPEN WED-MON 5PM-10PM ★

Karoo Brew is situated in the heart of pretty Montagu

There's been a brewery on Montagu's restaurant-dotted Bath Street since before the craft beer boom began, but somehow it's always struggled to take off. The initial concept was adopted from Sneeuberg Brewery in Nieu-Bethesda (page 118) – an extract brewery in a small-town setting. The brewery has changed hands several times over the past few years, but the three beers remain the same – a pale ale, a honey ale and a roasty dark ale. They're served in the bar at The Mystic Tin, an affordable guesthouse in pretty Montagu, but the best place to taste them is at the bar's beer garden out the back. When I visited for this book, the brewery had again just been taken over and there were no brews on tap, but hopefully under its most recent management the venture will finally find its feet.

SAGGY STONE
BREWING CO.

Amandalia Farm, Agtervinkrivier, Robertson; saggystone.co.za; 083 453 3526

★ OPEN FRI-MON 11AM-4PM ★

Adrian Robinson's CV must be an interesting read. He has worked as a geography teacher, a warehouse worker, a soldier, a fruit farmer and, of course, the reason he belongs in this book – a brewer. Of all the earlier jobs, it was his 12-year stint baking bread in his own Cape Town bakery that was most helpful in learning to brew, for beer is really just liquid bread after all. But there would be a few steps that Adrian would take to get from bread to beer, starting with a life-changing motorbike accident in 2002. 'I almost died. I had an epiphany and decided I wanted a change. I was making lots of money, but just chasing my tail – I was working insane hours and never saw my wife,' Adrian explains. 'Then one day I was sitting in a Jacuzzi with my brother, Phillip, drinking red wine, and we decided to buy a wine farm!' Adrian's farm sits in the Nuy Valley, just west of Robertson. There he grows grapes and other fruit; the former to sell to local wineries, the latter for export. He decided not to try and enter the highly competitive wine market, but then, in 2007, he and Phillip began to experiment with homebrewing.

After a couple of kit beers, Adrian decided it was all-grain or nothing, and for the next three years the brothers brewed for themselves and their buddies before deciding to make a business out of it. Phillip had spent time in Australia and noticed a healthy smattering of breweries in among the vineyards there, yet among Robertson's wineries there wasn't a sole beer being brewed. And so the idea was born. 'We didn't originally want a brewpub,' admits Adrian. 'We were just going to distribute our beer to other pubs, but then we decided we wanted to see how the customers reacted rather than just delivering and not knowing what they were saying about our beers.'

Since launching in 2010, Saggy Stone has proved to be more successful than Adrian or his brother could have imagined. The brewhouse has expanded four-fold, extra beers have been added to the range and are now being bottled as well as kegged, the pub's opening hours have been extended and plans are underway to add a rooftop tasting room to the pub, so that drinkers can enjoy the wonderful views on the Robinsons' farm.

The story behind the brewery's unusual name is as cute as the Saggy Stone brewpub itself. 'I had built a stone lapa out on the farm. I was trying to make it look really natural and it looked great until the baboons came and jumped on it, then it sagged in the middle,' Adrian explains. 'My daughter, then 10 years old, called it a saggy stone lapa and it just came off the tongue nicely. We googled it to see if anyone else had the name and all it came up with was saggy boobs, so we thought it was a sign from God!'

Adrian built the pub himself, giving up his weekends for a year to create the dry stone walling effect and the wooden deck. He was aiming for a building that would blend with the environment and he's rightfully thrilled with the result. 'Our philosophy is very basic,' says Adrian. 'We want it to be really accessible; we want people to come and drink the beer that they like. You might not like all of them, but hopefully you'll like one of them.' And you'll certainly love the setting and the laid-back, family-friendly vibe that the Saggy Stone team is successfully striving for.

BEER MENU
★

CALIFORNIA
STEAM (5%)

BIG RED ALE
(4.5%)

DESERT LAGER (4%)

DARK HORSE LAGER
(4%)

Brewer Adrian Robinson gave up his weekends for a year to build the gorgeous Saggy Stone pub

SAGGY STONE BREWING CO.

WESTERN CAPE CONTRACT BREWERIES

Contract brewing is an arrangement where a company will pay to produce its beer on another brewery's equipment. People have different reasons for starting up in this manner, but it's usually a way to set up a beer brand for those who can't yet afford to invest in the equipment and premises required to start their own brewery. Some contract brewers insist on brewing the beer themselves, others employ the services of the in-house brewer. The contract breweries are listed separately in this book simply because they don't have official taprooms that you can add to your itinerary, though each comes with a recommendation on where you'll likely be able to find their brews. The breweries here are listed alphabetically.

BROTHERS IN ARMS
BREWERY

biabrewery.co.za

★ BROTHERS IN ARMS DOESN'T HAVE A TASTING ROOM, BUT TO SAMPLE THE BEER HEAD
TO REDEMPTION BURGER IN WOODSTOCK OR ROELAND LIQUORS IN CAPE TOWN. ★

BEER MENU

★

WINGMAN'S WEISS (5%)

SUNSET SESSION BLONDE ALE (5%)

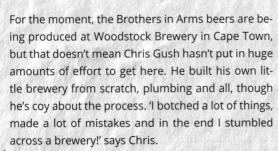

For the moment, the Brothers in Arms beers are being produced at Woodstock Brewery in Cape Town, but that doesn't mean Chris Gush hasn't put in huge amounts of effort to get here. He built his own little brewery from scratch, plumbing and all, though he's coy about the process. 'I botched a lot of things, made a lot of mistakes and in the end I stumbled across a brewery!' says Chris.

The leap from home-brewing to microbrewing kind of happened by accident, as Chris explains: 'I was happy with my beer and I'd had really good feedback so I started to research licensing and before I knew it I was half-way through the process!' The licence was fixed to a small unit in a Gordon's Bay industrial area, but Chris soon realised that the limits of a day job in IT and a fully-functioning but tiny 75-litre system were going to hinder the progress of the Brothers in Arms brand, so when Wood-stock Brewery opened in 2014, Chris approached them to produce his Wingman's Weiss under contract.

The beer's name, much like the brewery's, speaks of close friendships and, in part, references the brewing buddy that Chris initially set up the business with. He has since moved to Durban, but the Wingman's Weiss remains and Chris would like to think that this is a beer that you can always depend on, that will be there for any occasion, be it breakfast, braaiing or a morning-after-the-night-before 'regmaker'.

While the beers are currently being produced at one of Cape Town's newest breweries, the dream is still to make brewing a full-time job. In the meantime, Chris continues to head out to his Gordon's Bay premises to work on new recipes for the Brothers in Arms range on the small system he built by trial and error.

CITIZEN BEER

Cape Town; citizenbeer.co.za

★ CITIZEN DOESN'T HAVE A TASTING ROOM, BUT TO SAMPLE THE BEER HEAD TO ROYALE EATERY, CABRITO OR NEIGHBOURHOOD IN CAPE TOWN. ★

Across the globe, people tolerate jobs they despise with only one thought in mind – the weekend and the blissful beers it might bring. Gary Pnematicatos decided that rather than making beer his weekend goal, he would bid farewell to an unfulfilling job and make beer his life.

'I started making champagne and wine with friends,' says Gary, 'when I overheard them discussing plans to make beer. I thought that sounded amazing and started brewing with them. About six months later I was sitting at my desk at work and I thought – I hate this. I'd been making beer every weekend and I realised that was what I wanted to be doing.'

Two years later, the dream Gary had conjured up at his desk was realised. Along with local restaurant entrepreneur Hugo Berolsky, Gary launched Citizen Beer in April 2012 with their debut beer, Alliance Amber Ale. Although brewed under contract at Boston Breweries (page 16), the recipe is very much Gary's baby and it took half a dozen brews for him to perfect it. 'When I initially quit my job, my intention was to build a 1 000-litre system, have lots of fermenters and brew every day, but we came up against licensing and the difficulty in getting equipment, so we decided to focus instead on the brand and the logistics of selling the beer. I'd already been speaking to Chris [Barnard, of Boston Breweries] about brewing in general as he's a very affable guy, so it just made sense to ask him to brew the beer for us.'

But that's not to say that the guys won't brew their own beer in the future. Three years down the line, Gary says that 'the desire to have our own brewery is still incredibly strong', but for the moment he and Hugo are happy to develop recipes in their R&D lab – the 30-litre homebrewery Gary built when he left the corporate world. Here they have worked on recipes for their two follow-up beers – an English IPA and a Bohemian Pilsner.

When Gary quit his job, the craft boom was very much in its infancy, but his brave gamble for a fun-filled working life paid off. 'I quit because I was passionate about making beer and I wanted a profession where I would love to wake up every day. Now this is all I do – and it's the best job in the world,' he says.

BUYING BEER TO TAKE HOME:
FIVE CRAFTY LIQUOR STORES IN THE WESTERN CAPE

Craft beer is becoming much more widespread in South African liquor stores; try one of these spots for a particularly impressive selection:

1. **Roeland Liquors**
    65 Roeland St, Cape Town; roelandliquors.co.za; 021 461 6397
2. **Liquor City Claremont**
    Palmyra Rd, Claremont, Cape Town; liquorcity.co.za; 021 674 1478
3. **Tops Spar Cape Quarter**
    27 Somerset Rd, Green Point; spar.co.za; 021 418 0360
    Other particularly good branches of Tops include Hout Bay, Rosmead, Stellenbosch and Vergelegen.
4. **Shorties Blue Bottle Liquors**
    2b Hou Moed Ave, Noordhoek; bluebottleliquors.co.za; 021 785 2546
5. **Bottelary Hills Wine Centre**
    Cnr Koelenhof & Bottelary Rd, Stellenbosch; bhwc.co.za; 021 865 2955

BEER MENU

★

ALLIANCE AMBER ALE (5.5%)

SABOTEUR ENGLISH IPA (5.5%)

DIPLOMAT CZECH PILS (5.5%)

JACK BLACK'S
BREWING COMPANY

Cape Town; jackblackbeer.com; 021 447 4151

★ JACK BLACK DOESN'T YET HAVE A TASTING ROOM, BUT TO SAMPLE THE RANGE, HEAD TO BANANA JAM IN KENILWORTH, WOODCUTTER'S ARMS IN HOUT BAY OR VAN HUNKS IN CAPE TOWN. ★

Meghan and Ross have built the Jack Black brand into a supremely successful beer company

If there's one beer that can be considered instrumental in launching a craft beer culture in South Africa, then Jack Black's Brewers Lager is it. The brand is now ubiquitous and the company clearly a huge success, but it took a lot of hard work to get here.

It all began in Canada in 2002, where Ross McCulloch and Meghan MacCallum met at a wine-tasting stand. 'There's an underground beer culture within the wine industry,' says Meghan of the business they used to be involved in. And drinking post-wine show pints is just how the two started dabbling in craft beer, a trend that was just beginning to show its face in Canada. As Meghan and Ross got deeper into the local beer scene, they couldn't help wondering if a similar hop awakening was happening back in Ross's home city, Cape Town. On trips back home, he found that there were some serious gaps in the market and by the middle of 2005, perhaps pushed along by the brutal Canadian cold, they started making plans to move to South Africa.

After researching – otherwise known as tasting – a host of beers, they decided to develop an all-malt lager and set about brewing test batches at a Vancouver brewery. They experimented with various recipes using traditional hops found in the USA during the pre-prohibition era, such as the cluster hop, and so Jack Black Brewers Lager was born. The name comes from an early 20th-century American brewer, John Jack Black, whose family had a flourishing farm in the hop-growing region of New York State.

With recipe in hand, Ross and Meghan moved to Cape Town in 2006, quickly realising that their beer would have to change a little to use locally available ingredients. 'We had to make natural changes because of what was available in raw materials,' says

Most exciting, though, is the plan to open a Cape Town taproom and, further into the future, a brewery of their own. There's often a lot of snobbery about contract brewing, but no-one could ever discount the years of hard work that Ross and Meghan have put in. Along with a few early players, like Boston, Mitchell's and Darling, Ross and Meghan have created a craft beer culture in South Africa, paving the way for the 100+ breweries that came after them.

Ross. 'We have also made some tweaks based on consumer preferences here, but we have remained true to a pre-prohibition style.'

So with a recipe, a name and enough capital to keep them afloat for a couple of years, Ross and Meghan set out to find a brewery that could help them achieve their dream. Jack Black was first brewed at Birkenhead Brewery, then moved to Boston Breweries in Cape Town. Ross and Meghan had allowed themselves two years, thinking that if it hadn't worked in that time they would return to Canada and the corporate world. It was touch and go at times, Ross admits, and they were starting to think that it wasn't going to work when suddenly things took off. 'We could see that it was going to be a success,' says Ross, who has been a key player getting South Africa's craft beer industry off the ground. Today, the beer is brewed at Cape Brewing Co., a brewery Ross and Meghan teamed up with before the brewhouse had even been installed. The beer range has also changed over the years, with three ales now featuring alongside the flagship lager and some innovative speciality brews in the pipeline.

BEER MENU
★

SKELETON COAST INDIA PALE ALE (6.6%)

BREWERS LAGER (5%)

BUTCHER BLOCK PALE ALE (5.4%)

LUMBERJACK AMBER ALE (6%)

BIG 5 PINT

JACK BLACK'S SKELETON COAST IPA

While it lacks a little of the full-on hop aroma associated with the style, Jack Black's IPA has an awesome lingering bitterness, not only from the American hops used but, also from the malt. It's a complex brew, far more balanced than you expect, with plenty of malt backing up the hops. Enjoy it with a blue cheese and bacon pizza.

KING'S CRAFT
BREWING CO.

kingscraftbeer.co.za

★ KING'S CRAFT DOESN'T HAVE A TASTING ROOM, BUT TO SAMPLE THE BEER HEAD TO BARRISTERS IN NEWLANDS, SPIRO'S IN HOUT BAY OR FIND THEM AT THE OLD BISCUIT MILL IN WOODSTOCK EVERY SATURDAY MORNING. ★

Cliff Fitzhenry and Will Battersby dabbled in homebrewing before deciding to try and enter the craft beer market, but they opted for a different approach to many of the country's brewing hopefuls. 'We decided we didn't want to go down the "homebrew and scale up" route,' says Cliff, so instead they approached Chris Barnard at Boston Breweries and in late 2012 the first batch of LionHeart Lager was produced.

'We always wanted a flagship lager to suit the palate of South Africans,' says Cliff, though now the brand is becoming established, there are plans to add further beers to the King's Craft family. Future beers will continue the regal theme and carry the carefully thought-out branding of LionHeart, which even follows through to the stylish four-pack cartons, a welcome departure from the standard shrink-wrapped plastic packaging.

Cliff has noticed a leap from tap to bottle in the years since he first launched his beer, though it can still be found on tap at a number of spots,

Head to the Old Biscuit Mill on a Saturday morning to sample the LionHeart beer

BEER
MENU

★

LIONHEART
LAGER (4.7%)

including the Saturday morning Neighbourgoods Market, King's Craft's biggest selling spot. Cliff and Will certainly ended up with the beer they sought to produce, with LionHeart being a crisp and moreish beer, ideal for sipping with a braai or enjoying with a game of cricket in the background.

'WE ALWAYS WANTED A FLAGSHIP LAGER TO SUIT THE PALATE OF SOUTH AFRICANS.'

KING'S CRAFT BREWING CO.

BEER
101

LAGER OR PILSNER?

A pilsner is a lager, but a lager – or more specifically a light lager – is not a pilsner. Confused? Here are the basic differences: while both use a bottom-fermenting yeast, the grain bill would likely differ, with pilsners rarely using adjuncts such as rice or maize. Flavour and aroma-wise, it's the hops that make the real difference, with pilsners boasting a much more pronounced noble hop character and a higher level of bitterness. Appearance-wise, they're both found in various shades of gold, though typically a pilsner keeps its head for longer.

STRIPED HORSE

stripedhorse.co.za

★ STRIPED HORSE DOESN'T HAVE A TASTING ROOM, BUT TO SAMPLE THE BEER HEAD TO ROELAND LIQUORS IN CAPE TOWN, THE FOUNDRY IN JOHANNESBURG OR ST FRANCIS BREWERY IN THE EASTERN CAPE. ★

If you're looking for 'the sort of beer you'd drink while catching tiger fish on the Zambezi', then the Striped Horse team might just have you covered. 'The important thing was to create a craft beer that acknowledged European roots, but that had an African feel,' says Charles Bertram, one of the partners in Striped Horse and a former game ranger. Along with Grant Rushmere, founder of the rooibos ice tea company Bos, Charles set out to create a premium lager brand for the South African beer scene.

'We felt that there was a dearth of lagers,' explains Charles. 'South Africa is a lager-drinking culture and people forget that sometimes people just want to drink a beer.' When it came to producing a fine lager, Charles said there was only one brewery they approached – Cape Brewing Co. (page 65), who now own a 25% stake in Striped Horse. While discussing recipes, brewmaster Wolfgang Koedel persuaded them to launch with not just a lager but a pilsner, too, and in late 2014, Capetonians got their first sip of Striped Horse.

Although the venture was still very much in its infancy when this book was being researched, the Striped Horse team already had plans to add further beers to the range once the two lagers are well-established. The end goal is to open a Striped Horse pub, but for now you'll find the beers on tap at a few select locations around Cape Town and Johannesburg, and in bottle stores scattered across the country.

BEER MENU

★

STRIPED HORSE LAGER (5.1%)

STRIPED HORSE PILSNER (5.2%)

COMING SOON...

AFRO-CARIBBEAN BREWING COMPANY

157 Second Ave, Kenilworth, Cape Town
It seems only natural that Cape Town beer mecca Banana Jam Café would open an on-site microbrewery and as this book was being researched, construction was underway. Beer buddies Greg Casey and Shawn Duthie are behind the brews, which will include some unusual flagships like coconut IPA and chocolate chilli stout. The Stone Crow brand will also be brewed here.

BEARD AND BARREL

Cape Town; beardandbarrel.com
Founder and beard-wearer Mitch Lockhart says that beards are arguably more important to the finished product than the barrels at this innovative, small-batch brewery. The flagship ale is still to be decided, but everything here will be fermented/aged in a barrel – which could be anything from a bourbon barrel to a white wine barrel with added *Brettanomyces*. Look out for their beers on tap at Banana Jam Café.

BEER FLY BREWING CO.

Cape Town; beerfly.co.za; 083 384 0294
Corné van Niekerk began brewing in 2011 and, along with his wife Chantell and brother Jaco, was about to launch BeerFly when this book went to print. Look out for their three beers, a honey ale, American IPA and a dry stout, hitting bars and bottle stores around the northern suburbs of Cape Town.

BIG CITY BREWING COMPANY
Cape Town

Rob Heyns, the brains behind League of Beers, has teamed up with Savage Brewing founder David Savage to produce a range of beers that 'pair the magic of the industrial jungle metropolis with the glory of craft beer'. Launching with a low-carb beer and an IPA, the beers can be found in select locations and, of course, via League of Beers.

BLOUBERG CRAFT BREWERY
Montague Gardens, Cape Town; bloubergcraftbrewery.co.za
Jan Langenhoven had brewed kit beers for more than a decade when he was gifted an all-grain brewing course for his birthday in 2013. He hasn't looked back and was about to launch his own microbrewery serving an IPA, saison, stout and a Belgian tripel. An on-site tasting room and off-sales will be available.

FOLK & GOODE BREWING COMPANY
Hermanus
Gordon and Bevan Newton Johnson, of the Hemel-en-Aarde wine estate of the same name, have teamed up with beer-loving friends Patrick Gold and Steven Brooker to sprinkle a bit of grain among all those grapes. On a South African-built brewhouse, the team will be brewing an IPA and a weiss that will initially be available from the tasting room at the winery.

LEOPOLD7 BREWERY
Cape Town; leopold7.com
Leopold7's inaugural brew, a Belgian ale, launched in South Africa in 2014, with early batches being brewed in Belgium, and imported. Plans to open a carbon-neutral Cape Town brewery are underway.

LONG MOUNTAIN BREWERY
Church St, Robertson; longmountainbrewery.com
Craig Marson is the brewer at the Robertson region's second microbrewery, based in the town's industrial area. There will be a small taproom on-site, or seek out the brews around Robertson.

OLD HARBOUR BREWERY

Hermanus; oldharbourbeer.com

The brewhouse for this Hermanus-based brewery was still on a ship when I was on my Beer Safari, but should be up and running by the time you read this. Alas, it will be based not in the Old Harbour itself, but in the town's nearby industrial area. Look out for their beers on tap around town.

OLD POTTER'S BREWERY

54 Glory Rd, Nooitgedacht, Greyton; oldpottersinn.co.za

If ever there was a small South African town that needed a brewery, then Greyton would be it. Trevor Gerntholtz and Alan Blain are behind Old Potter's, based in a heritage building at the guesthouse of the same name. Expect to find a blonde ale, weiss and an IPA on tap at the brewery, with bottles possibly being released at a later date.

PLEBS

Durban Rd, Mowbray; plebs.co.za; 082 065 0296

This bar and live music venue was under renovation when *Beer Safari* was being researched, but pop in to find out if their on-site brewery is back up and running.

ROCA MICROBREWERY

Uitkyk St, Franschhoek

Although the microbrewery at the Dieu Donné winery has been functioning on and off for several years, they've never quite managed to get their beers off the ground. Check back now and then to see if things have finally taken off, for this would be a glorious spot to sit and sip a beer.

ROCK KESTREL BREWERY

Stellenbosch; rkbrewery.com

Brothers Johan and Nico Latsky are behind this Stellenbosch-based brewery. On the brew sheet is a blonde and an Irish red.

SEDGEFIELD CRAFT BREWERY

Scarab Village, N2 Highway, Sedgefield; sedgefieldbrewery.co.za

After a few years of retirement, Tony Hunter decided that rather than giving all his homebrewed beer away to ale-loving friends, he'd have a go at a second career. 'My hobby is now my job and my friends have to pay!' says Tony. The Hop Garden brewpub, situated next to Sedgefield's Scarab Village Craft Market, serves Tony's IPA, APA, blonde and Irish red ales in a family-friendly setting.

STELLENBOSCH BREWING CO.

Klein Joostenberg Farm, R304, Stellenbosch; stelliesbeer.com; 021 884 4141

Long-time homebrewer Bruce Collins has travelled the world in search of great beer and has the IBD diploma under his belt. The brewery has been a long time coming, but production was about to begin as this book went to print. Bruce, along with wife Karen and co-brewer Andrew Birss, will produce a Bohemian pilsner, pale ale, weiss and stout.

VILLAGE BREWERY

R304, Stellenbosch

Something has been brewing on the Vredenheim wine estate for several years, but the brand is struggling to get moving and when I visited there was no beer to taste. Check in to see if there's anything on tap, or look out for their bottled ale, which occasionally makes its way into local liquor stores.

ZEBONKEY BREWERY

Delvera, Cnr R44 & Muldersvlei Rd, Somerset West; zebonkey.co.za

The fact that German-born Jan Schmidtborn is launching a microbrewery will be welcome news to anyone who has tasted his superlative weizen at a SouthYeasters meeting. Jan and wife Mignonne will be serving their signature brew from a taproom at the brewery, along with an interesting range of beers, including a schwarz weizen, a brew using buchu-smoked malt, and the highly innovative Poseidon, a weissbier brewed with salt water.

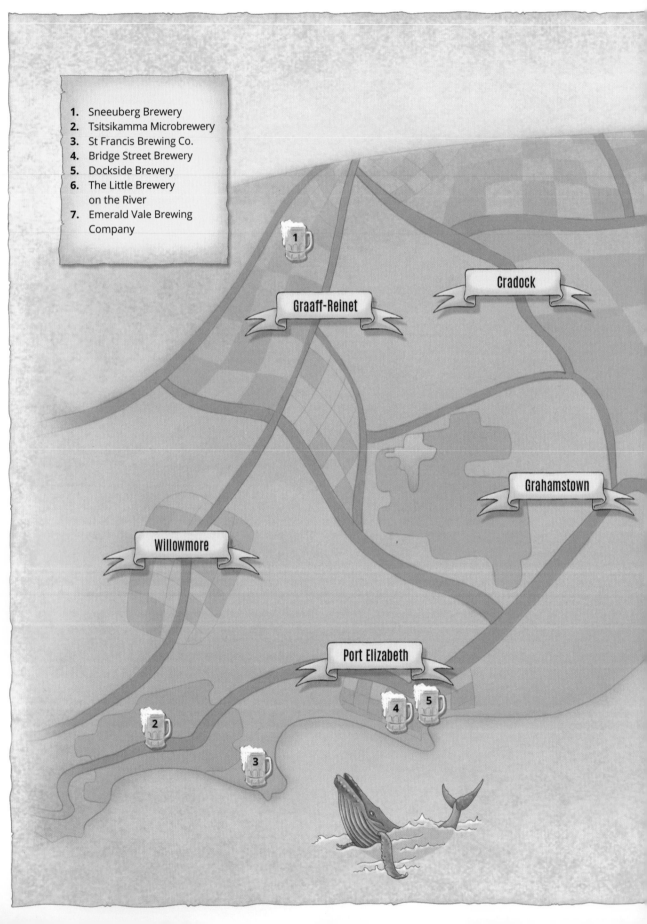

1. Sneeuberg Brewery
2. Tsitsikamma Microbrewery
3. St Francis Brewing Co.
4. Bridge Street Brewery
5. Dockside Brewery
6. The Little Brewery
   on the River
7. Emerald Vale Brewing
   Company

Cradock

Graaff-Reinet

Grahamstown

Willowmore

Port Elizabeth

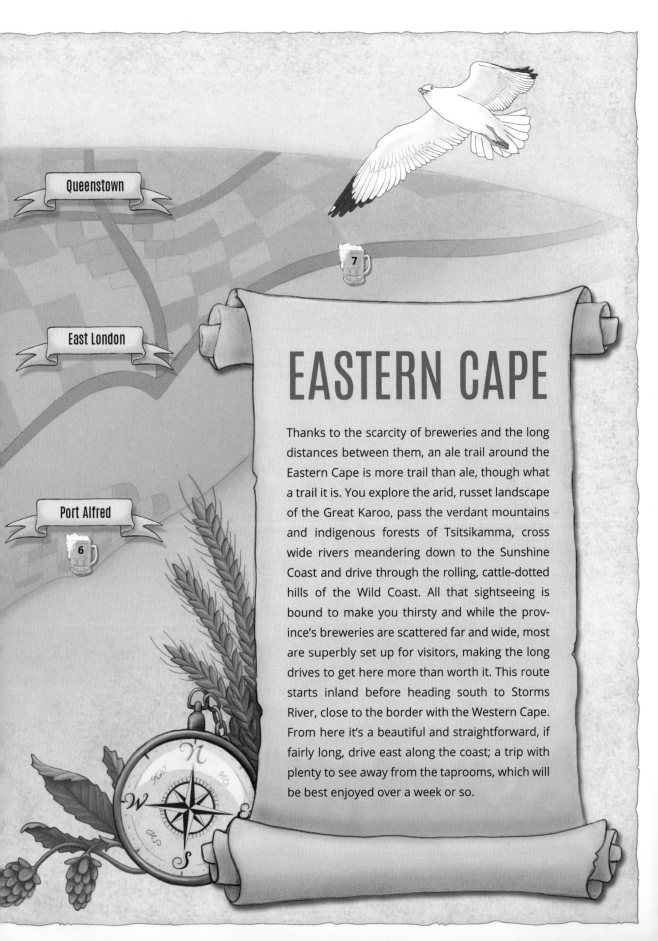

Queenstown

East London

Port Alfred

6

7

EASTERN CAPE

Thanks to the scarcity of breweries and the long distances between them, an ale trail around the Eastern Cape is more trail than ale, though what a trail it is. You explore the arid, russet landscape of the Great Karoo, pass the verdant mountains and indigenous forests of Tsitsikamma, cross wide rivers meandering down to the Sunshine Coast and drive through the rolling, cattle-dotted hills of the Wild Coast. All that sightseeing is bound to make you thirsty and while the province's breweries are scattered far and wide, most are superbly set up for visitors, making the long drives to get here more than worth it. This route starts inland before heading south to Storms River, close to the border with the Western Cape. From here it's a beautiful and straightforward, if fairly long, drive east along the coast; a trip with plenty to see away from the taprooms, which will be best enjoyed over a week or so.

SNEEUBERG
BREWERY

Pienaar St; Nieu-Bethesda; thebrewery.wozaonline.co.za; 049 841 1602

★ OPEN MON-SAT 11AM-5PM, SUN 11AM-3PM ★

BREWER
Spotted on
_____
Date
_____
Signature

Despite its remote location, Sneeuberg counts on a steady stream of thirsty travellers

Sometimes when you get to a brewery you just want to ditch the car and settle in for the afternoon, and where better to chill out for a day than the dusty Karoo dorp of Nieu-Bethesda. This mountain-fringed town is best known for its community of artists – in particular Helen Martins of Owl House fame – but at the Sneeuberg Brewery and Two Goats Deli you can also sample something I like to think of as 'edible art'. André Cilliers is not only a brewer – if the only paved road out of town got washed away, he'd be able to survive for some time on his homemade bread, cheese, pickles and, of course, a beer or two to wash it down.

The sandy goat farm is a far cry from André's former life as an economics lecturer in Cape Town, but there is no longing for the city here. When asked if he ever yearns for Cape Town, he looks around the peaceful, pretty surrounds and smiles – 'Would you?' He's often asked if he gets lonely living out in the sticks, but André laughs at the idea. 'I wish I could get lonely!' he says, referring to the near-constant stream of visitors who come to taste his produce.

After moving here in 2001, André quickly realised he would need an extra source of income to support his family and he instantly turned to brewing. 'I had brewed kit beers for my friends while I was at Rhodes,' says André. 'I'd always enjoyed it so I thought a little brewery would be a nice project.' Sneeuberg – named for the nearby mountain range – was established two years later, first using malt extract and later changing to partial mash brewing (see box). André has no plans to switch to all-grain brewing in future, largely due to the elevated transport costs involved in getting sacks of grain to this offbeat spot. And if it ain't broke, as they say, don't fix it – the brewery's

BEER 101

PARTIAL MASH BREWING

The 'partial' bit of this brewing style refers to the fact that only a small part of the sugar required to make beer is derived from the mash – as opposed to 'all-grain' brewing, where the grain provides all of the sugars during mashing. It's ideal for those with less space in which to brew since partial mash brewing requires a smaller mash tun than its all-grain equivalent. The malt is usually placed in a muslin bag and steeped – exactly like a giant teabag. This converts the starches into fermentable sugar, but extra sugar is then added in the form of dry or liquid malt extract.

popularity has steadily grown through the years and André is finding that he needs to brew his modest 100-litre batches with increasing frequency. 'People come to visit the town, but they've already seen the Owl House,' he explains. 'We're finding that more people are coming here specifically for us, which is great.' Initially, locals were a little hesitant about the brewery, perhaps envisioning a factory billowing smoke over their untouched town, but now André counts on support from them as well as tourists.

But it's not just the beer that keeps people coming back – it's the marriage of beer with two of its most compatible partners: bread and cheese. The eye-catching platters are as tasty as they are pretty, featuring a range of goat's and cow's milk cheeses, freshly baked bread and plenty of preserves and pickles, all made on-site. Only the smoked kudu salami comes from out of town, but despite André's pleas for the recipe, the Graaff-Reinet butcher who produces it won't spill his secret.

André's laid-back brewing philosophy perfectly suits the surrounds. 'I don't get too bogged down with details,' he says, referring to both his brewing style and the way he makes the cheese. 'I've got lots of goats and cows to be fed and to milk and lots of other things to do, so I'm not too worried about a degree or two of temperature here or an extra few minutes there.'

This ethos clashes with the way many brewers produce their beers, but with each sip of homemade ale and each mouthful of homemade cheese, you easily adapt to Nieu-Bethesda's sleepy pace of life, following André's lead to not sweat the small stuff – at least while you're in town.

BEER MENU

★

ROASTED ALE
(3.5%)

KAROO ALE
(3.5%)

HONEY ALE
(3.5%)

With everything in Nieu-Bethesda within easy strolling distance, the 'brewery shuttle' doesn't see much action

TSITSIKAMMA
MICROBREWERY

Darnell St, Storms River; tsitsikammamicrobrewery.co.za; 042 281 1711

★ OPEN MON-FRI 10AM-5PM, SAT-SUN 10AM-9PM ★

BREWER
Spotted on
_____
Date
_____
Signature

'...I AM GOING TO MAKE SURE THAT WE HAVE BEER DELIVERIES!'

There's just something about the Tsitsikamma Microbrewery that makes you want to stick around all day. It could be the darling little brewpub with its log cabin theme, it could be the gorgeous setting in the tiny town of Storms River, or it could be the cheery brewer, Chris Sykes, but something just makes you want to smile a lot and order another beer.

Chris is a novice brewer and he won't try and tell you otherwise. He started brewing in 2014 and his unofficial job title is 'Master Apprentice'. The rest of the Tsitsikamma team comprises Pine Pienaar ('Master Beer Lover') and former SAB engineer Johan Stumpf ('Master Brewer'). When Pine and Chris came up with the idea to start a microbrewery, Johan came to their aid – he had a 150-litre brewery lying around and happily taught Chris and Pine how to use it. One of the first things Chris did, once the brewhouse was installed, was to pretty it up. 'I think a lot of people forget that a big part of brewing is tourism,' says Chris. 'People want to see where the beer is brewed, they want to learn how it's made –

'Master Apprentice' Chris Sykes has infectious passion for the craft brewing scene

and of course they want to sit somewhere nice while they taste it.'

The Tsitsikamma Microbrewery certainly sits somewhere nice. Storms River, which has a permanent population of around 1 500, is a darling little town in a spectacular setting. A hub for tourists looking for outdoor adventure, its quiet streets are lined with guesthouses and restaurants and there's nowhere that you can't walk to in a couple of minutes. Chris has a hospitality background and runs the two businesses that the brewery is sandwiched between – the Tsitsikamma Village Inn and Marilyn's 60s Diner, a quirky, American-style eatery complete with classic cars and a free jukebox.

The brewery is about as visitor-friendly as they come, the wood-panelled vessels visible through large windows in the bar, where a range of South African craft beers are found on tap alongside Tsitsikamma's approachable ales. Outside sits a bicycle that is used for beer deliveries within the village. 'We don't have milk or newspaper deliveries in Storms River,' explains Chris, 'but I am going to make sure that we have beer deliveries!' When you visit, seek out Chris – his enthusiasm for both the brewery and the town in general is infectious, and make sure you set aside a couple of days to sip, wander and take in the surrounds.

With carefully chosen décor and a bike for beer deliveries, Tsitsikamma is one of the country's cutest brewpubs

BEER MENU

★

REDWOOD AMBER ALE (5%)

TSITSIKAMMA ALE (5%)

ST FRANCIS
BREWING CO.

167 St Francis Dr, St Francis Bay; 063 274 3743

BREWER
Spotted on

Date

Signature

A life-changing surfing accident inspired Lance Kabot to venture into the microbrewing scene

'You know you're a beer fanatic when...' It's the start of many a T-shirt or Buzzfeed-type list, but no-one can quite complete the sentence like St Francis brewer Lance Kabot. You know you're a beer fanatic when you come around from a near-death experience and the first words you utter are: 'Can someone get me a beer?'

Lance feels like he has found his calling in life, though beer isn't a new passion for him. He fell in love with ale in the USA back in the nineties, just as the craft beer scene was really taking off there. This was in the middle of an enviable seven-year trip around the world, in which he and his wife Linky worked in a host of different jobs in order to raise the funds to keep travelling. It was while working 'as a skivvy' in a couple of US breweries that Lance began to develop a passion for the industry. 'It was very inspiring to see how the brewers were all working together,' he recalls. 'They were all sharing ingredients and knowledge, bouncing ideas off one another.'

While it was the couple's passions for surfing and snowboarding that largely influenced their itinerary, Lance is quick to add that beer was always a big part of their trip and time spent in Europe introduced them to the vast range of beers coming out of Belgium. By the time Lance and Linky returned to South Africa, they were so used to having a range of beers available that they simply couldn't go back to just drinking light lager, and limited beer styles available at that time left them with no option but to brew their own.

BEER MENU

★

WILDSIDE IPA (6%)

STORMRIDER STOUT (5%)

BEACH BLONDE ALE (4%)

LIGHTHOUSE ALE (5%)

There's regular live music at the laid-back brewpub

Lance started homebrewing regularly in 2003, but it wasn't until he had a serious surfing accident that beer would become a much bigger part of his life. 'I hated hospital with a passion,' says Lance of his remarkably short recuperation time following the accident. 'They wouldn't give me any beer!' As soon as he was back at home he started brewing again, saying that he'd always found the process a prime way to relax (because you can't really carry out a homebrewing session without having a beer in your hand).

The surfing accident gave Lance and Linky a 'life is too short' moment and they opted for a lifestyle change that saw them move to St Francis Bay in 2013. Lance decided to make a go of his passion and set about creating a business plan. He cites many industry players in South Africa as being a source of inspiration and in early 2014 he finally decided to model his brewery on an American brewpub.

Today, the bar sits in a St Francis shopping arcade, the open-air seating, slouchy couches and surfboard décor making it a perfect match for the laid-back seaside town. Alongside Lance's four beers, drinkers will find a vast range of beer from around South Africa, plus a few from abroad. Lance decided to sell what are essentially competing brands when he realised he'd otherwise be opening a beer-less bar in St Francis's peak season. His brewing licence hadn't arrived in time, so he was left with the option to serve others' brews or nothing at all. In Lance's signature silver-lining style, he sees the delayed licence not as a hindrance, but a blessing. 'I'd never have been able to keep up with demand,' he says of the insanely busy first month. 'I'd have run out of beer and ended up with angry customers.' And now he plans to keep other craft beers on tap to lighten his own brewing load, for the reason for moving to St Francis was not to create more stress, but to cut back on it. And, of course, to split his time equally between brew kettle and surfboard.

You'll find beers from a selection of breweries on tap, as well as St Francis's own range

BRIDGE STREET
BREWERY

1 Bridge St, Port Elizabeth; bridgestreet.co.za; 041 581 0361

When the Bridge Street Brewery opened in 2012, it was like the official rebirth of South African craft beer, for the brewer at the helm of the stylish Port Elizabeth brewpub was Lex Mitchell – the founder of the country's first microbrewery, Mitchell's (page 96), way back in 1983.

Since selling Mitchell's in 1998, Lex had been absent from the South African brewing scene, but that's not to say that he wasn't looking for a way to get back into the brewhouse. In fact, he'd long been looking far and wide for a new brewing venture – as far and wide as the remote islands of Mayotte and St Helena – before finding the answer right under his nose.

'I was quietly sitting at home looking at other ventures when I was approached by Gary [Erasmus – the landlord of the building and partner in the brewery],' Lex explains. 'My involvement was simple – he asked if I'd be interested and I said yes!' Lex had already been brewing up some business plans of his own and while his vision to open an English-style pub didn't transpire, some of the ideas live on in the names of the beers.

Brewery assistant Sonny Ncanywa prepares the brewhouse

The beers are true to Lex's brewing inspiration – the United Kingdom. The trio of beers that Bridge Street launched with still remains, along with a cider and a few seasonal ales. The flagship Celtic Cross

Premium Pilsner is by far Bridge Street's biggest hit, not only with the drinking public, but also with judges at the 2014 National Craft Brewers Championship – a national competition where Bridge Street took second place.

Lex can't take all the credit for that win, though, for he no longer makes the beers alone. In fact, these days it is brewer Phumelelo Marali who spends the most time in the brewhouse. Phume, as he is known, has a background in hospitality and it shows, his infectious smile and evident passion drawing drinkers into the glass-fronted brewery behind the bar. He was thrilled about the win, though he wasn't as surprised as his brewing mentor was. 'I put so much love into my beers, I just knew they were going to win something,' he grins.

Bridge Street has become one of PE's most bustling bars, filled with families, lunching businessmen and night-time boozers. Perched on the edge of the Baakens River, the pub has helped kickstart regeneration of the neighbourhood and manages to marry classic beers and modern décor. The food is upmarket pub fare, the beers all sharing the same easy-drinking profile. And while you might not see Lex around too much, if you do, try to stop and shake the hand of the man who was brewing craft beer before the term had even been coined.

BEER MENU

★

CELTIC CROSS PREMIUM PILSNER (4.3%)

BLACK DRAGON DOUBLE CHOCOLATE STOUT (5%)

BOAR'S HEAD BEST BITTER (4.3%)

The stylish Bridge Street brewpub has become a top watering hole in PE

BREWER
spotted on
_____
Date
_____
Signature

DOCKSIDE
BREWERY

17 Horton St, Port Elizabeth; docksidebrewery.co.za; 083 273 7505

★ OPEN BY APPOINTMENT ONLY ★

'KARL KEPT ON BREWING AND EVERY TIME HE COMPLETED A BATCH HE'D SAY "I WISH I COULD DO THIS FOR A LIVING".'

BREWERS
Spotted on

Date

Signature

Karl and Jane Schlaphoff plan to keep their fledgling brewery small and intimate

One of the most inspiring things about the craft brewing industry is watching people grab hold of their dreams, and seeing a start-up business eventually blossom. When I visited Dockside Brewery, husband-and-wife team Karl and Jane Schlaphoff were just at the start of their journey and there's nothing more uplifting than following a brand, new venture as it grows.

Although the first commercial brew was yet to take place, Karl and Jane had already put in a lot of work to get here. The company name was registered back in 2007, though the brewing journey began much earlier. Karl learnt to brew through an old friend who had spent time in the USA and become passionate about homebrewing. 'I remember the first time he brought some beer to taste,' says Karl. 'I was sceptical, thinking about those guys who ferment pineapple juice and it explodes! But then I tasted it and I was impressed!'

'Karl kept on brewing and every time he completed a batch he'd say, "I wish I could do this for a living",' Jane continues. 'So one day, in late 2013, I said to him – okay, do it!' They took the plunge and set about researching how to put the brewery together on a budget. Over the next year or so, Karl literally made

BEYOND THE BREWERY:
THREE PLACES TO FIND CRAFT BEER IN THE EASTERN CAPE

1. **Beer Yard**
   1 Cooper St, Richmond Hill, Port Elizabeth; 041 582 2444
   There are rumours of a brewery opening at PE's premier craft beer spot. Until then, there's a good range of local, national and international beers on tap, plus more in the bottle.
2. **Beer Shack**
   Dolphins Leap Centre, Beach Rd, Port Elizabeth; 041 582 2354
   Under the same ownership as Beer Yard but with better views, Beer Shack is a nice spot for a pint and a gourmet burger overlooking the ocean.
3. **Prestons Liquor Stores**
   Cnr Genadendal & Buffelsfontein Rd, Mount Pleasant, Port Elizabeth; prestonsliquors.co.za; 041 368 5759
   Probably the liquor store with the best beer selection in town. There's also a good branch on Main Road in Walmer.

everything from scratch, learning on the job as he rolled and welded sheets of stainless steel to build his own mash tun, kettle, liquor tanks and fermenters.

The brewery sits in a small unit in an industrial complex near PE's harbour. A tasting room was in progress – decked out with 'steampunk' furnishings, all made by Karl. The area doesn't look much now, but the Dockside duo are convinced that it's an up-and-coming part of the city. A regeneration project is underway that will see the Baakens River developed into a visitor-friendly part of town, and with Bridge Street Brewery a short walk away, Dockside will be part of a mini brew route.

You can't help rooting for the Schlaphoffs, though they'll be the first to tell you that they don't want to get too big too soon. 'We don't want to make beer that we think people want,' says Karl, 'we want to make beer that we *know* they want. We want to find out what they like. We want to know the names of the people who drink our beers.' It's a charming concept, though with a bit of luck, by the time you read this, the business will have grown to the point where Karl can't remember the name of every drinker who passes through his brewery, for there will simply be too many.

BEER MENU

★

AFRICAN IPA
(4.8%)

PATIENCE PALE
ALE (4.4%)

BLOOD, SWEAT &
TEARS BELGIAN ALE
(6.4%)

DOCKSIDE BREWERY

THE LITTLE BREWERY
ON THE RIVER

20 Wharf St, Port Alfred; littlebrewery.co.za; 046 624 5705

★ OPEN MON-FRI 8.30AM-5PM, RESTAURANT OPEN TUE-SUN 11AM-10PM ★

The Little Brewery on the River sits in a building with a fascinating history

The eminently affable Ian Cook doesn't mind admitting that he 'bumbled into the whole brewery thing', though it might seem more like fate guided him to take over Port Alfred's long-standing but somewhat beleaguered brewery. After a brief but successful search for a semi-retirement business in small-town South Africa, Ian moved from Johannesburg to the Eastern Cape coast.

'I was initially interested in the Pig and Whistle, South Africa's oldest pub,' Ian explains. 'I was trying to work out how to make money and I thought we could stick a brewery in it!' With the new idea in mind, Ian started scouting around for second-hand brewing equipment and learnt about the vacant brewery in Port Alfred. Although established in 1998 as the somewhat successful Coelacanth Brewery, the setup had changed hands several times and hadn't been functioning for six years when Ian clapped eyes on it. Once he saw it in situ, the plan changed, for Ian fell instantly in love with the mid-19th century building in which the brewery resided. 'I could really see us doing things with it,' says Ian, 'and by the end of the weekend I called the owner and said I don't want the equipment – I want the whole shooting match!'

Thanks to Ian, the building had finally found its purpose. It started as the harbour-master's offices and warehouse during Port Alfred's heyday years during the Frontier Wars, then became the town hall, but it was always destined for a career in entertainment. After stints as a bottle store, cinema, restaurant and nightclub, the building finally became a brewery, but it took a few brewers to help the old build-

FIVE PRETTY PLACES FOR A PINT

These breweries, brewpubs and taprooms dotted around the country are particularly scenic places to sit and sip:

1. Emerald Vale Brewing Company (Eastern Cape)
2. Cederberg Brewery and Ceder Brew (Western Cape)
3. Brauhaus am Damm (North West)
4. Wild Beast Brewing Co. (Western Cape)
5. Mitchell's Brewery (Western Cape)

ing achieve its potential. 'It's a nice old girl,' says Ian, looking around at the high ceilings and thick stone walls, clearly glad that he opted to stick around when he first spent a weekend here in 2008.

Following a tip-off, Ian tracked down Colin Coetzee, a retired brewer living in nearby Kenton-on-Sea, and The Little Brewery on the River completed its first brew in 2009. Colin says his foray into brewing was simple – he flunked university and applied! But it was obviously the right path since he stayed with his post-varsity employer, SAB, for a further 34 years, working at breweries throughout Africa. You can quickly tell that Ian and Colin enjoy a friendship rare to people who have only known each other a few years. 'I haven't played one game of golf since I started here,' Colin mock-complains, referring to his retirement being cut short by Ian's venture. But it seems that Colin was just waiting for someone to

urge him back to the brewing scene. 'I didn't take much convincing,' Colin confesses. 'I got on an ego trip – I wanted to know that I could still do it.'

He couldn't do it without the help of the two assistant brewers, Bethwell and Alert Dube, brothers from Zimbabwe. Today, the two teetotal brewers take charge of the majority of the brewhouse happenings as Colin enjoys his semi-retirement, perhaps attempting to get a few more hours on the golf course.

The brewery has finally witnessed the kind of success it had been waiting for since it was first installed back in the nineties. The light, easy-drinking beers are found on tap throughout the town, as well as in neighbouring Kenton and Bathurst. For takeaways, you'll have to visit the brewery shop, which also stocks glasses, beer-infused edibles and toiletries, plus a range of light-hearted beer T-shirts that epitomise the cheery nature of this coastal brewpub.

The best place to sample Little Brewery's beers is at the Wharf Street Brew Pub, adjoining the brewery

BEER MENU

★

KOWIE GOLD PILSNER (4.5%)

SQUIRES PORTER (6.5%)

COIN ALE (4.5%)

EMERALD VALE
BREWING COMPANY

Off Cintsa East Rd, Cintsa; emeraldvalebrewery.co.za; 043 738 5397

★ OPEN MON–SUN 11AM–7PM – BOOKINGS ESSENTIAL ★

When I first met Chris Heaton, his brewery had been open for only a month. His rudimentary 75-litre system must have looked familiar to many homebrewers and although he was only supplying a couple of outlets, he couldn't keep up and was all out of beer when I got there.

Three years on, much has changed. In fact, the brewery is barely recognisable to someone who visited in the early days. Gone are the plastic fermenters wrapped in homemade insulation. Instead there's a shiny 500-litre stainless-steel brewhouse, each piece of equipment labelled to aid with the constant trickle of tourists wanting to take a brewery tour. The building itself has expanded upwards and outwards, and building works continue as the incredibly popular brewery constantly outgrows itself.

Even Chris is surprised with how well it's all gone. 'It got much bigger a lot faster than I had ever imagined,' he admits. The idea started in 2010 when Chris started making kit beers. Once he moved to all-grain brewing, he began to toy with the idea of

Emerald Vale's spent grains are used on the farm as animal feed

BEER MENU

★

PALE ALE (5.6%)

DARK ALE (5.6%)

GOLD ALE (5.6%)

AMBER ALE (5.6%)

'It got much bigger a lot faster than I had ever imagined,' says Chris Heaton

opening a brewery on his family farm, just outside Cintsa. The idea was to help boost tourism in the area, and it's definitely done that, with South African school holidays seeing the tasting room filled with domestic tourists and other months counting on a constant trickle of thirsty travellers from Europe, North America and Australia.

You can understand the attraction. For a start, Emerald Vale, which shares its name with the 380-hectare farm that the brewery is based on, is a simply beautiful spot to sit and sip a beer. But there's more to it than just a pretty panorama. It's a real destination brewery, with guided tours and tastings on offer and a restaurant serving simple, unfussy food. There's even a bring-and-braai option, with braais set up for customers to use. You can bring your own meat and wood to braai with – the only thing you can't bring, of course, is your own beer.

Emerald Vale has four flagship brews, all flavourful yet easy-drinking ales with names that Chris acknowledges aren't entirely true to what you find within the bottle, or glass. 'The Pale Ale is actually an American blonde ale,' he says. 'The Gold is a pale ale, the Amber is actually an English brown ale and the Dark Ale is a sweet stout.' I look at him, bewildered. 'Why?' is the obvious question. 'Because I didn't know anything about beer when I started,' he laughs, 'I just gave them names without knowing about the styles!'

The recipes have remained largely unchanged and Chris has decided to keep the names. 'The beers have a following,' he explains. 'People know which one they like, so I don't want to change the names.'

A lot has changed at Emerald Vale and a lot more is set to change – Chris is already thinking about a larger brewhouse, and there were plans to complete the tourism experience with on-site accommodation. But for all that had changed, one thing remained the same – when I visited, Emerald Vale had just come through a busy phase and once again, there was very little beer left for me to taste.

COMING SOON...

DAXI'S CRAFT BREWERY

3 Brooklyn Rd, Westbrook, East London; 082 492 4545

Craig Mayhew was just beginning to navigate the red tape as *Beer Safari* was being researched. Current plans are to start brewing on a small scale from an East London industrial park and, hopefully, to later go down the brewpub route.

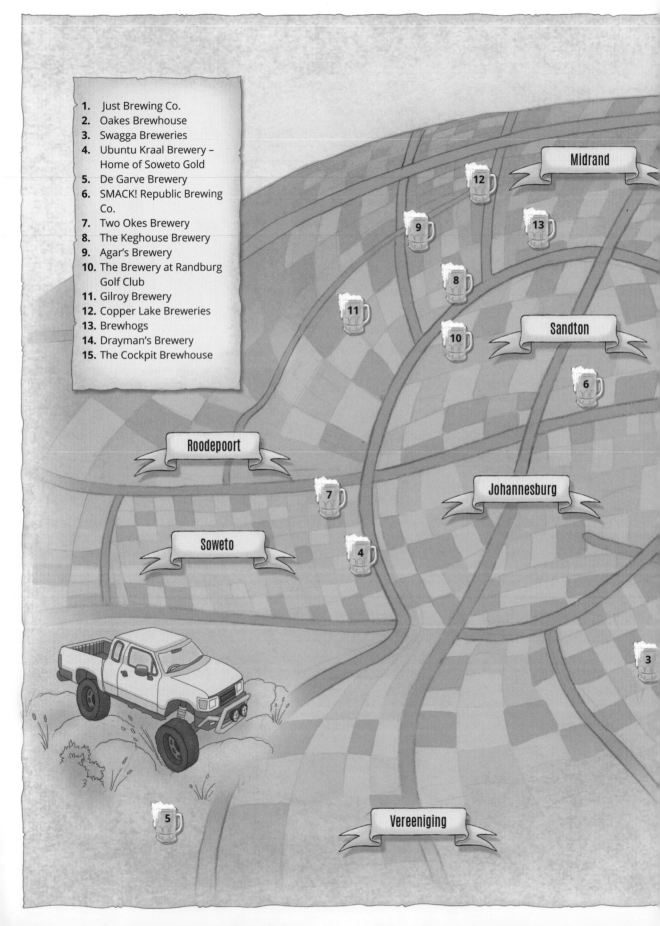

1. Just Brewing Co.
2. Oakes Brewhouse
3. Swagga Breweries
4. Ubuntu Kraal Brewery – Home of Soweto Gold
5. De Garve Brewery
6. SMACK! Republic Brewing Co.
7. Two Okes Brewery
8. The Keghouse Brewery
9. Agar's Brewery
10. The Brewery at Randburg Golf Club
11. Gilroy Brewery
12. Copper Lake Breweries
13. Brewhogs
14. Drayman's Brewery
15. The Cockpit Brewhouse

Midrand

Sandton

Roodepoort

Johannesburg

Soweto

Vereeniging

Cullinan

14

15

2

Kempton Park

1

Boksburg

Alberton

GAUTENG

South Africa's smallest yet wealthiest province has seen an explosion of microbreweries since 2012 and while many are popping up in rather obscure industrial areas skirting the cities, that doesn't mean they're not worth a visit. On the contrary, most of these small setups are making the most of their locations with simple tasting rooms and access-all-areas brewery tours. Visiting small mom and pop-type breweries is inspiring, making you want to take a chance on your dream as well. There is also an increasing number of brewpubs, particularly in the leafier areas of Johannesburg and Pretoria. The breweries in this chapter are scattered far and wide, though in this small province you can usually budget to visit three or four in one day. This route starts at O.R. Tambo International Airport and heads south, before backtracking briefly into the city centre. It then visits the breweries along the western edge of Joburg as it creeps north towards Pretoria. As the contract breweries aren't actually visitable, they're listed alphabetically at the end of the chapter (page 168), with recommendations on where to go to taste their beers.

JUST BREWING CO.

220 Van Dyk Rd, Boksburg; justbrewing.weebly.com

BREWERS
Spotted on
_____
Date
_____
Signature

★ OPEN BY APPOINTMENT ONLY ★

Kyle Pienaar is shy on first meeting. At 19 years old, he is certainly one of the country's youngest commercial craft brewers and with the brewery's doors only having recently opened when I visited, he seemed a little wary of having his beers critiqued. But a few minutes into the conversation his obvious passion for his newfound career emerged and suddenly he became a different person, animated about his family's new venture.

Just Brewing launched quietly in May 2014, their beers first being tasted by the general public at a local acoustic music festival. Since then, the trio of brews has trickled onto the market, featuring at various events from massive beer festivals in Cape Town and Johannesburg to smaller music and food festivals in the East Rand. 'The idea was to build up a following before selling to bottle stores,' explains Wendy Pienaar. Wendy handles the backstage stuff – social media, marketing and event organising – but it's her son, Kyle, who mans the kettles. As he neared the end of matric, Kyle started contemplating a culinary career. Around the same time his father, Julian, got a homebrewing kit and the two began brewing together. Gradually they brewed bigger batches and as Kyle started designing his own recipes, he realised he'd found his niche.

BEER
MENU
★
JUST PORTER (5%)

JUST PALE ALE
(4.5%)

JUST CHOCOLATE
COFFEE STOUT
(4%)

Kyle Pienaar takes care of the day-to-day brewing, but the whole family pitches in, especially at beer festivals

Based in an industrial complex near O.R. Tambo International Airport, Just Brewing shouldn't really be the cosiest place to sit and sip beer, but there's something about the family atmosphere that instantly relaxes you and makes you want to stick around for another brew. It's clear that the Pienaars are a close-knit family and they somehow manage to extend the family feel to drinkers, festival-goers and any homebrewers who cross their path. 'We're very supportive of the homebrewers,' Wendy says. 'They're the ones who come up with cool ideas and clever solutions. It's an exciting community to be involved with.'

Community is a big deal for the Pienaars, and it's not just the homebrewing population that they support. They also spread the love outside of the beer community by way of their spent grains. Most are sent to a local park, where the nutritious grain gets fed to the animals in the free-to-visit petting farm.

The rest Wendy uses in her frankly awesome biscotti recipe, then sells the goodies for charity.

What with schlepping the entire family to Cape Town to exhibit at the 2014 Festival of Beer, planning a world-class brewing workshop and generally spreading a lot of brewing love around the country, the Pienaar's company name actually sells them a little short, for there really is a lot more to this family than just brewing...

OAKES
BREWHOUSE

33 High St, Modderfontein; oakesbrewhouse.co.za; 011 608 0612

★ OPEN TUE-SAT 10AM-7PM, SUN 8AM-5PM ★

'This is not just a job for me,' says Happy Sekanka, 'it's kind of my baby.'

Happy Sekanka was well named. She beams as she pours tasters and pints for those who come to taste her beer and seems so at ease, you could easily imagine that she's been in the beer industry for years. But Happy, the perpetually smiling brewer at Oakes Brewhouse, is not only new to brewing, she's actually a recent convert to beer. 'I wasn't a beer drinker before,' she confesses. 'I even hated the smell of it!' But that all changed when she was approached to join the all-girl team at Oakes in 2014. Happy has a background in the hospitality industry and scored a full-time job as a butler at the USA embassy in Pretoria. Her contract was coming to an end when Thea Blom, a chef and former colleague of Happy's, approached her and asked her to come on board with a new venture – a microbrewery based at Thea's Modderfontein restaurant, 33 High Street.

Happy had her doubts – aside from the fact that she had never brewed beer before, she would have to leave her young family, commuting back to see them for just one day a week. In the end, with her family's blessing, Happy decided to give brewing a try. 'For me, brewing is like cooking. I love cooking and now I love brewing just as much. This is not just a job for me,' she says, 'it's kind of my baby.'

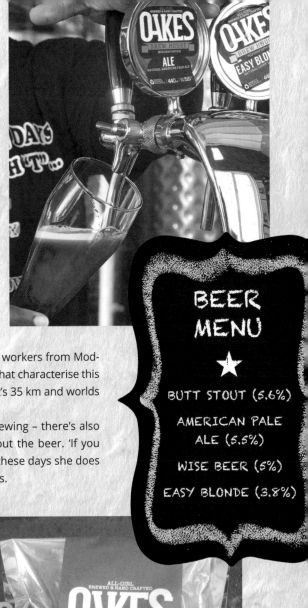

Her baby has received plenty of press since the first pint was poured. Happy is used to dealing with surprised customers who want to meet the brewer and calmly explains that yes, she did brew the beers they're tasting, her genuine smile never faltering. 'I do like to point out that, traditionally, African women have always brewed the beer, which makes people realise it's really not that strange,' she adds.

Two of the partners in the brewery were actually regulars in Thea's restaurant and were sitting under the century-old oak tree that dominates the grounds when the idea hit them – wouldn't this be the perfect place for a brewery? It is. The vibe is relaxed and family-friendly, with a jungle gym, live music and cute little pub in the basement. The restaurant serves flavourful Portuguese cuisine either outside or within the 120-year old heritage building in which it resides. The tasting room sits in a house once occupied by workers from Modderfontein's dynamite factory and overlooks the leafy lawns that characterise this corner of Johannesburg, a short hop from the main airport. It's 35 km and worlds away from the city's gritty centre.

Beer isn't the only thing that the ladies at Oakes are brewing – there's also a coffee roastery close by. But for Happy, it's really all about the beer. 'If you taste craft beer, you'll never go back,' she says, adding that these days she does indeed drink beer. 'It's part of my job description!' she laughs.

BEER MENU ★

BUTT STOUT (5.6%)

AMERICAN PALE ALE (5.5%)

WISE BEER (5%)

EASY BLONDE (3.8%)

The Oakes girls also brew coffee at the nearby roastery

SWAGGA
BREWERIES

31 Barium St, Alrode; swaggabrewery.co.za; 011 864 5056

★ OPEN MON–FRI 9AM–4PM ★

BREWER
Spotted on
_____
Date
_____
Signature

Justin Goetsch checks on a batch of Blonde Ale

Swagga Breweries began the way some of the world's greatest inventions probably begin – at the end of an evening drinking beer. 'We were having one of those discussions where you solve the world's problems,' explains Chris Botha, one of the partners in the brewery. 'All the great ideas you have in those conversations usually die right there with the last lager...but this one never did.'

The idea was a simple one – the three friends would build a small brewery at home, so that they would never again run out of beer while putting the world to rights. As Chris recalls how he, and the other founding partners Les Midgley and Corné Pretorius, agreed to each put in R6 000 to build the brewery, he looks around the room. The team didn't end up with a modest homebrewing setup in the garage of one of the friend's homes. They ended up with a 1 000-litre brewhouse consisting of shiny stainless-steel tanks shipped over from China. No-one is quite sure how they wound up running a sizable commercial brewery in an industrial area of Johannesburg. It started with some basic maths: 'It doesn't cost much more to make a slightly larger pot or a slightly larger fermenter,' says Chris. 'We started with the idea of doing 50 litres, then it went to 100 litres, then 200 and suddenly here we are!' It's not just the equipment that expanded – there are now seven partners involved in the brewery, which launched in April 2014.

It had only been a year since the fateful tipsy conversation on Les's stoep, and in that year Chris even travelled to China to check out equipment in

Bottles get filled with Swagga beer ready to hit Johannesburg's bottle stores

BEER MENU

⭐

SWAGGA IRISH RED ALE
(4.8%)

SWAGGA BLONDE ALE (4.8%)

SWAGGA ENGLISH ALE (3.8%)

SWAGGA PORTER (4.8%)

SWAGGA KRYSTAL WEISS
(4.8%)

SWAGGA ENGLISH IPA (5.8%)

person. With a 1 000-litre brew length finally settled on, a brewhouse was ordered and the team decided to set up shop in the stainless-steel workshop they already worked in together. It's a slightly odd arrangement, but it somehow works – the cavernous space is half alloy workshop, half brewery, but the picnic tables set up to face the brewhouse make it easier to forget you're in industrial Alrode. In fact, of the many Joburg breweries that have made their homes in industrial parks skirting the city, Swagga is one of the ones where you're likely to linger longer.

Since launching, the beers have quickly found a following. The focus is on drinkability, with the range of session ales devised by former SAB brewer Andrew Downes. These days, paramedic-turned-brewer Justin Goetsch is at the kettles, brewing the set range, a few contract beers and using the team's original 50-litre system to test out new recipes. Along with the rest of the team Justin, who is currently studying for the Diploma in Brewing with the Institute of Brewing and Distilling (IBD), would like to see Swagga moving to a brewpub in the not-too-distant future.

Swagga hasn't quite ended up being what the team had envisaged on that night when the beers ran out before the ideas did, but it's undoubtedly been more successful than any of the partners could have imagined. As Les points out, the beer is flying out of the fridges as quickly as they can brew it. In late 2014 they were awarded a kashrut certificate, making it the first kosher craft brewery in South Africa, which, Les says, opens up a whole new market for the Swagga team.

But despite all of the success, Les, Chris and Corné still find themselves faced with the same problem. 'We started this thing so that we'd have beer to drink,' says Les, 'but we sell everything we brew. Even after getting a brewery that got bigger and bigger, we still don't have any beer to drink!'

UBUNTU KRAAL BREWERY
HOME OF SOWETO GOLD

Senokoanyana St, Orlando West, Soweto; sowetogold.co.za; 079 890 8321

★ OPEN DAILY 10AM–10PM ★

The guys at Ubuntu Kraal have kind of become the rockstars of South African brewing. Everyone wants to interview them, their stands are guaranteed to have long line-ups at festivals and their shiny beer shirts have become a must-wear for fashion-conscious beer lovers. This is, in part, to the brand's hip image and the beer's undeniable drinkability, but it is mostly down to the location that gives the beer its name: Soweto.

It was a smart move to set up a brewery in such a well-known part of the country, a place that many South Africans hold dear to their hearts, that has such an important place in the nation's history. Brewer Ndumiso Madlala doesn't hail from this part of the country, but he still feels a special bond with the Johannesburg suburb. 'Soweto gave so much to us that it feels like home,' he says.

Ndumiso is new to the craft beer scene, but he's no novice when it comes to brewing. After completing his Master's thesis, which looked at methods of beer filtration, Ndumiso was scouted by SAB and ended up in a training programme with the brewing giant. He 'fell in love with the whole brewing process' and worked for them for a further three years before being headhunted by Heineken in 2008. Later returning to SAB, he spent time travelling Africa and got inspired to start up his own brewery. Along

the way he met Swedish-born Josef Schmid, a hospitality expert whose boundless energy is matched only by his grand plans for the brewery. The original idea – to start up a series of jazz club microbreweries was put on hold – 'it was way ahead of its time,' says Josef – but the brewery concept endured and, in October 2013, the first pint of Soweto Gold Superior Lager was served to the public at the annual Soweto Beer Festival.

There were many reasons that Ndumiso and Josef decided on Soweto – the name would be instantly recognisable, they saw a gap in a market that wasn't targeting the black middle class and, of course, in an urban area with a population topping 1.2 million, they wouldn't be short of customers.

The Ubuntu Kraal Brewery – named for the complex where it is located – predictably launched with a standard lager, but there are some interesting beers in the pipeline, including a coffee and cinnamon stout and a selection of fruit beers to accompany their existing apple ale. Situated close to the famous Vilakazi Street, the brewery is likely to attract plenty of tourists, though the team very much hopes to corner the local market. 'We want this to be a township project,' says Josef. 'We want this to be a catalyst for local economical upliftment. What we'd really like to do is to

SOWETO GOLD SUPERIOR LAGER

The usual words to describe a premium lager all apply here – Soweto Gold's debut pint is clear, it's crisp and it's refreshing. It's a very drinkable pint that's perfect for a South African summer's day.

take it back to beer's roots and have female brewers, to train local women to brew with us.' They've certainly captured a township vibe, with the brewery's corrugated steel exterior mimicking an early she-been, its façade dotted with photographs of Sowetan cultural, sporting and struggle heroes. A particularly nice touch is the traditional sorghum brewing paraphernalia adorning the terrace – artefacts that belong to the grandmother of their landlord.

Josef's eyes light up as he discusses the plans for the brewery – a canning line, a vegetable patch so the kitchen can grow its own food, increased capacity for the brewhouse and no lack of ambitious building plans. 'It's been a fun journey,' he says, 'and we're just at the beginning. We really believe this is going to be amazing.' Judging by the response from the public so far, the amicable Swede might just be right.

BREWERS
spotted on

Date

Signature

BEER MENU

★

SOWETO GOLD
SUPERIOR LAGER
(5.2%)

SOWETO GOLD
APPLE ALE
(4.5%)

Ndumiso Madlala and Josef Schmid toast their incredibly successful brand

UBUNTU KRAAL BREWERY – HOME OF SOWETO GOLD

Spotted on
_____
Date
_____
Signature

DE GARVE
B R E W E R Y

Olga Kirsch St, Vanderbijlpark; degarve.co.za; 082 428 8657

★ OPEN BY APPOINTMENT ONLY ★

BEER MENU
★

HAPPY MONK (6.5%)

JOLLY NUN (6.5%)

RASPBERRY DELIGHT (4.5%)

MALT & WALTZ AUSTRIAN STYLE ALE (5%)

GOLDEN BLONDE (4.5%)

PREMIUM BITTER (4.5%)

PICKLED HORSE PORTER (5%)

If homesickness can be defined as missing your home, then Patrick and Goedele van den Bon were almost definitely suffering from 'beersickness' when they arrived in South Africa in 1980. The Van den Bons hail from Belgium, and leaving a country with a cornucopia of beers to live in what was then a land of lagers was not an easy leap. It was 1982 when Patrick took up brewing – a year before the country's first microbrewery was launched and two Trappist-less years away from his beer-filled homeland.

'The early beers were... drinkable,' laughs Patrick, not willing to give much more detail on the subject. 'But in time the quality of the beer improved dramatically.' Well, there was plenty of time for them to get better, for it would be more than two decades before Patrick would decide to turn his 'hobby that got out of hand' into a small business.

Once the decision was made, Patrick decided that a little training in a commercial environment would be a good way to prepare for producing beer on a larger scale and he sought out the expertise of a fellow Gauteng brewer, Moritz Kallmeyer of Drayman's Brewery (page 164) in Pretoria. 'I spent a week with Moritz and learnt quite a lot about brewing commercially,' says Patrick. 'Then in September

2007 we were ready.' De Garve Brewery was born in an unlikely location on a farm outside of Vanderbijlpark, its name from the Flemish for 'sheave', referring to the bundles of barley harvested to make malt for brewing.

The brewery and tasting room are found at the Van den Bon's home, where empty bottles from around the world bear testament to the couple's shared love of beer. The De Garve range covers styles from a quartet of countries, but their flagship ales are unashamedly Belgian in style – a brave first for a South African craft brewery. But it's not all about the beer for Patrick and Goedele. Food also plays a pivotal role in the De Garve experience, with pairings offered to small groups with advance bookings. 'I always tell people that when it comes to beer pairing the rules are that there actually are no rules,' Patrick says. 'Having said that, we tend to pair a lighter beer with lighter food and a more full-bodied beer with something more flavourful.' You can quickly sense Goedele's shared passion for pairings as she shows off her collection of cookbooks featuring the kind of elaborate pairing you might normally expect with wine. But many of the Van den Bons' pairings come from experimentation rather than books, like the time a lactose-intolerant friend almost quashed Patrick's craving for pancakes. 'Then we thought maybe we could swap the milk for beer and a new De Garve dish was born.'

When Patrick first brewed De Garve's saison, it was meant to be a one-off brew to commemorate

De Garve's tiny tasting room sits in the Van den Bons' house

the birth of their grandson. That beer is now a permanent fixture on the beer menu and it looks like the same will happen with Raspberry Delight, which celebrated the arrival of their granddaughter. The fruit beer has become such a hit that Patrick has had to invest in a deepfreeze so he has year-round access to the berries. With the beer scene booming, Patrick has plenty of plans for the future, declaring that 'whether there's another grandchild or not, there will be new beers on the menu!'

THE DIVERSITY OF BELGIAN BEERS

While German beer styles have long been stifled by the Reinheitsgebot, Belgian beers have never been subject to such limitations, giving a range of ingredients found in no other beer culture. Expect herbs and spices, fruit of all types and the liberal use of candi sugar. But the one thing that gives Belgian beer its unique aromas and flavours is the yeast used, driven by higher fermentation temperatures than are the norm. For imported Belgian beers, check out the Belgian Beer Company (belgianbeercompany. co.za) or belgianbeers.co.za, or head to Den Anker at the V&A Waterfront in Cape Town. To taste local versions, try Clarens Brewery (page 210), Honingklip Brewery (page 84) and, of course, De Garve.

SMACK! REPUBLIC
BREWING CO.

Arts on Main Building, 266 Fox St, Johannesburg; smackrepublic.com; 084 491 0779

★ OPEN SUN 10AM–3.30PM ★

'If we didn't love beer, we'd have given up,' says SMACK! Republic brewer Drew Williams of their journey from homebrewers to Johannesburg's first inner-city craft brewers. Craft breweries are popping up so rapidly that you tend to forget the money, effort and massive amounts of time that it takes to set up even a small brewery, and chatting to the SMACK! team serves as both a reminder of the hard work required and also an inspiration that it can be within reach. All three partners are under the age of 35 and two of the three manage to hold down full-time jobs while brewing, bottling, cleaning, distributing, serving and marketing on the side.

Drew is what most would consider the lucky one, leaving his job in corporate communications to become the brewery's only full-time partner. But it wasn't always that way. Drew, older brother Dave and friend Grant York all recall the days when they would come to the brewery after a long day at work, brew until 2am and then be up again for the day job just a few hours later.

The brewery is based in the Maboneng Precinct in downtown Jozi and its position in a regenerated neighbourhood of the long-neglected city centre is an important part of SMACK!'s identity. 'When we were setting up, the craft beer scene was dominated by the Cape,' explains Drew, 'and we felt that inner-city Joburg had a gap. We wanted to be the quintessential inner-city brewery.'

'Essentially SMACK! is a collision between this awesome location in a historic building and this new inner-city movement,' Dave continues. 'We wanted to be right in the middle of that coming together of old and new Joburg.' That, in part, explains the name, though the main reason was that the guys wanted a name that people wouldn't forget. 'Some people don't like the name,' Drew concedes, 'but they'll all remember it.'

FERMENTERS

BEER MENU

★

MABONENG MAVERICK
BIERE DE SAISON (4.1%)

BRAAMFONTEIN BRAWLER
IPA (5.5%)

HILLBROW HONEY (5%)

BREE STREET BELLE
GOLDEN ALE (4%)

The beer names likewise reflect the brewery's location, each named for a central Joburg neighbourhood or street. The striking labels, whose original design was hand-drawn by an artist friend, seem in keeping with SMACK!'s location at the Arts on Main precinct and the beers within reflect a desire to break barriers and do things differently. The range contains staples like South Africa's first commercially available rooibos beer as well as occasional brews such as the chocolate stout infused with bourbon-soaked vanilla.

It's clear that the team is having a lot of fun and if you spend much time with them, you could imagine yourself setting up something similar with a group of close friends. But then you're reminded of the hard work that goes into the venture. 'We were self-funded,' says Drew, 'which basically means we were broke, so our model was to start small and then grow. People often ask us why we're not open more, but the honest answer is that we just can't – we don't have staff.'

The SMACK! team struggles to keep up with demand, even with the tap-room only open for one day a week, but the guys believe that this actually helps to fuel their desire to keep experimenting. 'We can't produce great volumes,' says Grant, referring to the fact that their beers are very hard to find, 'so to drink our beer people have to come back to the brewery. And if they're going to come back, we need to have something new for them when they get here.'

And as if it were scripted, our chat and tasting session is soon cut short – it is Sunday morning and there are literally people banging on the door for a post-breakfast beer to sip as they live and breathe the renaissance of South Africa's largest city.

MALTED BARLEY

Smack's small brewery is well set up to teach beer novices all about the process

SAB WORLD OF BEER

Gerard Sekoto St, Johannesburg; worldofbeer.co.za; 011 836 4900
Open Tue–Sat 10am–5pm; tours on the hour

If you needed proof that South Africa's beer culture is thriving, you only have to take a look around Johannesburg's Newtown district. There, in the city's revamped tourist/cultural quarter, sits what is definitely the city's most light-hearted museum, SAB's World of Beer. This homage to the amber nectar opened in 1995 to celebrate SAB's centenary and serves as a whirlwind lesson in the history, production and appreciation of beer.

The exhibits are delightfully tongue-in-cheek and at times borderline baffling in their silliness, perfectly portraying the down-to-earth nature that beer prides itself on. The 90-minute guided tour begins with a voice from beyond the grave as Charles Glass, founder of SAB's forerunner, the Castle Brewery, welcomes you. Audiovisual exhibits then take you through the early history of beer, beginning with an enjoyably cheesy 'holographic video' set in ancient Egypt. Things then go local, with the slightly sour smell of sorghum beer filling the air as a video fills you in on the history and culture of traditional South African beer. There's a chance to taste the murky brew from a communal clay pot before delving into European beer lore. You're quickly transported back to South Africa, though, with a mid-tour beer stop in a gold rush-era tavern and a walk through a mock-up sixties shebeen.

Part two of the tour introduces novices and know-it-alls alike to beer's ingredients and gives an overview of the brewing process that's informative without being too technical. Even in the most science-laden parts of the tour, the sense of fun remains, with comments like 'Can you feel the heat? Well that wort certainly can as this is the hottest part of the process' emblazoned on the information panels. There's plenty of chance to munch on malt as you peek into copper kettles and press buttons to release the heady aromas of each stage in the brewing process.

The tour naturally ends up in the on-site pub, where your ticket entitles you to two beers of your choice as you take in the brilliantly bizarre whirlwind tour of beer that has just been presented to you. It's not every country that can boast a museum dedicated to beer and the World of Beer is a perfect place to begin your education – or further it.

TWO OKES
BREWERY

Cnr Slingsby & Cartwright St, Stormill Ext. 9, Johannesburg; twookesbrewery.co.za

★ OPEN BY APPOINTMENT ONLY ★

'It was love at first sight,' laughs Hennie Kloppers, referring to the first homebrewing kit he received for Christmas in 2010. 'I went from having one bucket to taking over half the garage. Then the dining room turned into a mini brewery!' At one point Hennie was making 300 litres a week, but somehow still didn't have any beer to drink himself as friends would regularly drop by to stock up. He started visiting local microbreweries and soon realised he had a viable business opportunity on his hands. Hennie saw those visits to Gauteng brewpubs in a way that most people would not. 'There's something idyllic about it – some people see themselves lying on a beach looking at the sunset. I could see myself in a microbrewery.'

It was on Heritage Day 2013 that things kicked into high gear. Sitting sipping a homebrew with his beer-loving friends and family, Hennie suddenly

Hennie's jerry can dispenser was borne out of necessity but has become a regular feature at beer festivals

decided that he was going to make a go of it and a business plan quickly evolved. Two Okes was up and running within the year, but Hennie waited until 24 September 2014 for the official launch, a year to the day that he decided to open his own microbrewery.

The shiny Two Okes brewhouse was originally installed in a brewery in China, though the system had not been used, the building in which it was positioned

BEER MENU

★

TWO OKES IRISH ALE (4.5%)

TWO OKES AFRICAN PALE
ALE (4.5%)

TWO OKES PILSNER (4.5%)

TWO OKES HEFEWEIZEN
(4.5%)

being condemned shortly after the brewery was commissioned. Hennie admits he made a slightly ridiculous offer and, surprisingly, the offer was accepted. 'All of a sudden I had equipment being loaded onto a ship and I didn't even have a site to install it in!'

Hennie of course found premises – a bright, airy workshop in a Joburg industrial park. 'I wanted to divorce the public side of the brewery and the actual brewery,' says Hennie, though he adds that 'phase two' would be a brewpub, once the brand is well-established.

Although there is a second, silent partner in the business, that's not where the name comes from. It's more about the idea of not wanting to drink alone. 'Beer is a social thing,' says Hennie, 'and the idea is that you'll always be able to find someone to drink a Two Okes beer with.'

Hennie is planning to sell his beers, based on recipes he has tweaked and tested over the homebrewing years, in select liquor stores and hand-picked restaurants around the city. He's looking for places with a focus on small menus featuring local ingredients and is happy for his business to grow organically. Hennie continues to work in IT, with his office on the first floor mezzanine that overlooks the brewery. Just like someone whose office sits within view of a heavenly beach, Hennie can sit at his desk between brews and look out over his own version of paradise.

The Two Okes tasting room is a great place to get up close to the brewhouse while sipping a beer

THE KEGHOUSE
BREWERY

Unit 4, Stand 126, Watt Place, Kya Sands, Johannesburg; thebeerkeg.co.za; 073 501 3803

★ OPEN MON-FRI 9AM-5PM, SAT 9AM-1PM ★

BREWER
Spotted on

Date

Signature

Vincent le Roux doesn't only produce beer, he teaches others to brew their own as well

It can't have been a surprise to people in the South African homebrewing community when Vincent le Roux decided to open a microbrewery. He was already a well-known name within Gauteng beer circles, having run a successful homebrewing supply store in Johannesburg for several years.

Vincent began his homebrewing career as many do, with a Cooper's kit beer. Shortly afterwards, the suppliers asked if he might be interested in distributing the kits in South Africa and so Vincent's business, The Beer Keg, was born. The company originally operated from his home and he tended to it in his spare time, but in 2011 he left his job in IT and took to selling brewing goodies – equipment and ingredients for all-grain brewing alongside the kits – full-time. Once The Beer Keg outgrew Vincent's home, the store moved to premises at Gilroy Brewery (page 156) before eventually finding a permanent home in Kya Sands, an industrial area to the west of Joburg.

The reason for this move is clear – it's a region in which obtaining a licence to brew is fairly straightforward, and Vincent had decided to take his brewing up a notch and turn that, too, into a business. In August 2013, The Keghouse Brewery poured its

BEER MENU

★

AMERICAN PALE ALE (4.5%)

JOLLY PUMPKIN ALE (6%)

BOTTLE BLOND (3.5%)

DUNKELWEISS (4.5%)

The popular Pumpkin Ale has aromas of nutmeg and cloves, with background flavours of toffee

first pint of pumpkin ale, a heavily spiced brew that Vincent describes as 'a love it or hate it beer'. Luckily, most of his customers love it and the unusual ale is actually Vincent's most popular beer.

'I fell in love with beer the instant I started home-brewing,' says Vincent, and it's a good job as these days Vincent's life is all about beer, beer, beer. If he's not brewing it himself, or selling the ingredients to make it, he's teaching people how to turn malt, hops, water and yeast into it at one of his regular brewing classes. For any beer fan looking to take the first step into brewing, the classes are a lot of fun, with Keg-house beer on tap, a braai fired up outside and the chance to take home a couple of bottles of the beer once it has fermented. Most importantly, though, you leave with a manual and a recipe, so that all you need to do is a little shopping on the way out and you have everything required to make your own beer at home.

BREWING A KIT BEER

Many hobbyist brewers get started with a kit beer, the easiest and cheapest way to brew-it-yourself and the one that requires the least amount of equipment. A kit will come with a plastic bucket with an air-lock for fermenting, a long-handled spoon, brewing sugar, a tin of pre-hopped malt extract and a sachet of yeast. To successfully make the beer, all you need is two litres of boiling water (plus another 18 litres of cold water to top up the fermenter) and half an hour to spare. Don't expect to end up with the best beer in the world, but kit brewing is a great way to learn about the all-important sanitation involved in brewing and to see the science of fermentation in action.

AGAR'S
BREWERY

Unit 102a, Kya North Park, Bernie St, Kya Sands, Johannesburg; agarsbrewery.co.za; 076 191 5331

★ OPEN BY APPOINTMENT ONLY ★

Michael Agar taps a taster of his saison from the tank

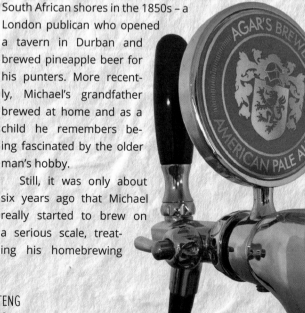

There are many breweries that carry a coat of arms on their beer labels, but, in South Africa at least, none seems quite as appropriate as that of Agar's. The brewery itself is one of Johannesburg's newest additions, but its roots go way, way back.

Michael Agar has been brewing for more than two decades, beginning the hobby when he lived in the USA near the start of their craft beer boom. But the family's beer history goes back considerably further. The first of the Agars landed on South African shores in the 1850s – a London publican who opened a tavern in Durban and brewed pineapple beer for his punters. More recently, Michael's grandfather brewed at home and as a child he remembers being fascinated by the older man's hobby.

Still, it was only about six years ago that Michael really started to brew on a serious scale, treating his homebrewing as though it was a professional microbrewery. He started taking steps that most homebrewers don't bother with – racking the beer to a bright beer tank, dabbling in filtration and swapping bottle-conditioning for force carbonation. The beers you find behind Agar's labels today are the fruit of many, many years of labour, based on recipes that Michael has refined throughout his homebrewing career. If the brewery's name seems familiar, you might well have seen Agar's at festivals in the early days of South Africa's beer boom, where they gave away samples to homebrewing enthusiasts while refining recipes and making plans to open a commercial brewery.

The brewery officially launched in August 2014, with Michael brewing on a purpose-built system designed and produced in South Africa by EJ Steel, a stainless-steel manufacturer that has recently added brewhouses to its repertoire. I visited only a month after the official launch and as Michael put it, 'we've only just started and we're already swamped!' After a quiet opening at the brewery, the brand launched to the wider public at the 2014 SA on Tap Craft Beer Festival in Pretoria. Considering the Agars' background in beer, it seemed only fitting that the entire family turned out to man the stand and it seems likely that there will be Agar ale enthusiasts for generations to come.

BREW TALK...
BRIGHT BEER TANK

Once the primary fermentation – that is, the part that creates the alcohol – is complete, most breweries transfer their beer to a secondary tank, also known as a bright beer tank. Here, the beer has a chance to clear up and, in some cases, this is where brewers carbonate their beers. The name – also sometimes spelt as 'brite' – comes from the fact that the beer is clearer since the yeast is no longer in suspension.

BEER MENU

★

BLACK MAMBA STOUT (5%)

AMERICAN PALE ALE (5.2%)

RED ALE (5%)

WHITE DOG SAISON (5.5%)

JOZI BLONDE (4.5%)

ENGLISH SPECIAL BITTER (4.5%)

Bottling and labelling is a hands-on process at this start-up brewery

THE BREWERY
AT RANDBURG GOLF CLUB

Setperk St, Randburg; randpark.co.za; 011 215 8600

★ OPEN TUE–SUN 9AM–10PM ★

Within South African brewing circles, Leon van der Westhuizen is well known for his association with fine brewing ingredients. His company, The Brew Master, has been supplying imported malt and hops since 2006, but Leon's initiation into brewing was actually characterised by a complete absence of any traditional brewing ingredients.

It's not the answer you expect when you ask the question, 'how did you get into brewing?' But when you think about it, Leon's reply does make sense: 'I spent a year in Saudi Arabia.' His first ever brew was a curious concoction cobbled together with what was available – water, some expired alcohol-free Budweiser, honey, sugar, Marmite and a sachet of dried yeast of the kind usually used in baking. You're probably recoiling in horror, but for one of the long-term expats living in a dry country cursed with year-round beer-drinking

BEER MENU

TPC SAWGRASS 17TH APA (4.7%)

AUGUSTA 12TH BROWN ALE (4.3%)

OAKMONT 1ST AMBER ALE (5.1%)

WHISTLING STRAITS 18TH WIT (4.3%)

LEGENDS 19TH ROBUST PORTER (6.1%)

ROYAL TROON 8TH BEST BITTER (4.3%)

Leon van der Westhuizen learnt to brew in the most unusual of places – Saudi Arabia

The range of ales rotates, so there will always be something new on tap

weather, Leon's unconventional brew was 'the best he'd ever had in Saudi'.

A year later and Leon was back in South Africa with a hankering to make 'some proper beer'. This was 2004, and when it came to ingredients, there wasn't a whole lot available here either. Sure, homebrewers weren't exactly resorting to tipping Marmite and honey into their fermenters, but the brewing supply scene was a long way off what it is today, so Leon decided to start importing small batches of speciality yeast and malt. This gradually morphed into the business now well known in South Africa as The Brew Master, and in 2012 Leon left his career in finance to focus on the brewing business full-time.

If there's one thing Leon loves about as much as beer, then it's golf, and by lucky chance he has managed to marry the two. He plays a couple of times a week at the Randpark Golf Club and one day was approached by a board member who had heard about his interest in beer. 'They had decided they wanted to do something different – you don't traditionally find a brewery at a golf club,' Leon says. His beers are brewed to strict BJCP styles and are exclusively available at the golf course. The beers are named for courses around the world – or more specifically, for holes within those courses that are particularly renowned for their difficulty. At any one time, you'll find four beers on tap at the Brewery, which is located in a small pub with outdoor tables overlooking the driving range. The beers have become so popular that Leon is installing two taps in the main clubhouse as well, and there are plans to add a beer garden to the club's facilities.

'I call us alchemists,' says Leon of himself and all his fellow brewers, 'we make liquid gold...from water!' You can see how passionate he is about his beers, though for the moment, brewing is still something of a side line. Along with his partner Heidi Palm, Leon's main job is one that's even more important than actually brewing – helping to grow the South African beer industry by supplying brewing ingredients and equipment to his fellow alchemists. Heidi sums up perfectly why they do what they do, and it's a sentiment I've often felt myself. 'It's wonderful when you've known a homebrewer for years and they come of age and eventually realise their dreams.'

GILROY
BREWERY

Cnr Beyers Naude & R114, Muldersdrift; gilroybeers.co.za; 011 796 3020

★ OPEN WED–SAT 11AM–10PM, SUN & TUE 11AM–6PM ★

BREWER
Spotted on
_____
Date
_____
Signature

Steve Gilroy entertains the Sunday lunch crowd with his topical poems

Steve Gilroy has been on the South African brewing scene, one way or another, for over 40 years and describes himself as 'like the granddad... well, a cross between a granddad and a naughty Father Christmas'. Never has a more appropriate description been tendered for this white-haired, long-bearded brewer who seems as innocent as a greeting card Santa... until he opens his mouth. Steve is known for his outspoken nature, his no-holds-barred opinions and, of course, for giving the finger to anyone who gets in his way – a challenge, he says, to other brewers to brew better beers than he does.

Locals and tourists alike flock to his Muldersdrift brewpub on weekends to soak up the raucous vibe, listen to live music, hear one of Steve's renowned poems and to join in his cheery toast of 'up yours'.

'A lot of brewers don't realise what business they're in,' Steve muses. 'It's the entertainment business. Entertainment is the backbone of any successful pub.' Of course, he is also in the beer business and has been brewing one way or another since he 'recently' moved to South Africa. By recently, Steve means 1970 – 'well, it was after the Boer War,' he adds. Hailing first from Ireland, but with a Liverpool and London upbringing, Steve was used to a certain style of beer when he came to South Africa and will tell you in no uncertain terms that he was, let's say, underwhelmed by the beer available. 'It doesn't take me long to get pissed off,' he says. 'And it took three months before desperation became the mother of inspiration.' Back in those post-Boer War days, equipment and supplies were almost impossible to come by, so Steve sourced malt extract wherever he could, often from relatives with a little extra suitcase space visiting from Europe.

Steve's working history is as chequered and colourful as his conversation – starting as a rock musician for controversial and oft-banned seventies rock band Suck, then moving from playing the guitar to 'playing the pornograph' (he worked for a while in the 'nudey photo business'). Eventually, though, his passion for brewing transformed from being a hobby to a profession and he decided to open his own brewpub. 'I didn't want to be in the rat race anymore,' he says. 'I wanted to have fun.'

When you look around the English-style pub sporting the occasional nudey photo, a range of newspaper cuttings showing Steve in his bow tie and waistcoat regalia and the Gilroy coat of arms featuring the famous outstretched finger, you sense that he definitely achieved this goal. The brewery and pub opened in 2008 and quickly developed a cult following of people keen to try the traditional English-style ales with a little English-style humour on the side. Steve seems like a natural publican, but he'd never worked behind bars before. 'I'd never been in hospitality, never run a pub or a restaurant, but sh*t you learn fast when you're losing money!' he reminisces.

The brewery was an almost instant hit, though, and Steve has since trained others to assist with the daily brews so that he can concentrate even more on being the frontman. Steve offers weekly beer experience tours, laced with his particular brand of wit, or if you like to keep your drinking sessions insult-free, drop in for a taster tray or a pint – just don't sit near the stage when Steve takes to the floor.

BEER MENU

⭐

LAGER (4%)

FAVOURITE PALE ALE (4%)

TRADITIONAL IRISH RED ALE (4.5%)

SERIOUS DARK ALE (5.5%)

THE WORT HOG BREWERS
worthogbrewers.co.za

The Gauteng-based brewing club is the country's largest, now with satellite chapters in Johannesburg, Hartbeespoort and the East Rand as well as the original club, which meets in Pretoria. All chapters meet every other month, usually at a brewery, so there's plenty of beer even if the homebrew runs out. The annual Summer Beer Festival has been going for over a decade and tickets are sought after in Gauteng beer circles. For instant advice, tips and general chat wherever you are in the country, join the Wort Hogs on Facebook.

COPPER LAKE
BREWERIES

Broadacres Shopping Centre, Cnr Valley & Cedar Rd, Broadacres, Johannesburg; copperlakebreweries.co.za; 079 686 6635

★ OPEN TUE 4PM–10PM, WED–SUN 11AM–10PM ★

Brendan Watcham built the Copper Lake brewhouse from scratch

The equipment at Copper Lake might look a little unorthodox, but there's a good reason for that. Pretty much the entire brewery – mash tun, fermenters, keg washers and all – was fabricated by hand; brewer Brendan Watcham's hands specifically. 'I built this brewery twice basically,' he laughs. 'Well, maybe that's a bit of an exaggeration, but I was learning as I was going along and a lot of things didn't quite work out, so I would change it and do it again.'

A metalworker and engineer by trade, Brendan was lucky enough to have the skills to build his own brewery once he decided to launch his beers commercially. His equipment has been gathered from a range of sources, including tanks from the Cullinan diamond mine, which he thinks were used to dispense beer to the workers. 'Each brewery gives the beer its own character and makes it unique,' says Brendan, making you eager to taste the beers originating in his idiosyncratic brewhouse.

'I actually first brewed beer in 1989,' he recalls, seeming surprised at the realisation that his first brew was over 20 years ago. It was kit beer that he brewed back then, though, working from a homebrew recipe book of his father's that he'd found lying around the house. A lack of available ingredients led Brendan to bow out of brewing soon afterwards, though his interest in fermentation had obviously been captured.

His next venture was homemade wines, including vintages made from rosehip, mint and, in an unlikely twist, beetroot – an experiment that Brendan perhaps under-exaggerates as 'not so good'.

The interest in hobbyist alcohol production then lay dormant until 2009, when Brendan stumbled across the Wort Hog Brewers club online. 'I decided to join as it had always been an interest in the back of my mind,' says Brendan. 'Then after a couple of meetings, I started brewing all-grain beer on a small system.' He soon graduated from an urn and a bucket to his homemade three-tier system, which he later began to manufacture for homebrewers who had outgrown the 'giant pan on the stove' approach. But it was a freak occurrence that convinced Brendan to bow out of steelwork and turn his hobby into a career. 'I had a motorbike accident and spent six months in bed,' he explains. 'I did a lot of thinking and realised I was tired of what I was doing and wanted to change my life. Brewing was what I enjoyed, so I decided to start brewing commercially.'

It was while Brendan was bed-ridden that he began studying for the Institute of Brewing and Distilling (IBD) Diploma in Brewing, later becoming the first independent brewer in Africa to be awarded the diploma – something he urges other brewers to do. 'Studying forces you to learn things that you might normally skip, like pH, minerals in the water and such. It gives you a great footing and background.'

Copper Lake was established in 2011, based in a workshop on Brendan's cattle farm a short hop from Lanseria Airport. After a couple of years without a real tasting room, Brendan and his wife Tracy were in the process of opening a brewpub in nearby Broadacres when this book was being researched. Beer-infused food will be on offer and, along with brewing courses, there will be a chance for groups to come and brew a bespoke ale on the in-house brewery. Brendan will also brew speciality beers here, though the bulk of Copper Lake's beers will still be produced at the farm.

BEER MENU

★

IPA (6%)

DARK LAGER (5%)

LIGHT LAGER (4.5%)

ENGLISH ALE (4.5%)

CHOCOLATE (6%)

Thanks to the brewery's sizable capacity ('He who dies with the biggest capacity wins', says Brendan, I suspect only partly in jest), Copper Lake's beers are now widely available and the brewery's mobile beer stand is a common sight at beer festivals. Actually, there's usually a lot more to it than just a stand – Brendan tends to put on a mini Copper Lake festival within the larger event, having waitresses deliver beers to those playing the outsized games he brings along to entertain his fans between pints.

BREWHOGS

Unit 50, Barbeque Corner, Dytchley Rd, Barbeque Downs, Kyalami; brewhogs.co.za; 011 466 0746

★ OPEN MON-FRI 9AM-5PM, SAT 9AM-1PM ★

Built in the UK, the Brewhogs brewhouse used to be on show at Gold Reef City

A lot of attention is given to the fact that Apiwe Nxusani is a black woman thriving in the South African craft beer industry, but perhaps more attention should be given to the fact that she's a bloody good brewer.

Apiwe's interest in brewing began early. 'I was always into the sciences,' she says, 'and when I was in standard nine I went to a career open day. I wasn't really sure what exactly I wanted to do within the sciences, but at the microbiology stand they had a can of Castle and a pot of yoghurt, which intrigued me. I started talking to them and they told me about fermentation science and I thought "that is what I want to do".' Following a BSc in microbiology, she was studying for

BEER MENU

★

NO. 2 ORIGINAL RED LAGER (4.5%)

NO. 1 PREMIUM PILSNER (4%)

NO. 4 INDIA PALE LAGER (5%)

NO. 3 BLACK IPL (5%)

Brewmaster Apiwe Nxusani pours a pint of pilsner at the Brewhogs tasting room

her Honours at the University of Pretoria when she learnt about a partnership between her department and the Institute of Brewing and Distilling (IBD), a UK-based organisation that offers training and education. Thanks to the partnership, students had the opportunity to incorporate the IBD's Diploma in Brewing into their degree – 'one of those things you don't pass up', as Apiwe puts it.

Apiwe walked out of varsity into a traineeship with SAB and worked for the brewing giant for seven years. Her roles were many and varied, but it was during her time working as 'craft brewer' at SAB's Chamdor plant that 'the lightbulb was switched on'. Free to brew something other than the lagers the company is known for, Apiwe's interest was piqued. 'Being able to create my own recipes, that's where another avenue opened up,' she says. In the same year she visited the second annual Cape Town Festival of Beer and was further inspired by the creativity and passion of the country's existing microbrewers.

Over time, Apiwe developed two new career goals – to help provide training to upcoming brewers, and to start her own microbrewery. In 2013 she left SAB and met Mike Martin and Patrick Ellidge, owners

of the Hogshead chain of pubs. Together they came up with the Brewhogs concept, although the original plan featured a far smaller brewery. But an offer too good to pass up came their way in the form of a disused brewhouse built in Burton-upon-Trent and used in the eighties and nineties at Johannesburg's Gold Reef City amusement park. By the time the Brewhogs got hold of it, the brewhouse was gathering dust in an SAB depot and needed some serious refurbishment before Apiwe brewed her first batch on it.

Today, the 4 000-litre system is in constant use, not only for Brewhogs' innovative range of lagers, but also to produce contract-brewed beers for other Gauteng brands. Ale is notably absent from the beer list, but Apiwe easily explains why. 'We shouldn't be following trends, we should be setting them. The point is playing around with lager, showing people that you don't have to make an ale to make an interesting beer.'

It's been a busy couple of years – as well as becoming a partner in her own brewery, Apiwe has completed the IBD's highest level of training, making her one of very few craft brewers in the country who can legitimately call themselves 'brewmaster'. There are plenty of plans for limited edition brews and Apiwe doesn't rule out the possibility of producing ales in the future, but for the moment South Africa's most famous female brewer is happily at the helm of a little lager revolution.

BEYOND THE BREWERY:
FIVE PLACES TO FIND CRAFT BEER IN GAUTENG

1. **Capital Craft**
   Greenlyn Village Centre, Cnr Thomas Edison & 12th St East, Menlo Park, Pretoria; capitalcraft.co.za; 012 424 8601
   Pretoria's premier craft beer hangout has a beer list as long as the food menu. Enjoy beers from across the country in the garden or join one of many beery events, including talks from local home- and microbrewers.

2. **The Griffin**
   Illovo Junction, Oxford Rd, Johannesburg; thegriffin.co.za; 011 447 9842
   This gastropub gives equal attention to beer and food, with some healthy dishes even appearing on the menu.

3. **The Wolfpack**
   21 4th Ave, Parkhurst, Johannesburg; 011 447 7705
   A low-key bar that keeps it simple with burgers 'n' beers. Look out for house brews available exclusively here.

4. **Beerhouse**
   1 Sunset Ave, Cnr Witkoppen Rd, Fourways, Johannesburg; beerhouse.co.za; 011 465 2402
   The '99 bottles of beer' model has been exported from Cape Town to Fourways, where revellers spill out onto the deck to drink a wide range of local and imported brews. The food is largely an afterthought – this place is really all about the beer, beer, beer.

5. **Foundry**
   Parktown Quarter, 3rd Ave, Parktown North, Johannesburg; foundrycafe.co.za; 011 447 5828
   As well as boutique beer, the Foundry's bar features a range of South African craft spirits. There's also a coffee roastery on-site.

DRAYMAN'S
BREWERY

222 Dykor Rd, Silverton, Pretoria; draymans.com; 012 804 8800

★ OPEN MON-FRI 8AM-1PM ★

If there's one name you hear over and over when asking people how they got into brewing in South Africa or how they went about setting up their microbrewery, it's Moritz Kallmeyer. This probably isn't

The Drayman's beers are all bottled by hand

too surprising, since it seems that Moritz was born to make booze. While most people trace their fermentation fascination back to their university days, Moritz's history with creating alcohol goes back much, much further. 'When I used to go fishing with my father, I collected the spent grains from the sorghum breweries to attract fish. I had some left over in a bucket and it started fermenting. That's when Philemon, one of the farm workers who was like my second father, explained how they made the beer and told me if I added some sugar it would start fermenting again. That was my exposure to fermentation – I must have been in grade seven or eight.'

It was the beginning of a lifelong journey to transform sugar into booze, starting with homemade wine. 'I made fruit wine long before I made beer,' says Moritz. 'I fermented it in the sock drawer of my cupboard! It was great exposure to the chemistry and hygiene side of fermentation.' From there it was a quick leap into spirits – furtively distilling his first schnapps in a camping kettle when he was 15 and sneaking it into a biology class where his classmates passed it around. 'I suppose that was laying the groundwork for my distilling career as well. Even though life took me in a different direction at first, I was going to come

DELIVERIES BY DRAY

Traditionally, beer was transported from the brewery to its neighbouring pubs on a dray – a flat-bedded cart pulled by a horse. Moritz got the idea for his brewery's name from a varsity brewing buddy whose father had worked as a drayman in the United Kingdom. In South Africa, as in most places, horse-drawn deliveries have died out, but on the first Friday of each month you can listen out for hooves on tarmac as three kegs of Castle Lager are delivered from Newlands Brewery in Cape Town to a trio of nearby pubs.

back to it in the end. It was meant to be. The passion was going to override everything else.'

A career as a biokineticist beckoned, but the urge to ferment stuff was always there and when winemaking fell away at varsity, it was beer that would take over, thanks to some university housemates with a brew-it-yourself kit. He continued brewing when he started working and used to advertise that there would be a 'malt tea' available at lunchtime in the gym. Here, Moritz would share his beers, ask for criticism and fine-tune the recipes – it's also where he met and converted Theo de Beer, now the brewmaster at Anvil Ale Brewery (page 202).

Eventually, the need to ferment won out and Moritz took a job at one of the country's earliest brewpubs, The Firkin in Pretoria. 'Unfortunately it died a quick death,' says Moritz. 'It was way before its time.' But graduating from his garage brewery had given him the push he needed and, in 1997, Moritz founded his own brewery, Drayman's. The brewery soon outgrew its original thatched home in Koedoespoort and moved to the Pretoria suburb of Silverton in 2000, where it remains to this day. Although successful now, the brewery didn't always flourish and Moritz turned to other types of fermentation to help make ends meet. In 2005, he started a small-scale whisky operation and four years later added mampoer to the catalogue of mostly German-style beers.

Today, the malty aromas from the mash tun mingle in the air with the sweet smell of distillation. The recent additions of honey liqueur and Tej – Ethiopian mead – are as much about Moritz's passion to ferment as anything else, since he admits that the brewing side has finally taken off. 'At last!' he enthuses. 'It took 15 years, but I'm so pleased that it's changing – we fought for a culture of beer and created a culture of flavour.' It's fair to say that Moritz played an important role in creating that culture, offering honest opinions of other brewers' beers, training people who would later become his competitors and helping to set up several other breweries. There's no doubting that Moritz has been one of the key players on the South African beer scene, so next time you're in Pretoria, drop into Drayman's and raise a glass of beer to him. Or a whisky. Or mampoer. Or wine. Or Tej...

BEER MENU

★

GOBLIN'S BITTER (4%)

JOLLY MONK RAUCHBIER (4%)

DÜSSEL ALTBIER (4%)

BERGHOF (4%)

EMPEROR INDIA PALE ALE (4%)

ALTSTADT WEISSBIER (4%)

THE COCKPIT
BREWHOUSE

80 Oak Ave, Cullinan; www.thecockpitbrewhouse.co.za; 012 734 0656

★ OPEN THU 12PM-9PM, FRI-SAT 11AM-9PM, SUN 11AM-4PM ★

BREWER
Spotted on
_____
Date
_____
Signature

André de Beer is known for his willingness to share brewing information

If there is one man who sums up the craft beer industry in South Africa, then André de Beer is it. The aptly named brewer is humble, welcoming and always willing to share his expertise with fellow 'beer nerds'. He also brews some pretty awesome beers.

Cockpit is a charming brewpub sitting in an equally charming town. Cullinan has managed to fuse diamond mining with tourism – a feat helped in no small part by the opening of the brewery in 2010. Cockpit sits in one of the old mine-owned cottages on Oak Avenue, though it was touch and go whether André would secure the property for a while. 'At first they thought I wanted to do a beer hall for the mine workers,' André tells, 'but I persisted and the GM – a teetotaller – saw the potential in the idea since they wanted to bring more tourism to Cullinan.' At first the brewpub relied on overflow from nearby restaurants, but within two years André and his team were having to turn people away. 'Every business manual says that nine out of 10 restaurants fail within the first year and 80 per cent of those left fold in the second year. We were breaking even from the very first month,' André beams.

It's not too tough to see why, with a great range of beers, a well-thought-out menu and a delightful building and gardens in which to enjoy it all. André brewed his first beer in 2002 and insists that his early success was aided greatly by Gauteng's homebrewing club. 'Without the Wort Hogs I wouldn't have reached the point of brewing decent beer as quickly as I did. The guys are very forthcoming with information and in some cases brutally honest about the taste of your beers!' In André's case, brutal honesty wasn't often a bad thing since the beers were undeniably good – he won the National Homebrew Championships a few years in a row, as well as a homebrewer of the year award.

MUSTANG IPA

There's a dose of tropical fruit on the nose here, thanks to the American hops André uses in his signature pint – think lychees, mango and granadilla. There's some caramel-like malt in the background, but as the style dictates, the flavour of this beer is mostly about the hops. That said, it's not a hugely bitter brew, making it a good introduction to IPAs for those who aren't yet mad about high IBUs.

About five years after he first dabbled in home-brewing, André started exploring the idea of setting up a brewpub. Following a nationwide search for the right spot, he ended up in the region where he grew up, providing Cullinan with a brand-new gem. The brewery's name comes from André's other passion, aviation. 'We wanted a theme,' he says, 'and I love aviation.' He used to co-own a plane with Triggerfish brewer Eric van Heerden and Stephan Meyer from Clarens Brewery, but decided to sell when he started brewing. 'The whole "12 hours bottle to throttle" rule didn't work for me when I was brewing!' he laughs, though his love of flying lives on in the beer names and pub's décor.

Cockpit has become a familiar and very welcome sight at the country's many beer festivals, with the

award-winning Mustang still a firm favourite. Along with the fixed beer menu, André continues to brew some occasional ales, many of which pack a serious flavour – and alcohol – punch. André is certainly not afraid of bold beer, a fact confirmed by the keg of 14.5% barley wine sitting in the brewery's cold room.

Alas, this particular beer is not for public consumption, though its story will put almost as much of a smile on your face as a taste of it would. André brewed the barley wine three months before the birth of his first daughter back in 2007 and each year on her birthday, he has one glass. The last glass – well, glasses actually – will be drunk on her 18th birthday when Gerda can join her father in a celebratory toast. This is one example of André's love for and dedication to beer. He brews it, holds gourmet dinners paired with it, and encourages others to make it. All you have to do is go there and drink it.

BEER MENU

★

MUSTANG IPA (6.2%)

BLACK WIDOW STOUT (5.4%)

SPITFIRE ENGLISH PALE ALE (3.6%)

TIGER MOTH BELGIAN DUBBEL (6.5%)

HELLES BELLES BLOND ALE (4%)

FOKKER WEISS (4%)

GAUTENG CONTRACT BREWERIES

Contract brewing is an arrangement where a company will pay to produce its beer on another brewery's equipment. People have different reasons for starting up in this manner, but it's usually a way to set up a beer brand for those who can't yet afford to invest in the equipment and premises required to start their own brewery. Some contract brewers insist on brewing the beer themselves, others employ the services of the in-house brewer. The contract breweries are listed separately in this book simply because they don't have official tap rooms that you can add to your itinerary, though each comes with a recommendation on where you'll likely be able to find their brews. The breweries here are listed alphabetically.

ACES
BREW WORX

acesbrew.com; 011 334 6410

★ ACES DOESN'T HAVE A TASTING ROOM, BUT TO SAMPLE THE BEER HEAD
TO THE WOLF PACK, THE GRIFFIN OR STEAMWORKS IN JOHANNESBURG. ★

It was South Africa's oldest microbrewery that got brothers Dyllan and Lliam Roach interested in beer. For almost four years they were the Gauteng agents for Mitchell's and when they got wind that the brewery was planning to take over the distribution themselves, the Roaches began to formulate a plan. By the time they lost the contract, they had a fully developed ace up their sleeve, hence the company's name.

The brothers were already running The Tap Room, a company that installs and services draught beer-dispensing equipment, so the infrastructure for their own beer brand was very much in place. Like most who contract brew, Lliam and Dyllan didn't have the finances to build their own brewery, though they are both keen homebrewers. 'We mess around on a 50-litre gravity-fed system,' says Dyllan, explaining how they develop recipes on their homebrew setup before contracting a local brewery to produce the beers on a larger scale. Somewhat unusually, the Aces team doesn't contract all their brewing out to the same brewery, with current beers being brewed at both Brewhogs and Swagga and others set to be produced at The 400 Brewing Company, Brickfields and possibly Nottingham Road.

With the beers recently launching in Cape Town and the Roach brothers looking for a partner in Durban, business seems to be booming, though that doesn't mean they have achieved everything they'd like to. The goal is to open an Aces brewpub. 'The brewery is on pre-order, and we're just looking for the right spot,' says Dyllan. 'The brewpub will only brew beers to be served on-site. All of our commercially available beers will always be contract brewed by different breweries.' The business model certainly ensures a vast capacity, ensuring that there will be plenty of Ace beer on tap throughout the country.

BEER MENU
★

PREMIUM LAGER (4%)

IRISH RED ALE (5.1%)

BARE NAKED BLONDE (4.8%)

KRISTALL WEISS (4.2%)

LAGER

100% HAND CRAFTED

MADE IN
SOUTH AFRICA

440 ml

HATE CITY
BREWING COMPANY

Johannesburg; hatecity.co.za

★ HATE CITY DOESN'T HAVE A TASTING ROOM, BUT TO SAMPLE THE BEER HEAD TO THE WHIPPET IN LINDEN OR ROELAND LIQUORS IN CAPE TOWN. ★

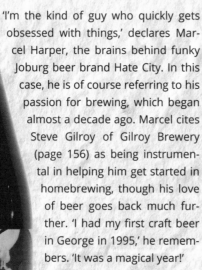

'I'm the kind of guy who quickly gets obsessed with things,' declares Marcel Harper, the brains behind funky Joburg beer brand Hate City. In this case, he is of course referring to his passion for brewing, which began almost a decade ago. Marcel cites Steve Gilroy of Gilroy Brewery (page 156) as being instrumental in helping him get started in homebrewing, though his love of beer goes back much further. 'I had my first craft beer in George in 1995,' he remembers. 'It was a magical year!'

By 2012, Marcel says he felt confident enough to start sharing his knowledge with novice brewers and he began writing one of the country's earliest brewing blogs, The Beginner Brewer. On it he shares recipes, brewing tips, posts beer reviews and writes occasional comment pieces on the South African beer scene.

BEER MENU

★

INSURRECTION STEAM BEER (5.4%)

BURNING BEARD BLONDE ALE (4%)

Soon after launching the blog, Marcel began to co-teach brewing workshops along with Vincent le Roux of The Beer Keg, a homebrewing shop that's now home to The Keghouse Brewery (page 150). It was here that Hate City was born. 'I wanted to

get into the mechanics of the brewery,' says Marcel, 'and to develop my own recipes.' He and Vincent invested together and Hate City's beers are now brewed at Keghouse.

So what about that name? It has various meanings, according to Marcel. 'It's partly about my love/hate relationship with Johannesburg,' he says, 'but it's also about having a hatred of bland beer and wanting to drink a handmade product instead.' Like most who start out as contract brewers, Marcel hopes to one day open his own brewery. 'When I'm brewing, I don't feel like I'm working at all – that's when I knew it was for me,' he says, his smile making you realise there really isn't much hate to be found in this start-up beer venture.

BUYING BEER TO TAKE HOME:
FIVE CRAFTY LIQUOR STORES IN GAUTENG

Craft beer is becoming much more widespread in South African liquor stores; try one of these spots for a particularly impressive selection:

1. **Hops, Scotch & Barrel**
    Shop 23, Honeycrest Centre, Beyers Naude Dr, Randpark Ridge, Johannesburg; h-s-b.co.za; 011 795 3222
2. **Norman Goodfellows**
    192 Oxford Rd, Cnr Chaplin Rd, Illovo, Johannesburg; ngf.co.za; 011 788 4814
3. **Locoliq**
    70 Conrad Dr, Randburg, Johannesburg; locoliq.co.za; 011 886 9108
4. **Liquor City Groenkloof**
    51 George Storrar Dr, Groenkloof, Pretoria; liquorcity.co.za; 012 460 6813
5. **Liquor City Northcliff Corner**
    183 Beyers Naude Dr, Northcliff, Johannesburg; liquorcity.co.za; 011 782 9281

LOXTON
LAGER

loxtonlager.co.za; 011 486 2297

★ LOXTON DOESN'T HAVE A TASTING ROOM, BUT TO SAMPLE THE BEER HEAD TO
THE LOCAL GRILL, THE FOUNDRY CAFÉ OR STANLEY BEER YARD IN JOHANNESBURG. ★

In many ways, the South African beer scene simply steals from craft beer culture elsewhere. Heavily hopped American IPAs are starting to become big business, bold Belgian ales are sneaking onto beer menus, some brewers pair their Reinheitsgebot beers with sausage platters or eisbein, while others offer pie and chips with their pints of English-style bitter. Of course, all of these international beer styles and more deserve a place at the South African table, but it's also refreshing to see something with a real local feel in our fridges.

'What I was looking to create was a true South African beer,' says Loxton Lager's founder Stuart Thompson. 'I didn't want to do an Irish red or a Belgian dubbel – I'm too bloody South African for that,' he asserts, referring to his family's deep-seated roots in the country.

Loxton Lager is not the only beer that's using endemic ingredients, but there is just something quintessentially South African about blending fynbos from the Karoo, buchu from the Cederberg and honey from the Sunshine Coast and adding it to that most South African of beers – lager. Stuart's main muse was the vast and arid Karoo, a place he has spent many years exploring on holidays. 'The Karoo is a place that's really bitten me,' he smiles, as the aroma of the medicinal Karoo plants he grows in his garden fills the room.

Finding the perfect ingredients for his unique lager was a lengthy task, with Stuart gradually stumbling across them along his travels. With buchu and honey sourced, the combination was complete when he discovered Karoo locals sipping tea brewed with an aromatic fynbos

A fynbos-infused beer and some biltong – it doesn't get more South African than this

species known as *kankerbos* (cancer bush). With indisputably South African ingredients selected, it was time to work on the recipe.

Through a process of trial and error – and no fewer than 34 batches of the beer fermented in buckets at his Johannesburg home – the lager was created. Now it just needed a name. 'The name actually came last,' admits Stuart, explaining that it was partly Loxton's location in the Karoo and partly its alliterative allure that made him name his beer after a town with a population numbering just over 1 000 people.

Although by this time Stuart was an accomplished brewer, he opted to have the beer contract brewed, first at Copper Lake and later at Brewhogs. 'I would love to do it myself one day,' he says. 'Though in a way I'm glad that I haven't bought the hardware yet – it's like buying shoes for a child.' He refers to the fact that he had no idea what kind of capacity he would need or how people would respond to what is admittedly a very unusual beer. As it turns out, the beer has been well received and has lived up particularly well to its tagline 'brewed for food', with a number of eateries and high-end restaurants choosing to stock the complex beer.

'My problem,' says Stuart, who has a certain way with words, 'is that I tend to drink all liquids at the same rate. So I can hold conversation for 20 minutes if I'm drinking spirits, 40 with wine and two hours with beer. I wanted to come up with a beer that I could enjoy in the evening and particularly with a meal – a great, complex beer.' He acknowledges that for some palates his lager is 'too interesting', but its popularity is growing and it's even on sale at Die Rooi Granaat, a coffee shop in the town that gave the beer its name.

Stuart has a long-standing relationship with the South African beer industry, working for many years as an investment analyst and completing detailed research on SAB, but it seems with Loxton Lager he has found his true calling in life. 'I rather love small businesses,' he says. 'A little business that washes its face – it's what I've always pined for.' The only other thing he seems to pine for is to move his little business to the little town whose name it shares and who knows, if he hurries, perhaps Loxton could become the home of the Northern Cape's first craft brewery.

BIG 5 PINT

LOXTON LAGER

It's not going to be to everyone's tastes, but in my mind you can't deny that this 4.8% brew is a superbly made beer. Buchu is a tricky herb – pungent and fairly unfamiliar to most, especially when it comes to beer – but the balance here is spot on. The aroma is minty and this follows through on the palate, giving a complex but refreshing beer with just a touch of sweetness. It will probably far surpass any expectations you have when it comes to sipping a light lager. Pair it with mildly spiced food like Cape Malay or some of the more delicate Thai dishes.

MAD GIANT

madgiant.co.za

★ MAD GIANT DOESN'T HAVE A TASTING ROOM, BUT TO SAMPLE THE BEER HEAD TO BEERHOUSE IN FOURWAYS OR CRAFT IN PARKHURST. ★

'For me, beer has always been the catalyst for stuff to happen,' says Eben Uys, though he's not referring to hitting the dance floor after a couple of pints or suddenly starting to speak a foreign language at the end of a night out. 'Whenever my career path changed, beer was there,' he adds.

Beer has certainly provided Eben with an interesting working background. He was studying for a PhD at Stellenbosch University when he first got involved in brewing. It was 2008 and, thanks to funding from SAB, Eben built the nanobrewery for Stellies' first intervarsity brewing team. 'SAB introduced me to craft,' he admits, adding something that many brewers and drinkers tend to forget: 'There's a lot you can learn from them.' Eben certainly had a lot to learn when it came to brewing, and he had to learn it quickly. Having completed his first brewhouse, he wanted to test it out. 'I started that first brew at 5pm,' he remembers

A brewery in central Johannesburg is on the cards for Eben Uys

BEER MENU

★

PUNK HOP PALE ALE (5%)

TRUE GRIT AMBER ALE (5%)

ELECTRIC WEISS (4.5%)

sheepishly, 'I thought I'd just throw something together – I had no idea how long it would take!'

Eben talks candidly about the mistakes he made and when asked what that first batch was like, he replies, 'Well, it was beer...' With the engineering and chemistry departments watching, he realised his pride was on the line and sought advice from experts – Denis da Silva, trade brewer at SAB Newlands, and Moritz Kallmeyer of Drayman's in Pretoria (page 164). 'He's a legend,' says Eben of Moritz, who has been instrumental in getting Mad Giant off the ground.

The brewery was a success and the Stellenbosch team fared well with Eben among their ranks. On completing his studies, a serendipitous meeting with wine giant Charles Back led to his next brush with brewing. 'I chatted to Charles at his Paarl wine estate and said "you should put a brewery in here". He smiled and said "it's already commissioned",' recounts Eben. 'I said I'd love to see it and eventually I was invited to work on installing the Cape Brewing Co.'s brewhouse (page 65).'

You get the feeling that this sort of thing happens to Eben all the time. He's instantly likable, a humble guy who could have a successful career in motivational speaking if the beer thing doesn't end up working out. After a 'year of being in a dream', Eben had to leave CBC to fulfil work commitments with Sasol, but beer was pretty much always on his mind.

Along with business partner Graham Smit, Eben began to develop the idea that would later become Mad Giant. Although they discussed starting with a small, affordable brewery of their own and gradually building up the business, both decided they would rather launch on a larger scale and opted to have the beer brewed under contract at Drayman's. Eben developed the recipes and was able to brew alongside Moritz at the start, but his chemical engineering job in Secunda keeps him fairly busy. The beer is bottled in Secunda, by aspiring brewer Mruti Ndlangamandla. Mruti was a little down on his luck and looking for work. 'He wasn't so successful at gardening,' Eben says, 'but Mruti now loves what he is doing. He literally sits there with a smile, bottling the beer, and in the evenings he's studying John Palmer's book *How to Brew*.'

Mruti has aspirations to be a brewmaster and, with a little help from Eben, you feel like he'll get there. 'What motivates me is people who follow their dreams,' he says. His dream is, of course, to open his own brewery and the search for premises was underway when we chatted. If it all goes to plan, I have a feeling that Mad Giant is going to be something pretty special.

BIG 5 PINT

PUNK HOP PALE ALE

This beautiful copper-coloured beer is clear enough to read through. There are earthy hops when you whiff, with a little resinous pine if you search for it. Sipping is like drinking liquid toast. Hops on toast. And the lingering but very pleasant hop-and-malt-derived bitterness means you can keep enjoying Mad Giant's maiden beer long after you've finished sipping.

THREE SKULLS
BREW WORKS

threeskulls.co.za

★ THREE SKULLS DOESN'T HAVE A TASTING ROOM, BUT TO SAMPLE THE BEER HEAD TO BEERHOUSE OR THE FOUNDRY CAFÉ IN JOHANNESBURG OR CAPITAL CRAFT IN PRETORIA. ★

It's fairly common for people to start off as a contract brewery while they establish the brand and save some cash, later moving production to their own brewhouse, but Three Skulls was never known for doing things the conventional way. Jonathan Nel launched his one-man brewery at the Clarens Craft Beer Festival in 2012 and for two and a half years he literally did everything himself – brewed, bottled, cleaned, marketed, distributed and kegged. In late 2014, he made a tough decision to turn Three Skulls into a contract brewery, with the beers now produced at Standeaven Brewery (page 226) near Durban in KwaZulu-Natal.

'Trying to operate a full-time brewery that can produce beer, bottle and distribute is extremely difficult when you're trying to keep costs down and doing all the work yourself,' Jonathan explains. There were worries about consistency, quality and brewing enough beer to actually make a profit, and then came the clincher – a job opportunity that

BEER MENU

★

BANSHEE IRISH RED ALE (5%)

GOLDEN SKULL IPA (5.8%)

GRAVEDIGGER AMERICAN BLONDE ALE (4.5%)

THREESKULLS.CO.ZA

INGREDIENTS: MALTED BARLEY, HOPS & WATER

5.8% RBV
440ML

ALCOHOL IS ADDICTIVE

Golden Skull
INDIA PALE ALE

THREE SKULLS BREW WORKS

saw the Nel family move to London in 2014. But the funky brand had already gathered a following and Jonathan decided to keep the beer on our shelves, ready for the day he eventually returns to South Africa.

Jonathan has a fairly long history with the South African brewing industry, working in SAB's various marketing departments for six years. Through work he got to attend the inaugural Cape Town Festival of Beer, which is where he was first introduced to craft beer. 'I suddenly realised that I had very little idea of how you actually make beer, so I asked my wife for a homebrew kit for Christmas,' he says.

That was in 2010 and Jonathan didn't wait long to get moving, making his first batch after lunch on Christmas Day. 'At the beginning I did two Cooper's kits – one was a spectacular failure and one was good,' Jonathan laughs, more than willing to explain the failure. 'It was because I didn't quite grasp that you have to ferment at a certain temperature and I left it by a large window. I came home one day and saw that the temperature was 29 degrees. I tasted it and it was basically nail polish remover!'

The brews improved and he soon upgraded to an all-grain system. 'I was still working at SAB then, so I used to take my beers to the SAB tasters – they really helped me to improve.' Not long afterwards Jonathan decided to leave the company and set up his own small brewery. 'I wasn't happy at SAB any-more. I learnt a lot there and I'm thankful for that, but I had to go and do it, to try it.'

Three Skulls was born soon afterwards, a concept that Jonathan came up with by 'taking every-thing I learnt at SAB and then doing the complete opposite'. He's quick to explain what he means by that: 'The rules of beer say that if you're going to re-lease a beer in South Africa, then the South African consumer wants a green bottle, a gold cap, gold foil, German heritage and hops they've maybe heard of or are at least easy to pronounce. So I looked at all of those rules and wanted to make something that you look at and say, "there's no way that's a beer brand and if it is, that's really rad".'

For the moment, Jonathan's more madcap brews are on hold – in the past he has added anything from lavender, passion fruit, cinnamon, chocolate and chillies to his beers – but despite the hardships in setting up a solo brewery, the Skulls continue to be familiar faces on the craft beer circuit.

The Three Skulls beers are currently brewed at Standeaven Brewery in KZN

COMING SOON...

BACKWARDS BEAN BREWERY

Johannesburg; backwardsbean.co.za

This father-son venture based in central Johannesburg has been struggling to get off the ground despite appearances at a couple of the city's major beer festivals. Brewer Graham Stansell counts a PhD in microbiology and some high-scoring entries in the National Homebrew Championships in his achievements. Beers include a premium bitter and an APA, which was being brewed exclusively for the Wolfpack in Parkhurst.

BOSHEUVEL COUNTRY ESTATE

54 Glory Rd, Nooitgedacht, Muldersdrift; bosheuvelestate.co.za

With luxurious rooms and a restaurant on-site, this is a good place to sink a few brews. The flagship beer is a pilsner, though beer fans prefer the Dark Silence – a high-alcohol sweet stout. It's a family-friendly place close to Gilroy Brewery (page 156).

BRICKFIELDS BREWING CO.

Newtown, Johannesburg; brickfieldsbrewing.com

Named for Johannesburg's late 19th-century brick-making industry, Brickfields is set to become a super-slick brewery with no lack of capacity. The range will consist of everyday-drinking beers plus some occasional ales brewed on a smaller brewhouse.

FRIAR'S HABIT CRAFT BREWERY

Pretoria; friarshabit.co.za

A trio of homebrewing friends in Pretoria has decided to make the leap to microbrewing. Plans were in the early stages, but the beer menu looks set to include a couple of less commonly found styles, including a rauchbier and a California common. Look out for the beers at Capital Craft in Pretoria.

MAINSTREAM BREWING COMPANY

Johannesburg; mainstreambeer.com

Ryan Zwankhuizen and Gavin White launched their brand in style in 2014, with the Mainstream Altbier scoring highly in the national Craft Brewers Championship. The beer was briefly contract brewed at Swagga (page 138) and Black Horse (page 188) while Ryan and Gavin put the finishing touches to their own brewery. As well as the Alt, look out for their cream ale, APA and IPA.

THE 400 BREWING COMPANY

Jeppestown, Johannesburg; facebook.com/The-400BrewingCompany

Named for the brewery's batch size, The 400 is a venture started up by five old friends. Brewer Carl Nienaber describes the upcoming beers as 'something yellow, light-bodied and lightly hopped, something red, medium-bodied and quite 'American' and then something black, full-bodied and roasty'. Look out for them in liquor stores, bars and restaurants throughout downtown Jozi.

STIMELA BREWING CO.

Johannesburg; stimelabrew.co.za

Tsikwe Molobye is a relatively recent convert to craft beer, but from the very first sip he was pretty much obsessed. His engineering background was handy when it came to building his own homebrewing system and just over a year of avid brewing later, Tsikwe was about to launch his own brand, Stimela.

THREE STAGS BREWERY

Edenvale, Johannesburg; tsbrewery.co.za

Eben Roux was happily 'living a dream' as he awaited the licence for his nanobrewery based near O.R. Tambo International Airport. Pilot brews were underway and he hopes to put in a small, rustic tasting room once he's up and running. If his enthusiasm runs over into his brews, you could be in for something special.

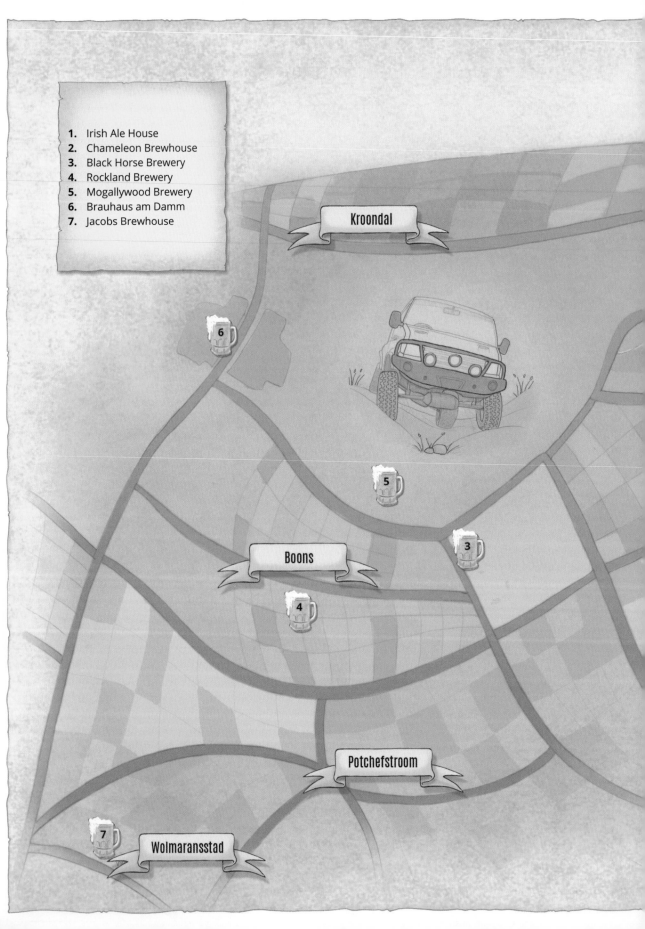

1. Irish Ale House
2. Chameleon Brewhouse
3. Black Horse Brewery
4. Rockland Brewery
5. Mogallywood Brewery
6. Brauhaus am Damm
7. Jacobs Brewhouse

Kroondal

6

5

3

Boons

4

Potchefstroom

7

Wolmaransstad

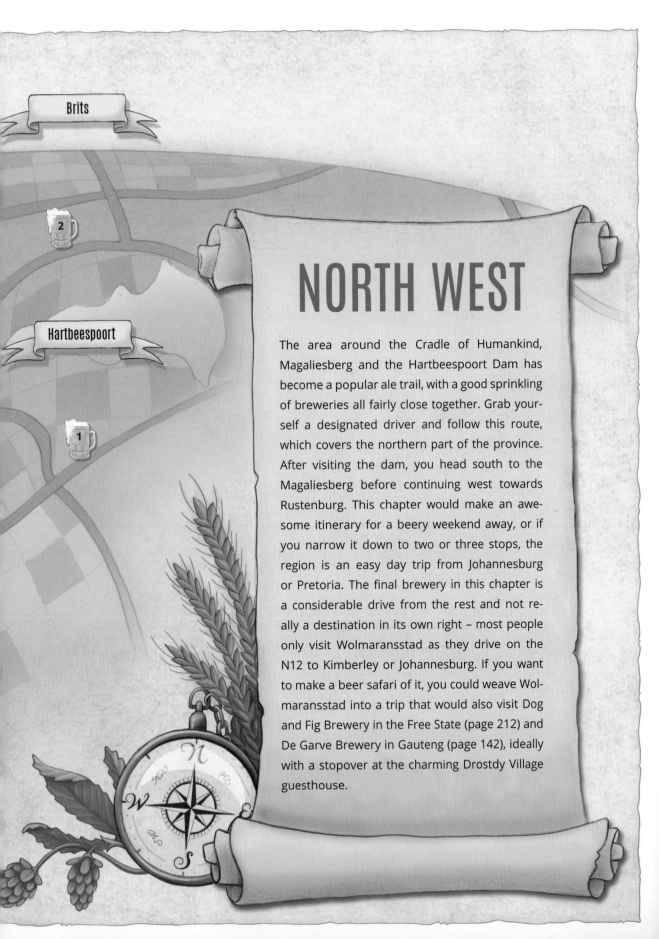

Brits

2

Hartbeespoort

1

NORTH WEST

The area around the Cradle of Humankind, Magaliesberg and the Hartbeespoort Dam has become a popular ale trail, with a good sprinkling of breweries all fairly close together. Grab yourself a designated driver and follow this route, which covers the northern part of the province. After visiting the dam, you head south to the Magaliesberg before continuing west towards Rustenburg. This chapter would make an awesome itinerary for a beery weekend away, or if you narrow it down to two or three stops, the region is an easy day trip from Johannesburg or Pretoria. The final brewery in this chapter is a considerable drive from the rest and not really a destination in its own right – most people only visit Wolmaransstad as they drive on the N12 to Kimberley or Johannesburg. If you want to make a beer safari of it, you could weave Wolmaransstad into a trip that would also visit Dog and Fig Brewery in the Free State (page 212) and De Garve Brewery in Gauteng (page 142), ideally with a stopover at the charming Drostdy Village guesthouse.

IRISH ALE

HOUSE

Bart Pretorius Rd, Broederstroom; alehouse.co.za; 082 464 9387

★ OPEN SAT-SUN 12PM-SUNSET ★

'I'm a style hillbilly!' proclaims Dirk van Tonder, referring to his penchant for flouting any guidelines that suggest what certain beer styles should and shouldn't look, smell or taste like. Dirk, well known for his maverick brewing style, runs the kettles at the very rustic Irish Ale House, sitting on a 4.5-hectare 'beer farm' amid a network of dirt roads in Broederstroom.

The farm does indeed produce beer, but at the moment it doesn't produce the barley needed to brew those beers. A 'plough to pint' experience is the long-term goal, and Dirk has already started buying unmalted barley to malt on-site. It's a fairly rudimentary process – he soaks the unmalted grain in his mash tun, aerates it with a fish tank pump, dries it in a traditional floor-malting process, then roasts the malt in his pizza oven. The whole thing takes around seven days and Dirk insists that he's seen vast improvements in his beers since he took on the role of micro-maltster.

Once the malt – which he's currently only producing in winter due to climate constraints – is ready, it heads off to the brewery to fulfil its destiny. The brewhouse is a small but shiny setup sitting in a one-room building, whose cement walls are washed

with local sand to blend in with the dusty surrounds. Here Dirk brews, in his words, 'whatever I can get my hands on'. His flagship beer, though, is a blonde ale, generously hopped, unfiltered and carbonated only slightly. This blonde is really more on the auburn side, and has heavier hop notes than the average blonde ale, but as long as you're not a stickler for styles, it's a highly recommended beer.

Tastings take place in the Ale House proper, a larger version of the building housing the brewery, with rustic fittings and dim but atmospheric lighting. The 'Irish' part of the Ale House moniker refers not to any beers available here, but to a little-

Dirk van Tonder tops up the mash tun

BEER
MENU

★

ALE HOUSE
BLONDE (4%)

ALE HOUSE
BUCHU (4%)

remembered piece of history that is close to Dirk's heart. His pub is part homage to beer and part homage to the Irish Brigade who sided with the Boers rather than the English during the Anglo-Boer War.

There are no TVs and Dirk is proud of the fact that no sports game, however important, will ever be shown in his pub. 'This place must be for getting away from life. As you sit, you must feel like you could have been here 100 years ago,' he says. The Ale House is a place for a tranquil sunset pint or a family afternoon, munching on pizza and getting acquainted with Dirk's donkeys, which are as much a part of the brewery as he is. When Dirk is brewing, the donkeys are never far away. 'They can smell the boil and they know they're going to get a good feed in a couple of hours – the spent grain is incredibly nutritious.'

This essence of stepping back in time is also the root of success behind Dirk's other baby, The Solstice Festival. Established in 2008, it is one of the country's oldest craft beer festivals and offers a totally different vibe to anything you'll find elsewhere. Bagpipes play, vendors sell chain mail and jester hats, and tipsy patrons pay to throw tomatoes at presumably equally tipsy participants. In short, it's a festival as quirky and offbeat as the brewer who organises it.

The diminutive brewery building blends perfectly with its surroundings

THE MALTING PROCESS

Usually referred to simply as 'malt', malted barley gives beer its colour, its body and much of its flavour. Barley, of course, starts its life in the field, but once the crop has been harvested, it's only halfway through the journey towards the mash tun. In South Africa, barley is largely grown in the region around Caledon in the Western Cape, as well as near Douglas in the Northern Cape. There are two major malting plants in the country, both owned and operated by SAB.

There is a lot of science in each sip of beer and this starts with the maltster, whose job is to encourage certain enzymes in the grain to expose starches that can be successfully converted into fermentable sugars.

Malting is a four-step process:

Steeping
After being sieved and sorted, the barley kernels are steeped in cool water for up to two days, though the grain is not soaked continually for this time, instead being drained at regular intervals and allowed air rests. Once the grain begins to sprout, or 'chit' as it is known in the industry, it is ready for the second step.

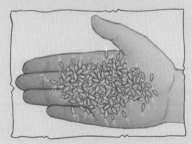

Germination
The grain is left to germinate for four to six days. It's kept at a constant and cool temperature and regularly turned to avoid too much moisture or heat and to stop each grain's roots from attaching themselves to their neighbours'. This is when the starches, which will later be converted to fermentable sugars, are formulated.

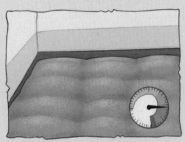

Kilning
The grain is next moved to kilns, where it's kept at around 76 °C to dry out the grain and to stop it from sprouting. Too much moisture will lead to rotten grain, while successfully malted barley can be kept for months, if not years. Kilning gives malt its characteristic sweet, biscuit-like flavour.

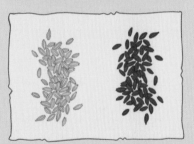

Roasting
Roasting batches of malt at different temperatures and for varying lengths of time gives a huge range of flavour profiles to beer – and offers different hues of gold, copper, brown or black to the final liquid product.

CHAMELEON
BREWHOUSE

Chameleon Village, R104, Hartbeespoort; www.chameleonbrewpub.co.za; 072 369 2309

★ **OPEN MON-FRI 10AM-5PM, SAT & SUN 10AM-7PM** ★

'It took one sip and we were hooked' – that's how Amanda van den Berg sums up the beer awakening that started on a journey to Germany in 2006, a journey that led her and husband Ruaan to open the Chameleon Brewhouse six years later.

'We visited Germany as part of a European tour,' explains Ruaan. 'It was then that we tasted weiss beer for the very first time in a small town called Weikersheim. We loved it and in the next town we went to we walked into a pub and asked for a Weiss. We were so stupid – we thought that weiss was a brand name!'

Then Ruaan and Amanda realised that they couldn't get the beer made just a couple of towns away, but that each little town had its own brewery. It was this realisation that stirred something within. 'We said we'd do anything to be able to have this beer at home – steal, borrow, import it ... but when we came back I couldn't find anybody selling weiss beer.' There was only one option for Ruaan to get his weiss fix – he decided he'd have to start making it himself.

Ruaan started brewing at home and over the next two years he and Amanda 'tasted' (or drunk) around 750 litres of homebrew – a fact he recalls with a slightly embarrassed grin. But he's quick to add that it was all for a good cause. 'You have to brew as much as you can – that's how you learn the trade and that's how you learn from your mistakes.'

BEER MENU

★

AMERICAN PALE ALE (5%)

INDIA PALE ALE (7%)

OATMEAL STOUT (4.5%)

WEISS BEER (3.5%)

IRISH RED (3.5%)

LAGER (3.5%)

BLOND ALE (3.5%)

WEISS, WEISSE OR WEIZEN?

This German wheat beer goes by many names. Most commonly used in South Africa is 'weissbier', often just referred to as 'weiss' on beer menus. You might also see it as weisse, weizen, weiß or hefeweizen, but it all refers to the same style. By German law, the beer must use at least 50 per cent wheat in the grain bill, alongside malted barley, and it is the wheat that gives the beer its name (weizen means 'wheat' in German).

The word weiss translates as 'white' and while some believe that this refers to the characteristic haze that the wheat lends to this beer, others insist that the name started out as weizen and became corrupted over time. It's not just the wheat that causes the typical lack of clarity – traditionally, weiss (or weizen) is an unfiltered beer – that is, with the yeast (hefe in German) still suspended in the pint. There is a filtered version as well, known as kristalweizen (or krystal weiss, or any number of variations on the theme).

Whatever you call it, it's a medium-bodied beer, typically with aromas and flavours of cloves and banana, and sometimes some bubble gum from the yeast. In South Africa, look out for fine examples at Cape Brewing Co. (page 64), That Brewing Co. (page 218) and Brauhaus am Damm (page 194) as well as Chameleon, of course.

And if you're not already sufficiently confused, there's also 'witbier', a Belgian beer also brewed with wheat, whose name also means 'white'.

The new passion also rekindled some old friendships in the form of André de Beer of The Cockpit Brewhouse (page 166) and Stephan Meyer of Clarens Brewery (page 210) – both old university buddies of Ruaan's. André and Stephan encouraged Ruaan to take the BJCP (Beer Judge Certification Program – page 251) test, an internationally recognised exam that qualifies you to judge beer in competitions. Although challenging, Ruaan encourages all brewers to take the exam. 'I've never learnt so much in such a short time as when I was studying for the BJCP. I think anybody in home-brewing or craft beer should do that exam, so that you have the ability to recognise off-flavours before you present your beers to anybody.'

It is usually Amanda who presents their beers to the public. She runs the brewpub that sits in the Chameleon Village complex, just north of the Hartbeespoort Dam. Attracting plenty of local and international tourists, it's the perfect spot to enjoy a beer in the sun, with outdoor tables nestled among curio stalls and one-off home décor shops. The pub has quadrupled in size since opening in 2012 and

its rustic, reed-roofed bar has something of a holiday resort feel to it. If you're a breakfast and beer person, there's a good range of morning meals, plus light lunches and beer-friendly snack baskets served throughout the day. On tap you'll find a solid range of beers, including the award-winning APA and, of course, a homage to the beer that set the whole thing in motion – the Weikersheim Weiss.

Chameleon's open-air brewpub is chilled during the week, while weekends get pretty lively

BLACK HORSE
BREWERY

Bekker Schools Rd, Magaliesburg; blackhorse.co.za; 082 453 5295

★ OPEN WED–SUN & PUBLIC HOLIDAYS 8AM–8PM ★

Author's note: Although Black Horse officially falls in Gauteng, it's right on the North West border and as you're likely to visit when exploring the breweries in this area, it made more sense to include it here.

It wasn't exactly in Nuschka Botha's plans to have a career in beer. Fresh out of university with a marketing degree in hand, her entrepreneur father, Bernard, launched a brewery and asked her to swot up on beer-making. In truth, the brewery wasn't entirely in his plans either – 'It just kind of happened,' says Nuschka.

In fact, the plan had been to build a small-scale brewery for Bernard to enjoy with friends, but a bunch of renegade builders saw to it that the home-brewery became something altogether more grand. 'In 2010 my dad decided he wanted to build a small brewery, so he told the builders what he wanted and then he went on holiday. When he came back, they had built this massive building!' says Nuschka, gesturing at the three-storey glass-and-brick build-

ing that now houses the Black Horse restaurant. But Bernard opted to run with it, expanding his plans to fit with the expanded structure. A larger brewery was ordered from China – in itself a bit of a headache since it arrived with assembly instructions only in Chinese – and Nuschka suddenly found herself having a career change.

A new 1000-litre brewhouse was being installed to handle demand for the Red Ale and Golden Lager

BEER MENU

⭐

AS WELL AS THE BEERS IN THE
CORE RANGE, THERE ARE
ROTATING BREWS, INCLUDING
WEISS, PORTER, IPA, PALE ALE,
DUNKEL AND BLONDE ALE.

RED ALE (4.5%)

GINGER BEER (2%)

GOLDEN LAGER (4.5%)

PINK DRINK (2%)

'My dad said, "Hey, Nuschka – learn how to make beer!" So I started reading a lot,' she says. After some hands-on training at a small brewery in the Cape Winelands, she completed a short apprenticeship at Heineken's Johannesburg plant and kept reading until March 2012, when she completed her first solo brew – the brewery's signature Red Ale. She knew her beers would then have to pass the first quality control test before she could hope to serve them to paying customers. 'My dad's a big beer drinker so if there's something wrong he's going to tell me,' she laughs.

The beer met Bernard's approval and Black Horse – named for the Friesian stud farm that the Botha family used to operate here – opened its doors a month later. The building might have been a mistake, but it's a charming place for lunch and drinks, whether you opt for the rambling, tree-studded garden or the glass-fringed main building. And although it was larger than it was originally planned to be, it turns out that the building wasn't nearly large enough. A new wedding venue has been added and a bigger brewhouse installed to keep up with the increasing demand both from the festival scene and from the day-trippers or weekenders who head to the pretty Magaliesberg region from Johannesburg.

'If someone had told me five years ago that I was going to be a brewer, I would have thought they were crazy,' says Nuschka, but despite initial plans to move into the marketing side of the business, she now seems to be a permanent fixture at the ever-expanding Black Horse Brewery.

Black Horse is a great spot for an alfresco lunch

ROCKLAND
BREWERY

Off the R509, near Magaliesburg; rocklandbrewery.co.za; 083 307 9566

★ OPEN BY APPOINTMENT ONLY ★

There are grand plans for the brand-new Rockland Brewery

James Viney sure does like a challenge. Not content with teaching himself to brew and turning the hobby into a small business, James also wants to grow his own barley. This in itself is a pretty bold goal, and that's without taking into account the reason behind the brewery's name. Speaking about the family farm where James lives, and where the brand-new brewery resides, James explains how he came up with the moniker: 'Wherever you want to plant anything here, you first have to move a wheelbarrow full of rocks out of the way!'

But James is adamant that, eventually, Rockland will produce its own barley – and he also intends to malt it on-site. 'I'm going to start with a hectare and I expect the first harvest to be in late 2015,' he says. 'The barley will be planted behind the brewery – I think it will give a great feel to the place for those coming to visit.' It's not the only harvest James is waiting for. He's also dabbling in viticulture, having planted some 400 vines on the property. It's an unusual location for a winery, being on the edge of the Magaliesberg, far from any wine-growing areas, so James is currently testing out cultivars to find out what will thrive in his rocky soil.

Having made both beer and wine, James believes the former is a more difficult process. He'd been brewing at home for five years before deciding to open a microbrewery, and admits that the earliest brews weren't great. 'As a homebrewer, you need a lot of friends to help you drink all the rubbish at the beginning!' he laughs. These days he's fine-honed a handful of recipes on the 300-litre system he brews on with his son, Hilton. The brews, which debuted in early 2014, are easy-drinking ales, designed to please the brewer's palate. He's working on a lager to complete the range, and there will also be seasonal beers available at the brewery.

Construction was in its infanthood when I visited, but once everything is complete, you can expect to find a small restaurant serving wood-fired pizzas from its open kitchen. Rockland is one of South Africa's more off-the-beaten-track breweries, but once you find it, it's set to be a family-friendly spot where you can sip on sessionable beers while watching home-grown barley blowing in the breeze.

BEER MENU
★
BLONDE ALE (4%)

BROWN ALE (4.5%)

WEISS (4.5%)

PORTER (5%)

BREW TALK...
SESSION BEER
A lighter beer designed to allow the drinker to have several in one sitting.

James Viney started as a homebrewer back in 2009

MOGALLYWOOD
BREWERY

Moddraspruit Farm, Maanhaarrand, Magaliesberg; 082 330 0646

'I've been brewing since I was eight years old,' insists Johannes Lodewikus Griessel, better known to all as Roeks. He goes on to explain that he dabbled in pineapple beer and moonshine as a boy. Although he took a hiatus from booze production after leaving school, he got back into brewing during a lengthy stint in the South African army. 'You always had a bucket and something to brew with,' he says of his military years.

Roeks has led an interesting life, filled with daring business deals and fascinating tales, pan-African travels and crushing misfortunes. It was after a particularly bad bit of luck that Roeks found himself financially crippled and deciding to turn to an old hobby to make ends meet. The result was Mogallywood Brewery, which produces Roeks Beer.

Roeks and his wife Lauran actually met at a beer festival, so it seems apt that the couple man their brewery's stand together at every event they attend. They are well known for their plastic 'help-yourself' keg setup and their brand's rather unusual logo, which features a dog named Sparky peeing on what appears to be an electrical socket. The devil-may-care logo and the atypical dispensing system speak of the 'take us or leave us' nature of the Griessels and their brand. The beer is brewed on a rough-and-ready plastic system on the couple's Magaliesberg farm and served on the deck of their rustic pub, with great views across the hilly region. The farm shares its name with the brewery – a name

There's a quintessentially African view from the stoep of Mogallywood Brewery

STOUT VS PORTER

Stouts emerged in the 1800s as a higher alcohol version of porter. Today, there are various versions of each style – robust, brown and Baltic porters; dry, sweet and Russian imperial stouts. If you're studying BJCP guidelines, stouts tend to be a little darker in colour and, as they tend to use more roasted barley, have more pronounced coffee characteristics and sometimes a slightly sour flavour. Common wisdom today though, suggests that if a beer is labelled a stout, then it's a stout. If it's labelled a porter, it's a porter. And if you enjoy drinking it, then it probably doesn't matter what it's called. Fine examples include Dog and Fig's Sturdy Stout (page 212), the dry stout from Apollo Brewing Company (page 82) or when available, Cockpit Brewhouse's Russian Imperial stout ((page 166). If you're looking for a porter, try the robust version from Red Sky Brew (page 80) or Long Beach Brewery's brown porter (page 42).

that Roeks came up with as a tribute to Lauran's lifelong yearning to become an actress. 'She never made it to Hollywood,' he says, 'so instead I built her Mogallywood.'

BEER MENU

★

RASPBERRY BEER
(4.5%)

ROEKS PORTER
(4.5%)

ROEKS BEER
(4.5%)

'I'VE BEEN BREWING SINCE I WAS EIGHT YEARS OLD.'

Roeks and Lauran Griessel always man their festival stands together

BRAUHAUS AM DAMM

R24, near Rustenburg; brauhaus.co.za; 087 802 5519

★ OPEN TUE-SAT 11AM-11PM, SUN 11AM-4PM ★

Every brewer has a story, but in the case of Brauhaus am Damm, the brewery itself also has a tale to tell. Described by brewer Imke Pape as 'the Rolls-Royce of breweries', the 1 000-litre system is indeed a fine specimen of beer equipment, but the copper kettles are more than just a pretty face. This system was the lifeblood of one of South Africa's earliest microbreweries, the much-loved Farmers' Brewery in Hattingspruit, KwaZulu-Natal. It helped realise the lifelong dream of a German expat, Otto Martin, who set up the brewery in 1993. It saw thousands of tourists and loyal locals pass through to sip on the oft-talked about Farmers' Draught and it was there in 2009 when the Farmers' Brewery closed its doors for the last time. But as Otto's son, Josef, was quoted in the most impassioned obituary you'll ever read for a brewpub, 'the brewery is not dead'.

It has been reincarnated in a grand setting on the edge of the Olifantsnek Dam near Rustenburg. Imke takes up the story where the Martin family left off: 'Very good friends of ours, Walter and Christine Stallmann, went to Hattingspruit in 2008. The beer they tasted was two years old, but it was the best beer they'd ever had!' Walter and Christine decided there and then that they wanted to buy the brewery, despite having no brewing knowledge or background. They headed home to try and get further backing for the brewery, which is where Imke comes into the story. 'They sat here and said we are going to buy this brewery together. We said no – we don't know anything about brewing; no, we're not doing this – but, of course, here we are!' she laughs.

Imke Pape never imagined herself as a brewer but she's utterly at ease at the controls of the brewhouse

BEER MENU

★

LOOK OUT TOO FOR
SPECIALITY BEERS,
INCLUDING KOLSCH, BOCK
AND OKTOBERFEST.

BRAUHAUS WEIZEN (4.5%)

BRAUHAUS DUNKEL (5.2%)

BRAUHAUS PILS (4.8%)

FARMERS DRAUGHT (4.2%)

Challenges rained down – they had no premises, no brewer and a brewery sitting almost 500 km away, but gradually the solutions appeared. The first job was to move the brewery, an event that Imke remembers fondly. 'We went down to Hattingspruit and labelled every part of the brewery. We also took thousands of photos because we didn't know where anything went and needed to know how to put it back together afterwards.'

The brewery was dismantled and placed into storage until premises were found. After looking around the Rustenburg region to no avail, Imke decided to sell a 10-hectare piece of the farm she was born on to the brewing consortium, ensuring that the pub and restaurant would always enjoy uninterrupted views over the dam. In July 2009, construction of the impressive, airy building began, its expansive deck and vast windows all helping to make the most of the brewery's picturesque setting.

Now there was just one problem left – the question of who was going to brew the beer. It was Imke who came to the rescue. 'I can cook but I didn't want

BREW TALK...
BREWHOUSE
This term is sometimes used to talk about the building or room where brewing takes place, though more commonly it refers to the machines used for the hot side of the brew – namely, the hot liquor tank, mash tun, lauter tun and kettle.

Brauhaus am Damm hosts an annual Oktoberfest on the picturesque deck

BRAUHAUS WEIZEN

Am Damm serves some great beers, but this is the best of the bunch. It's orange-gold to look at with a dense white head on top, and being mit hefe (with yeast), it's virtually opaque. Banana hits first as you inhale, with the characteristic spice and bready aromas lingering in the background. This is what I call a 'chewy' beer, but not in a 'what's this floating in my pint?' sort of way. It's a medium-bodied beer – a proper example of liquid bread. Flavour-wise expect more banana, cloves and bread, with an up-front sweetness that's replaced by a pleasant dry aftertaste when you swallow.

to cook in a restaurant, so I decided to turn my hand to brewing,' she says. 'For two years I read, slept and drank beer. When I finished the books, I turned back and read them again.' With the theory covered, it was time to brew. Imke started small – with a pot on the stove – before brewing with Heiko Feuring, a close friend and qualified brewmaster, with whom she devised the Dunkel recipe that is one of Am Damm's flagship beers today.

After a week-long stint brewing and learning the all-important cellar work at Hanover-based micro-brewery HBX and a gruelling fortnight in Vienna, brewing eight times on the same system that the Am Damm team had bought from Hattingspruit, Imke headed back to Rustenburg ready to brew. Brauhaus am Damm then had three of their flagship recipes sorted – the Dunkel developed with Heiko, a Pilsner recipe from Hanover and the beer that started it all – the Farmers' Draught, which was bought from Hattingspruit along with the equipment.

In November 2011, Brauhaus am Damm opened its doors, serving German-style beers and hearty food to match. In fact, the German backing is evident throughout – from the food and beer to the hi-tech and über-organised cellar housing fermenters and shiny tanks from which the draught beer is pumped directly in this keg-free operation. Imke is rightly as proud of the equipment as she is of the beers, and the brewhouse is on show for patrons to admire.

Since launching, Brauhaus am Damm has been showered with accolades, from people's choice awards at major festivals to being a finalist in the National Craft Brewers Championship in both 2013 and 2014. Their beers are found in an increasing number of bars and bottle stores around Gauteng and the brewery hosts regular festivals and special events. The team breathed new life into an old brewery and, this time, it seems that the kettles are set to have a long, happy and healthy life.

JACOBS
BREWHOUSE

4 Leask St, Wolmaransstad; drostdyvillage.co.za; 083 262 0387

★ OPEN MON-FRI 9AM-7PM, SAT 9AM-5PM, SUN 9AM-2PM ★

Gert Jacobs brews and distils in the far-flung town of Wolmaransstad

Gert Jacobs is one of South Africa's most isolated brewers. It's some 180 km to the closest microbrewery and even further should he wish to browse the shelves of a brewing supply shop. There's no homebrewing club with whose members he can compare recipes or share ideas, and few beer enthusiasts venture to this maize-farming town to offer feedback on Gert's brews.

But the far-flung, frontier-like feel is exactly what's most alluring about a visit to Wolmaransstad. The brewery is part of the Drostdy Village, run by Gert and his wife, Wilna. It sits at the north-eastern entrance to the town and comprises a pub, restaurant, charming guesthouse, a theatre hosting shows by Afrikaans pop stars, a pizzeria, distillery and, of course, a brewery. Most people stopping over in the town are doing so en route to or from Johannesburg, but the quaint and cosy feel of the Drostdy might just tempt you to stay a second night.

It could be the corrugated iron structures, the fact that you've driven through hours of tumbleweed-strewn flatlands to get here, or perhaps it's because Wolmaransstad clings on to its alluvial diamond-digging past, but you feel like you've stepped into the Wild West here. Diamond diggers congregate in Gert's pub and discuss recent finds, and once a week the town's accommodation fills with international diamond buyers, here to eye up the latest discoveries.

Topping off the frontier feel is Gert's brewery/distillery, where he makes a trio of ales plus a range of moonshine that would put hairs on even the most ruthless outlaw's chest. Gert bought his brewhouse in 2008 from the Highlands Brewery in Rhodes (East-

BEYOND THE BREWERY:
WHERE TO DRINK BEER IN THE NORTH WEST

River Café, Potchefstroom
2 Calderbank Ave, Potchefstroom; rivercafe.co.za; 079 093 7403
The selection is largely imported, but alongside a lot of lager you'll find the likes of Paulaner, Kilkenny and Duvel, plus a few South African brands. Head here for happy hour between 2pm and 3.45pm.

ern Cape), which closed its doors just as the first rumblings of the craft beer revolution were underway in Cape Town. With email and telephone help from Dave Walker from Highlands and from Dirk van Tonder of Irish Ale House (page 183), Gert began to brew his own beer. 'I learnt through trial and lots of errors,' he chuckles, though at least those errors would turn out to be profitable. It was because of a couple of bad batches that Gert decided to moonlight as a distiller, transforming failed brews into his first vintage of moonshine.

These days he distils mealies into moonshine and turfs any brewing flops, saying that it's not worth the effort to convert them into hard liquor. Gert brews once a week on his 150-litre system, and distils once a week on the still he inherited from a local nonagenarian moonshine-maker who had been distilling for close to five decades. And despite being as far from his nearest brewing neighbour as virtually any commercial brewer in South Africa can get, he's been inspired by the craft beer boom – Gert is thinking about exhibiting at his first festival and planning to start bottling his brews in the near future, so you can take a little piece of wild Wolmaransstad home with you.

BEER MENU

★

DARK MOON STOUT (4%)

FARMERS PALE ALE (4%)

DIGGERS IRISH RED ALE (4%)

COMING SOON...

PILANESBERG CRAFT BREWERY
Sun City; pilanesbergbrewery.co.za
Set to be based at Sun City, this brewery has long been planned, but brewer Tim Dawson has hit a few snags along the way. If it comes to pass, the concept is an awesome one – a pint at the brewpub will be the prize for beer lovers who make it to the end of the Maze of the Lost City.

THE LAZY LIZARD INDEPENDENT BREWHOUSE
Broederstroom; lazylizardbrewhouse.co.za
Due to open in mid-2015, this rural brewpub promises to be a family-friendly retreat. Food will focus on local produce, though there was no word yet on which beers would make it onto the menu.

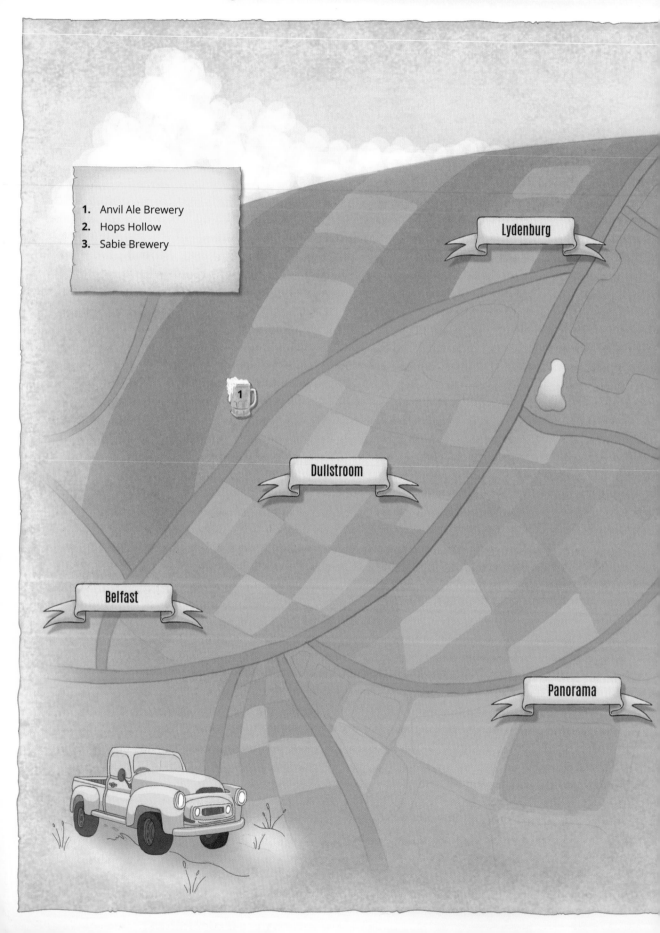

1. Anvil Ale Brewery
2. Hops Hollow
3. Sabie Brewery

Lydenburg

Dullstroom

Belfast

Panorama

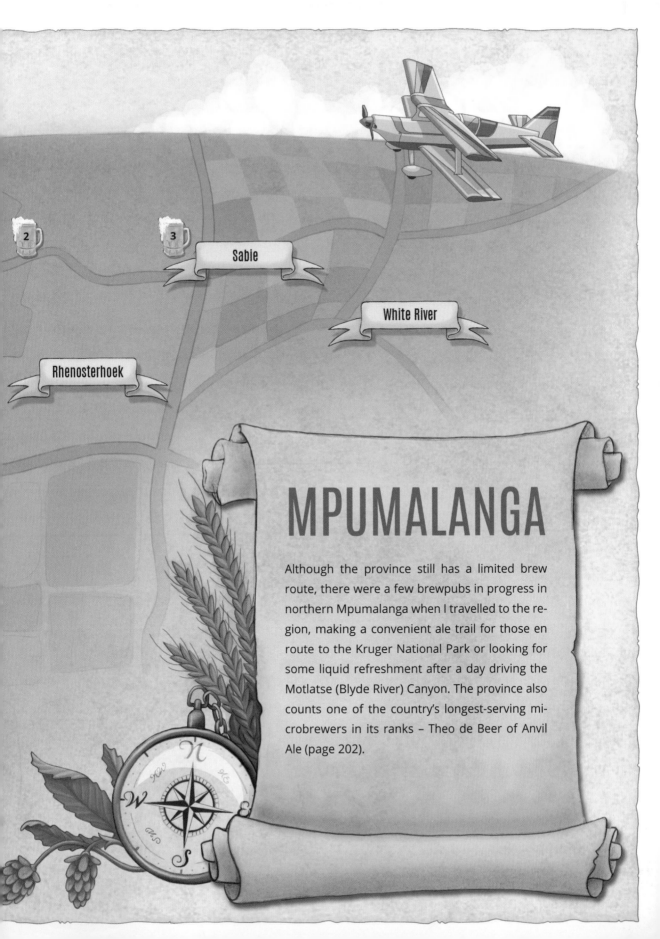

2

3

Sabie

White River

Rhenosterhoek

MPUMALANGA

Although the province still has a limited brew route, there were a few brewpubs in progress in northern Mpumalanga when I travelled to the region, making a convenient ale trail for those en route to the Kruger National Park or looking for some liquid refreshment after a day driving the Motlatse (Blyde River) Canyon. The province also counts one of the country's longest-serving microbrewers in its ranks – Theo de Beer of Anvil Ale (page 202).

ANVIL ALE
BREWERY

Main Rd, Dullstroom; anvilbrewery.com; 073 168 6603

★ OPEN SUN-THU 8AM-4PM, FRI & SAT TO 5PM ★

Fate is a funny thing. If Theo de Beer hadn't suffered a serious back injury, he would never have met Moritz Kallmeyer of Drayman's (page 164). If he hadn't met Moritz, he might never have got into homebrewing. And if he hadn't started homebrewing, he never would have ended up running two successful brewpubs.

It all started after Theo and Moritz crossed paths during Moritz's former life as a biokineticist. 'I'd had a back op and Moritz did my rehab,' Theo recalls. 'He had me captive on an exercise bike, all the time yapping at my side about beer.' By the end of the rehabilitation, Moritz had converted Theo from a hobbyist winemaker into a homebrewer. This was over 30 years ago and Theo hasn't stopped brewing since.

It had always been just a hobby, but when a career change beckoned, Theo and his wife, Sarie, fancied starting a business in the hospitality industry – an industry they somewhat knew after years working in nature reserves. That's how Theo ended up with his first brewpub, Hops Hollow on the Long Tom Pass.

Hops Hollow flourished, but Theo and Sarie sold in 2008 with a plan to move to New Zealand and set up a brewery in that country's thriving craft beer sector. But fate stepped in again and with the world's economic crash that year, the De Beers felt

their cash was just not enough to take the chance and instead opted to stay in South Africa.

'By that time we had sold the place lock, stock, and barrel – including the recipes. We literally walked out of there with our clothes!' says Theo, his face crestfallen at the memory. 'We squatted for a year in a friend's flat and after looking around at our options, we decided to do it all over again. In fact, when we started Hops Hollow, Dullstroom was where we'd

FIVE BREWPUBS AND TAPROOMS YOU WON'T WANT TO LEAVE

1. Devil's Peak Taproom (Western Cape)
2. The Cockpit Brewhouse (Gauteng)
3. Clarens Brewery (Free State)
4. Anvil Ale House (Mpumalanga)
5. L'Abri Fountain Brewery (Limpopo)

BEER MENU

⭐

WHITE ANVIL (4%)

BLACK ANVIL (4%)

BLOND ALE (4%)

PALE ALE (4%)

BIERE D'SAISON (4%)

BREWER
Spotted on
_____
Date
_____
Signature

Theo de Beer has been brewing for more than 30 years

originally wanted to be.' And that's exactly where they ended up with their second brewery, Anvil.

The brewery and pub sit on the edge of the town, a roaring fire in place for Dullstroom's cold winters and outdoor tables catering for the summer months. The range of beers likewise caters for all weathers, with a crisp and refreshing witbier (White Anvil) ideal for sunny days and the roasty oatmeal stout (Black Anvil) helping to keep out the winter chill. In fact, the Black Anvil and its white counterpart used to rotate on a seasonal basis, but they became so popular they can be found on the menu year-round now. A more recent addition is Bookoo, a buchu-infused ale. It's currently brewed once a year, though Theo is considering making it a permanent fixture. 'It sold so quickly it makes you wonder if we should do it all the time!' he says. But by the sounds of it, he might not have the space to add another permanent beer as there are plans for some interesting seasonal brews and one-off beers – keep an eye on the taps.

Opening another brewery in South Africa might not have been plan A, but watching Theo talk about his ideas for future beers, you can see that things worked out pretty well in the end.

BIG 5 PINT

WHITE ANVIL

This beer has a simply amazing aroma. So much coriander it almost smells like biltong, and yet the dried naartjie peel used to spice this traditional witbier is also abundant. So lots of fruit and lots of spice – it's a real sniffer's beer. But this beer is also made for sipping; a crisp, refreshing brew that's perfectly balanced. Try it with a delicate cheese like Brie or a soft goat's milk cheese – the high carbonation works wonderfully with something creamy.

HOPS HOLLOW BREW PUB

Old Bull Bitter

The Highest Brewery

HOPS HOLLOW BREW PUB

Blacksmith's Brew

The Highest Brewery

HOPS HOLLOW BREW PUB

Diggers Draught

The Highest Brewery

HOPS HOLLOW

Long Tom Pass, between Mashishing (Lydenburg) and Sabie; hopshollow.com; 013 235 8910

★ OPEN WED–SUN 8AM–6PM ★

Sitting on the Long Tom Pass, Hops Hollow is one of the best-located brewpubs in South Africa. It was founded in 2001 by Theo and Sarie de Beer from Anvil Ale House, but since they sold the business in 2008, the brewery has been struggling to find its feet. When I visited, a new brewer had been appointed – Colin Ntshangase, formerly of Old Main Brewery in KwaZulu-Natal (page 236). The beer names remain the same as when Theo was at the kettles, and hopefully the beers themselves can be restored to their former glory with a little TLC from a new brewer. It's a gorgeous spot, with great views, simple accommodation, a kids' play area and an atmospheric pub.

BEER MENU
★

DIGGERS DRAUGHT
(4%)

OLD BULL ALE (4%)

MAC'S PORTER (4%)

BLACKSMITH'S BREW
(4%)

There are guest rooms alongside the cosy Hops Hollow pub

SABIE
BREWERY

45 Main Rd, Sabie; sabiebrewery.com; 013 764 1005

★ OPEN DAILY 11AM–10PM ★

It was a simple lack of ales that pushed friends Shaun McCartney, Walter Comley and James Sheard towards opening their own brewery. 'We were sitting up at Misty Mountain Hotel [owned by James] about five years ago, lamenting on how sad it was that we didn't have a hand-crafted brewery in the Lowveld,' says Shaun. 'The guys in Gauteng and Cape Town were having all the fun. We wanted real ale and that got us moving in the right direction.'

They missed out on buying Hops Hollow from Theo de Beer by a mere matter of days, but unperturbed, the team set about sourcing equipment, opening bank accounts, applying for a licence and settling on a name. Then there was just one small matter left to deal with – the fact that none of them knew how to brew! They turned first to Theo and, just as he had been mentored all those years ago by Moritz Kallmeyer, so he shared his expertise with the Sabie team. In 2012, Shaun took extended leave from his job as CEO of a Limpopo game reserve and headed to the United Kingdom for a three-week course at Brewlab, followed later by a two-month distance-learning course on the chemistry of beer, taken through Oklahoma University in the USA. 'I told the guys, if we are going to start a brewery, at least one of us should know how to make the stuff,' says Shaun. 'At that stage I was not anticipating being the brewer, but when we couldn't find a brewer I put my hand up and have been dabbling ever since.'

The brewpub opened in November 2014 to much local acclaim. As well as taking its name from the town in which it resides, the Sabie Brewery also honours local history in its beers, each one named for a local character or historical event. The easy-drinking brews are served in the brewpub, based in a 1920s trading post, but can be increasingly found throughout the region. One thing is for sure, the people of the area now have a truly local beer to drink at the end of a steamy Lowveld day.

Sabie Brewery's beers are all named for local characters or events

BEER MENU

⭐

GLYNN'S GOLD (5%)

LONG TOM LAGER – DUNKEL (5%)

DRAVIDIAN DRAUGHT ENGLISH IPA (5.5%)

SHANGAAN STOUT (4.7%)

WHEELBARROW WEISS (4.7%)

COMING SOON...

BRILOU'S BRAUHAUS
Nelspruit; 083 754 5391
The brewery was due to move when I visited the area, so keep an eye on these guys to find out where they'll be taking their brewpub.

MOUNTAIN STREAM BREWERY
59 President St, Graskop; 084 708 5877
A brewery was in the early stages, set to be based in the Firebreak Pub.

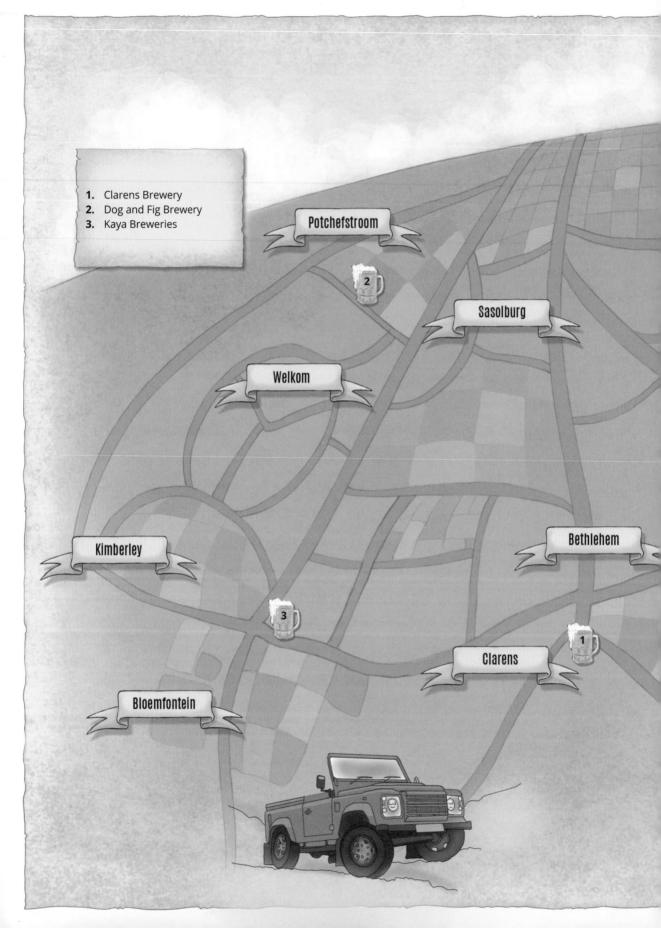

1. Clarens Brewery
2. Dog and Fig Brewery
3. Kaya Breweries

Potchefstroom

Sasolburg

Welkom

Kimberley

Bethlehem

Clarens

Bloemfontein

Bethal

Standerton

FREE STATE

The Free State is home to a mere trio of breweries, but it's also the staging post for one of the country's largest and most popular beer events, the Clarens Craft Beer Festival, so if you can plan a trip for late February, you'll be well-rewarded. At any time of year though, while there isn't an abundance of breweries, there are some interesting – and award-winning – beers being produced in the province. The breweries make up a triangle and with 300 km between each one, it doesn't really matter which order you tackle them in - this route begins in Clarens, heads north towards the Vaal River, then ends in the province's capital and largest city, Bloemfontein.

CLARENS
BREWERY

326 Main St, Clarens; clarensbrewery.co.za; 058 256 1193

★ OPEN DAILY 10AM–6PM ★

Natalie and Stephan Meyer preside over their ever-growing brewery in the pretty town of Clarens

Strangely enough, it was a hankering to make cider that eventually led Stephan and Natalie Meyer to open a brewery. 'We had an apple and cherry farm and started making cider, but we battled for about four years to get it sorted,' says Natalie. She credits a Gauteng homebrewing club with the eventual success of their cider, claiming that they would 'never, ever have sorted it out without the help from the Wort Hogs'. It was while mingling with fellow hob-byist booze-makers that Stephan developed a side-line passion that would soon take over – brewing.

'We went to the Wort Hogs meetings for three years,' Natalie recalls. 'Stephan had never expressed an interest in brewing and then one day he just said, "I think I'll brew" and the beers were really good!'

Eric van Heerden, childhood friend and brewer at Triggerfish Brewing (page 78), claims that 'Stephan turns everything he does into a business', so it was only a matter of time before the brewery went commercial. True to Eric's words, Stephan didn't delay in turning his latest hobby into a profession, and in 2006 the Clarens Brewery was launched.

'We thought we'd concentrate on the cider and just do a little bit of beer, but it turned out to be the other way around,' says Natalie of their first outlet in the town of the same name. Their beers were an instant hit, but the business didn't take off at the start, as Stephan explains: 'People liked the beer, but we didn't make any money...'

A larger brewery followed, along with an outlet at the town's popular Clementine's Restaurant. Then, in 2008, Natalie and Stephan opened a small tap-room tucked away in the corner of the Clarens village square. The brewery, supposedly for the short term,

CLARENS CRAFT BEER FESTIVAL
clarenscraftbeerfest.com

It might seem a surprising location for a major beer festival, but, in fact, the compact nature of Clarens makes this pretty town the perfect spot for an annual homage to hops: you can leave the car keys behind, you can wander the square looking for a sit-down meal or non-fest toilets and, if the tasting gets to be too much, a booze snooze at your guesthouse is just a few minutes' walk away! The first festival was held in 2011 and doubled in size the following year. It now takes over the entire village square and for two days in late February, beer shirt-clad ale enthusiasts come to taste, to chat with the brewers and to take copious notes on the beers on offer. Book early as accommodation and tickets sell out in advance.

remained on the couple's farm while Stephan made a few upgrades. But thanks to a constant demand for the beer, dismantling and moving the brewery became unfeasible and it remained on the farm until 2012, when it moved to a new and larger building in a prime spot on the square.

Although Clarens is one of the country's best-known and respected breweries, the Meyers are far from being stuck in their ways. As well as getting new premises, rebranding the bottles, playing around with the existing recipes and adding some new beers to the brew sheet, there's a lot going on behind the scenes. Stephan and Natalie have made hefty investments after being inspired by their fellow South African microbrewers. On a tasting trip to the Cape, it quickly became apparent that where brewing is concerned, quality and consistency is largely down to equipment, equipment, equipment, so the Meyers opted to upgrade. They've also added an on-site distillery and the whisky and Calvados (apple brandy) they're producing is now available alongside the beer and cider.

Of all the hobbies Stephan has turned into professions, it seems that brewing was the one he was waiting for. I suppose when you consider the homework, it's not an unpleasant industry to be involved in. 'We keep drinking other breweries' beers as much as we can,' Stephan admits, knowing that research is key. 'We're always experimenting with recipes,' he adds, sipping on a pint of his latest creation, the well-hopped 1912 American Pale Ale.

BEER MENU

★

CLARENS 1912 APA (4.5%)

CLARENS IPA (6.5%)

CLARENS RED (4.5%)

CLARENS BLONDE (4.5%)

CLARENS STOUT (5.5%)

CLARENS ENGLISH ALE (4.5%)

CLARENS WEISS (4%)

Free tasters of the Clarens beers are on offer to visitors

DOG AND FIG
BREWERY

Kopjeskraal, Parys; dogandfigbrewery.com; 076 180 6521

★ OPEN TUE–SUN 10AM–7PM ★

BREWER
Spotted on
_____
Date
_____
Signature

If you like your brewers to know their science, the Dog and Fig Brewery just outside Parys is the place for you. The five partners count between them two PhDs, two Master's degrees and an Honour's degree, all in chemistry. They also share a love of beer and a determination to produce unusual beer styles from across the globe.

In fact, it was researching world beers that got co-brewer Sean Barradas hooked on the amber nectar – though not necessarily drinking said beers. 'I suppose my passion for beer started when I finished varsity in '92, when I started collecting beers,' says Sean. 'Initially I bought two of each so I could drink one and keep the other, but that got too expensive so a lot of them are still full.' With close to 1 000 beers from around the world in his collection, you can imagine that some beer boffins would pay a great deal to sip some of those bottles, even if they are a couple of decades old. And it's surprising that they've survived, especially since Sean set up a beer appreciation club at work not long after he started his collection.

'There were about 10 guys and we'd meet to do a tasting at each other's houses,' says Sean. 'Then one of the guys, Johan [Huyser – one of the Dog and Fig partners], brought some of his own beer to one of the tastings and it was brilliant. So one week we started brewing in someone's garage.'

It could have been an 'aha' moment for Sean, but that early brew didn't go entirely as planned. He laughs when he thinks back: 'It was terrible, like sour Champagne!' It would be a few years before Sean attempted homebrewing again; then in 2004 the beer-loving buddies put on a small Oktoberfest event. Speaking about his homebrew, Sean remembers how 'people loved it, even though it was terrible!' Luckily, Sean and university friend Johan graduated from kit brewing to all-grain in 2007 and even Sean admits that they finally started making some really good beers.

A year later the seeds that would grow into the Dog and Fig Brewery were planted, though Sean wasn't exactly a part of that momentous decision. 'I was away in New York but my wife, Morné, was pregnant and couldn't fly. One night I called and she was having dinner at Johan and Michelle's place and they said they had big news for me, and that's where the whole concept of this brewery came from.'

Sean, Morné, Johan and wife Michelle were joined by Cathy Dwyer – another varsity friend. And it's not just the partners who came from the University of Johannesburg – the brewery's name also has its roots at varsity. 'Boys at that time were called 'dogs', girls were called 'figs', and although we went through a couple of names before deciding on this one, they all had dog and fig in them somewhere,' says Sean.

Once the concept and the name were established, the beer ideas just started to flow. Perhaps their most notable beer is the Boisterous Buchu, South Africa's first commercially available buchu beer. They took an interesting approach to recipe development, as Sean explains: 'We originally tried adding the buchu to Black Label to test how much we would need to add. What we wanted was to taste it, but for it not to be overwhelming.' Once the balance was right, Sean and Johan brewed an English IPA to use as the base for this speciality beer, which continues to be a hit with their more adventurous customers. But it is their stout that gets the most attention, a rich brew which won first prize in the

inaugural National Craft Brewers Championship in 2013 and has taken the top spot in numerous other competitions.

The biggest challenge has always been keeping up with demand, particularly since the beers started winning awards, so the team has taken the plunge and upscaled the brewhouse. The new 1 000-litre system is being installed in a snazzy purpose-built brewery just out of town, where light meals will also be on offer. Finally, fans of the much sought-after stout will be able to stop searching in vain for the hard-to-find brew.

BEER MENU

★

STEWIGE/STURDY STOUT (7%)

BALDADIGE/BOISTEROUS BUCHU (7%)

WAFFERSE/WICKED WEISS (5%)

AARDIGE/AGREEABLE ALE (6%)

ALTERNATIEWE/ALTERNATIVE ALT (5%)

VYL ALE (4.5%)

BIG 5 PINT

STEWIGE/STURDY STOUT

Jet black and topped with a creamy head the colour of a strong cappuccino, Dog and Fig's stout sure is pretty. But as nice as it is to look at, it's even better to sniff. And better still to sip. Expect aromas of freshly roasted coffee and dark, dark chocolate. It's a warming, full-bodied beer full of roasty coffee and cocoa bean flavours – think coffee liqueur wrapped in dark chocolate and you get the idea.

'WE NEED TO TAILOR THINGS TO OUR CROWD... IT'S ALL ABOUT WHAT OUR MARKET WANTS.'

KAYA
BREWERIES

Bloemfontein; kayabreweries.co.za

BREWER
Spotted on

_____
Date
_____
Signature

★ BREWERY CLOSED TO THE PUBLIC ★

If one of the forerunners of South Africa's craft beer revolution heard Phillip Coetzer and Marcus Meunier's story, it would definitely feel like déjà vu. The brewers behind Kaya might have started several years after the pioneering Cape Town craft breweries opened, but as the first microbrewery in Bloemfontein, it's like launching the revolution all over again. Just as in Cape Town circa 2008, Kaya first unveiled their beers to the public at an artisanal market. Just as in Cape Town, they had to begin with a lager in order to woo beer drinkers and lure them away from their familiar pints. And just as in Cape Town, they're having to educate their customers, one palate at a time.

'A lot of people in Bloem have not been exposed to craft beer, or different styles of beer, so our first challenge is to explain what beer can taste like, what beer can be,' explains Phillip. 'The best place to do it is at the market, where we can explain what we are doing and how we are doing it.' The market he refers to is the Volksblad Food and Art Market, held on the last Saturday of every month. It was here that Kaya sold its first pint in August 2013, though the brewery has been around a lot longer than most Bloemfontein beer buffs realise. In fact, the pair applied for their licence way back in 2009, but a series of mishaps and misfortunes meant that the brewery didn't actually pour its first pint for another four years.

It was over a pint that the Kaya concept was born – a pint of the black stuff. Phillip and Marcus would meet each week to drink Guinness at the only place in Bloem where the stout was available on tap. Phillip had recently dabbled in kit beer, while Marcus was making cheese, and the two soon started all-grain brewing together. They quickly decided to turn the hobby into a business and so began the four-year battle with some particularly sticky red tape.

Once they were finally free to pour that first pint, the beers were well received, though Phillip admits that they've had to make some sacrifices to cater to the city's current beer tastes. 'We cannot brew the beers we love for Bloem right now,' he says, referring to his preference for heavily hopped, bitter ales. 'We need to

BEER MENU
★

CASCADE BLONDE
(4.5%)

DARKMOON STOUT
(4.5%)

MYSTIC ALE (4.5%)

CZECK LAGER (4.5%)

tailor things to our crowd...it's all about what our market wants.' Things are changing, though, and quickly. Around half of the customers on market day used to approach the Kaya stand and ask, 'What do you have that tastes most like Black Label?' These days, people actually ask which ales are available, though Phillip admits that they'll never convert everybody.

The brewers themselves describe Kaya's range as 'middle-of-the-road' brews and at the moment the easy-drinking beers are available in select spots. The brewery is not currently open to the public, though Phillip and Marcus hope to open a brewpub in the city in the near future – let's just hope it doesn't take another four years to get the licensing sorted!

COMING SOON...

DE JAGER BROUERIJN
Rooikraal Farm, Roadside; 082 578 3051
This family-run venture is set to be part of a larger development featuring a restaurant, accommodation, conference facilities, bakery, deli, wine boutique, art gallery, curio shop, fuel station and a wild cat sanctuary. Four beers are planned – amber ale, IPA, stout and lager – plus a fifth beer that will rotate each month. An exciting addition to the Free State beer scene!

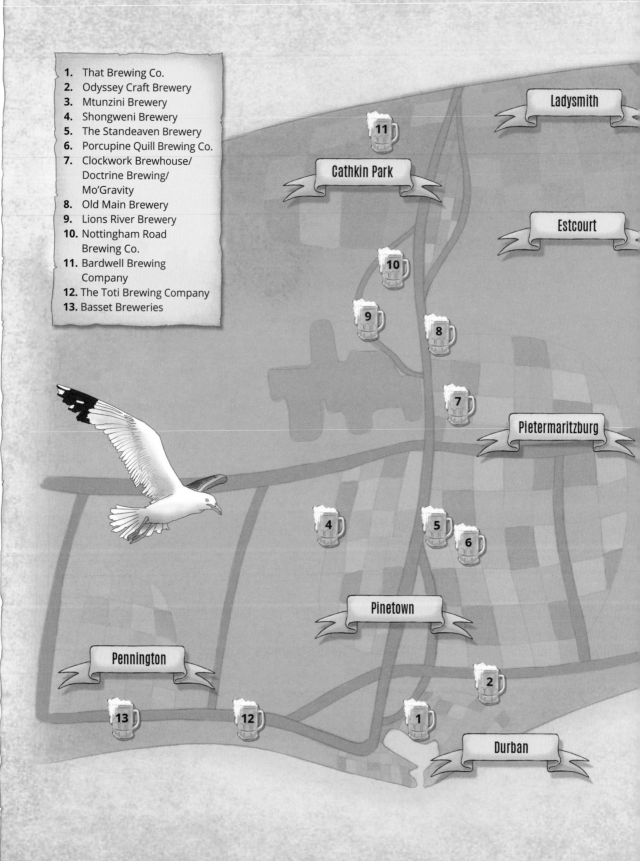

1. That Brewing Co.
2. Odyssey Craft Brewery
3. Mtunzini Brewery
4. Shongweni Brewery
5. The Standeaven Brewery
6. Porcupine Quill Brewing Co.
7. Clockwork Brewhouse/
   Doctrine Brewing/
   Mo'Gravity
8. Old Main Brewery
9. Lions River Brewery
10. Nottingham Road
    Brewing Co.
11. Bardwell Brewing
    Company
12. The Toti Brewing Company
13. Basset Breweries

Ladysmith

Cathkin Park

Estcourt

Pietermaritzburg

Pinetown

Pennington

Durban

KWAZULU-NATAL

KwaZulu-Natal has long had its own brew route, though many of the breweries that flourished in the late nineties and early 2000s have since closed. Luckily, as beer has begun to blossom, KZN has enjoyed something of a renaissance and there are now more beers on offer than ever. There are mini routes to follow in the Valley of a Thousand Hills and along the Midlands Meander. That said, brewpubs are popping up all over the province – this chapter sees you starting in Durban, heading briefly up the Zululand coast before trekking inland through the Valley of a Thousand Hills and the Meander and up into the Drakensberg, before backtracking to Durban and ending on the South Coast.

THAT BREWING CO.

Silvervause Centre, 117 Silverton Rd, Musgrave, Durban; unitybar.co.za; 031 201 3470

★ OPEN MON–SAT 12PM–MIDNIGHT ★

BREWERS
Spotted on
_____
Date
_____
Signature

(L-R) Paul ten Hoorn Boer, Sean Roberts and Mpho Cele are having a blast in their start-up brewery

It reads like every homebrewer's dream, but when restaurateur Sean Roberts approached Paul ten Hoorn Boer at a homebrewing festival and asked him to be the brewer at his start-up brewery, Paul took some serious persuading.

Paul had been brewing for five years when he presented his ales at a Beer and Burger Festival held at Porcupine Quill Brewing Co. (page 228) in 2011. He had started as a 'beer appreciator', tasting whatever he could get his hands on. Soon he was brewing kit beers and while he acknowledges that they're a great starting point for understanding fermentation, he was happy when he completed his first all-grain brew. 'It tasted like beer!' he laughs, recalling the less-than-awesome result from the kits.

Sean, meanwhile, was on a mission to build up Durban's first craft beer bar, Unity. He'd started as a waiter at the adjoining restaurant and seen a string of restaurants fail in the unit that is now home to his very successful pride and joy. Unity opened in 2011 as a brasserie and bar, though Sean felt there was a crucial ingredient missing. 'I don't know why, but I wanted to have my own beer,' he says, remembering how he called various breweries in the Cape, begging them to brew for him. At the time he couldn't understand why someone wouldn't brew him a house beer, or let him rebrand an existing beer of theirs, though he admits that 'if someone asked us the same thing now, I'd say "not a chance!"'

Luckily, someone a little closer to home did say yes and Unity soon had their own in-house brew, Cowbell, brewed at Shongweni Brewery (page 224). When the brewery changed hands, though, production stopped for a while and Sean discovered he had created a monster – or indeed a horde of them. 'We didn't have beer and the customers wanted to fight with me!' Sean tells. 'Brian at Shongweni said there would be nothing for three months, so I needed to make a plan.' He con-

THAT APA

The perfect shade of amber-gold, this pint gives you a hit of fruit salad when you sniff – think un-derripe peaches and apricots, with a twist of fresh citrus squeezed on top. It's a medium-bodied brew, with plenty of hop character that's well-backed up with malty notes. Very drinkable.

tacted the Cape brewers again and set about 'import-ing' various bottled beers from some of the longer-established breweries there. It was the birth of what is now Durban's premier craft beer hangout.

Soon afterwards, Sean and Paul would cross paths, with Sean instantly falling for Paul's would-be-brewer's red ale. 'I tasted everything there and that was the beer that won me over. So I gave him a business card and said something like, "I've got this bar and I want you to brew for me. Come and see me." Six months later he finally walked in here.' Paul laughs at his own scepticism, but is quick to defend himself. 'Who does that? Who comes up to you and says: "I'm going to build you a brewery and pay you money to work in it"? It sounded awesome, but this is the real world.'

Eventually, Paul could see that Sean was serious and he gave up his job lecturing music to take a leap of faith into the brew kettles. In 2012, That Brewing Co. was born. The beers were largely left up to Paul. 'My only brief was that I wanted sessionable beers,' says Sean. 'They have to sell!' First on the brew sheet was the red ale that had spoken to Sean at the Beer and Burger Festival and while he claimed he knew nothing about beer back then, he obviously had a palate for the good stuff, for the red ale is now the brewery's biggest seller.

That Brewing Co.'s beers are approachable and easy-drinking, but still manage to offer variety and plenty of flavour. And with Unity Bar acting as the brewery's tasting room, Paul – along with assistant brewer Mpho Cele – has plenty of opportunity to ex-periment with new and seasonal brews. It might have taken a while for the whole thing to come together, but Sean has no regrets. 'It's definitely the best thing that we've ever done,' he states simply as he goes back for another sip of the ale that built a brewery.

BEER MENU ★

THAT APA (4.8%)

THAT GOOD ADWEISS (4.8%)

THAT BLONDE (4%)

THAT IRISH RED (4.8%)

THAT BREWING CO.
219

ODYSSEY CRAFT
BREWERY

Unit 7 Cypress Park, 19 Cypress Dr, Glen Anil, Durban; odysseycraftbrewery.com

BEER MENU

★

CHOCOLATE COFFEE PORTER (4.7%)

PALE ALE (4.7%)

GOLD ALE (4.7%)

PILSNER (4.7%)

They say watching too much TV is bad for you, but in the case of Ashton Barske, a TV show changed the course of his life. It was 2012 and he had just graduated with an honours degree in accounting when he started watching *Brew Masters* on the Discovery Channel. The documentary series followed the team at US brewery DogFish Head as they thought up more and more inventive ways to brew beer.

'My father had retired and I thought it would be fun to do something together,' says Ashton. 'After watching *Brew Masters* I went to him and said I'd like to try my hand at brewing beer. He told me he used to make pineapple beer at university and I said, "well I never had that experience so let's try brewing together."' Ashton, along with his dad, Raymond, skipped the homebrewer's usual first step – kit beer – instead launching straight into a 60-litre all-grain system that Raymond built.

'I loved it straight away,' recalls Ashton, 'but I wanted to learn more. I couldn't find any formal training available in South Africa, so I just googled "beer universities" to see what came up.' What Ashton found was the World Brewing Academy (WBA), a US-based programme run by the prestigious Siebel Institute of Technology and, as serendipity would have it, when he happened upon their home page, they were advertising a scholarship for one international student. To date, Ashton is the only brewer in South Africa with a diploma from the WBA.

'It all just came together at once,' Ashton explains. 'After just four or five batches of beer, I realised I didn't want to go into the nine-to-five grind that accounting would entail and we decided we wanted to turn the hobby into a profession. Around the same time, I got the scholarship and we found premises for the brewery.' In fact, the

thumbs up from the WBA came on the very day Raymond and Ashton were up before dawn to drive to Clarens to collect a tank for their up-scaled brewery.

The brewery – also built by Raymond – sits on an industrial complex in north Durban, where they are now making beer full-time. The plan is to open a brewpub in the city, with the dream being to have three breweries across the country. 'I love Durban and want to stay here,' says Ashton, 'and I'd also love to open a brewery in Grahamstown. I would love to link up with the WBA and run satellite courses from Rhodes (his alma mater).' And the third location? 'It would be great to open something up in Cape Town, because my dad really wants to move there,' Ashton adds, demonstrating the close relationship this father-son team has.

Ashton Barske pours a taster at Odyssey's on-site bar

BEYOND THE BREWERY:
FIVE PLACES TO FIND CRAFT BEER IN KZN

1. **Unity Bar**
   117 Silverton Rd, Durban; unitybar.co.za; 031 201 3470
   Durban's first craft beer bar has eight local brews on tap and another 30-plus beers from across the country available in bottles. They serve awesome gastropub-type food and it's great for lunch, dinner or late drinks.

2. **Remo's Fratelli**
   Flanders Mall, 14 Flanders Dr, Mount Edgecombe, Durban; remos.co.za; 031 539 5955
   Remo's stocks the Baladin range of beers imported from Italy and there were plans to put a couple of South African brews on tap. There's also a branch in Umhlanga.

3. **The Tap House**
   Davallen Centre, 22 Davallen Rd, La Lucia; thetaphouse.co.za; 031 572 3674
   As well as having Odyssey's beer on tap, there's draught beer from the Cape and a rotating range of bottled brews at this cool little pub.

4. **Franks Speakeasy**
   Accord House, 2 Golf Course Dr, Mount Edgecombe; franksspeakeasy.blogspot.com; 031 502 2221
   There's a great selection of local, national and imported beer and a small menu featuring classic bar food. Look out for beer-themed events.

5. **Pizzology**
   The Edge Lifestyle Centre, 120 Victoria Rd, Pietermaritzburg; pizzology.co.za; 033 345 0024
   This funky artisan pizza joint had just moved to new premises and the liquor licence was still pending, but once in place there should be a dozen beers on tap, featuring a wide range from Clockwork, Doctrine and Mo'Gravity, plus bottles and occasional guest taps from breweries around the country.

MTUNZINI
BREWERY

Fourwinds Farm, Mtunzini; 082 444 7690

★ OPEN BY APPOINTMENT ONLY ★

'I'm the kind of person who likes to do things myself,' declares Ivan Beukes, brewer-owner at Mtunzini Brewery. So when the idea of making beer occurred, he quickly launched himself into the hobby.

'I always liked beer and I starting doing a bit of homework into how to do it myself,' says Ivan. He didn't mess around – after two kit beers ('it was horrible') Ivan leapt straight into a 100-litre all-grain system. Two years down the line, he decided the system – three or four times the batch size of the average homebrew setup – was too small and upgraded to a 200-litre brewhouse. 'It's an odd size,' he admits. 'It's too big for a homebrewer and too small for a commercial brewery.' But he has been brewing on it for the best part of a decade and when asked how he managed to get through all the beer he brewed, Ivan's answer is simple: 'I suddenly found myself with a lot of friends!'

Ivan has also got plenty of fans, and his stand is hotly awaited each year at the Clarens Craft Beer Festival. Hot is the operative word here, since the brew that beer fans are eager to taste each year is Ivan's Chilli Beer. Ivan made his debut at Clarens in 2011, back when the event featured homebrewers as well as commercial breweries. In fact, it was the response at the inaugural festival that started Ivan thinking about taking his Chilli Beer – and the others in his repertoire – to market. Now he's upgrading his system and hoping to one day leave his metallurgist background behind in favour of brewing full-time. Seasonal brews are definitely going to feature and Ivan has been experimenting with other additions, including honeybush, but for beer – and chilli – enthusiasts, there's one thing that Ivan will always be associated with and that's a nice cold, hot blonde.

'I SUDDENLY FOUND MYSELF WITH A LOT OF FRIENDS!'

BEER MENU
★

CHILLI BEER (4%)

RED IRISH (4%)

BLONDE (4%)

GROZNE STOUT (5.5%)

BIG 5 PINT

MTUNZINI CHILLI BEER

'It's not to everyone's taste,' says Ivan of his most talked-about beer, but if you're a fan of chilli (and beer), you'll love it. The base beer is a blonde, with chillies added in the boil – just the right amount, leaving a beer that has quite a kick, but that is still very much in touch with its blonde roots.

SHONGWENI
BREWERY

B13, Kassier Rd, Shongweni Valley; shongwenibrewery.co.za; 083 250 7193

★ OPEN BY APPOINTMENT ONLY ★

Sometimes the brewer goes to the brewery and sometimes the brewery comes to the brewer. In the case of Brian Stewart, the latter was very much the case. Although he had been happily making beer at home for 20 years, he had no plans to turn it into a commercial enterprise. Then a local brewery came up for sale and Brian is now making beer at one of KwaZulu-Natal's longest-running craft breweries.

Shongweni Brewery was founded by British beer enthusiast Stuart Robson in 2006. A microbiologist

BREW TALK...
BOTTLE CONDITIONING
Using a fermentable sugar to carbonate the beer in the bottle. Used with many Belgian beers and in some South African microbreweries. It's a traditional method and a natural way to carbonate.

Johanes Mahlaba checks the gravity of the brew

BEER MENU

★

UPRIGHT IRON MONKEY
[APA] (5.9%)

WEST COAST ALE (5%)

EAST COAST ALE (5%)

HAMMER OF THOR (8.3%)

DURBAN PALE ALE (5.7%)

by trade, Stuart had worked for various European breweries before setting up his own, smaller version not far from Durban. The beer range carries his surname, something that Brian hasn't changed due to the label's loyal following. He also kept the same assistant brewer Johanes Mahlaba, who has been with the brewery since it was born. Brian also had to move the brewery – a mere 2 km down the road, in fact, to its new home on Brian's duck farm.

Today, the brewery has a homely, welcoming feel thanks to Brian's renowned friendliness, Johanes's infectiously cheery demeanour and nice touches like a couch in the corner of the brewery where you can sit and taste the beers.

Since Brian took over, equipment has been upgraded, production has increased by 300 per cent, beer recipes have been tweaked and new brews have been added. The labels, too, received a much-needed overhaul and now feature KZN icons such as the Moses Mabhida Stadium, the beachfront rickshaw drivers and, of course, Durban's most famous foodstuff, Bunny Chow.

With collaboration brews in the pipeline, national awards under his belt and international distribution underway, Brian is ensuring that one of the province's longest-standing breweries is set to keep thriving long into the future.

Brian Stewart toasts another successful brew day with son Donn and assistant brewer Johanes

SHONGWENI BREWERY

225

THE STANDEAVEN
BREWERY

Alverstone; thestandeavenbrewery.co.za; 031 777 4685

If you meet the Standeavens at a festival and spend even a moment longer with them than it takes to order a beer, you'll be struck by the fun this family seems to have together. The brewery sits on the family farm, the beers bear their surname and festivals are a group affair, with the entire family even schlepping the 1 700 km down to the Mother City each November for the Cape Town Festival of Beer. Having said that, the brewery is really the baby of Shaun Standeaven, who works full-time brewing his very popular range of lagers and ales.

It all started on a cruise ship back in 2010. Shaun, who had trained as a chef and studied hospitality management, turned his hand to cocktail-mixing for two years on ships cruising the Caribbe-an, Europe and the United States. Every time Shaun was away from the cocktail shaker, he was sampling beers from whichever port they were docked in and once a love for the amber nectar was born, it didn't take long for Shaun to realise that his foodie leanings were going to end up taking him into a brewery. 'Although I trained as a chef, I realised that being stuck in a kitchen and not being able to get out there and talk to people was not an option for me,' says the affable brewer. 'I love cooking and I love cocktail-making, and brewing seems to almost be a blend of

The Standeaven beers can often be found at festivals around the country

BEER MENU
★

NO. 7 AFRICAN PALE ALE (4%)

NO. 5 PRESS CLUB STOUT (4%)

NO. 11 BEST BLACK GOLD (5%)

NO. 13 LAGER X (5%)

NO. 3 BOHEMIAN PILSNER (4%)

NO. 9 UNCONVENTIONAL WEISS (4%)

the two. It's alchemy, mixing ingredients together, but it's also cooking. I can cook, put it in a bottle and see the looks on people's faces when they drink it.'

Shaun can't emphasise enough how important it is to him to be able to see people drinking his beers and to chat to them, citing the country's vibrant beer fest scene as one of his favourite aspects of the industry. His eyes light up as he talks about 'converting people' and challenging their perceptions of 'what beer should be and what beer can be'.

'It's alchemy,' says Shaun Standeaven when talking about brewing beer

When the Standeavens decided to launch a commercial brewery, Shaun hadn't brewed a beer in his life, but he's certainly made up for lost time. The beer first launched at Durban's Good Food & Wine Show in 2011, and in the run-up, Shaun had to brew three times a day, four days a week in order to stockpile enough beer for the event.

Despite the brewhouse receiving an upgrade soon afterwards, he has still struggled to keep up with demand, brewing at least four times a week, though with the arrival of a 2 000-litre setup from the UK, Shaun should be able to relax a little. Not that he minds the long brew days. He calls the farm, a 30-acre former mushroom farm that now specialises in instant lawn, his little piece of paradise. 'This is my bliss,' he says, and as you witness the views he has when he steps out of the brewery for a brief break, you can see what he means.

PORCUPINE QUILL
BREWING CO.

Old Main Rd, Botha's Hill; craftbrewers.co.za; 031 777 1566

★ OPEN WED–SUN 8.30AM–4PM ★

Thanks to the on-site chef's school, visiting the Porcupine Quill brewery is a foodie delight. There's a cheesery, fresh produce from the student-run delicatessen, a constant supply of baked goodies straight from the oven and, of course, a range of microbrewed beers.

The brewery itself is a simple system that owner John Little imported from the United Kingdom when he started up back in 2010. He didn't follow the usual route of graduating through the homebrewing ranks before opening a commercial brew-

BREWER
Spotted on

Date

Signature

Beer tasters at the taproom are poured by students of the adjoining culinary school

ery, instead launching straight into all-grain brewing on a large-scale system. 'I did a brewing course in Manchester,' says John, 'but more importantly I went and worked with commercial guys who had the exact same system as mine.'

There are now 12 beers to choose from, including the extreme range, Dam Wolf. 'I like to do my own thing with regard to the beers,' says John. His personal favourite is the Karoo Red from the flagship Quills range, though he admits that the 8% Yellow Eyes is great 'if you're looking to get fired up'.

His beers are now in kegs as well as bottles and John hosts regular meetings of the East Coast Brewers (page 232), ensuring that a new generation of brewers will be found at Porcupine Quill, whether it's the homebrewers moving up the ranks, or the latest graduate from his chef school who decides to swap the saucepan for a mash tun.

BEER MENU

★

PORCUPINE QUILL
KAROO RED (5.5%)

PORCUPINE QUILL
KALAHARI GOLD (5.5%)

QUILLS BLONDE ALE (4.5%)

PORCUPINE QUILL BLACK DOG
BITTER (6%)

PORCUPINE QUILL
FLAT TAIL ALE (6%)

AFRICAN MOON IMPALA
LIGHT (5%)

AFRICAN MOON WHITETAIL
PILSNER (5%)

AFRICAN MOON
AMBER ALE (6%)

AFRICAN MOON BLACKBUCK
BITTER (7.5%)

DAM WOLF YELLOW EYES (8%)

DAM WOLF HOWL & CRY (9%)

DAM WOLF WOLF IN SHEEP'S
CLOTHING (9%)

CLOCKWORK
BREWHOUSE

Willowton, Pietermaritzburg; clockworkbrewhouse.co.za

Megan Gemmell is well known in KZN brewing circles, though when people refer to her, they're not singling her out for being the only female commercial brewer in the province. She's not referred to as 'the girl' or 'the chick' or even 'the brewster'. When people talk about Megan, they refer to her as 'The Yeastie'.

Just polishing off her PhD in the microbiology field as Clockwork Brewhouse launched, Megan understands beer in a way that most brewers – and virtually all drinkers – do not. Yeast management or brewing science did not form a part of her formal studies – the doctorate looked at river water used for agricultural purposes – but her scientific background sets her apart from many of her peers when it comes to the fermentation side of things. And while beer didn't directly feature in her university qualifications, it did play a significant part in her time spent at the University of KZN – and not just in the way beer usually stars in the average university student's life...

It was a lengthy trip around Europe that first introduced Megan to beer, and on her return to Pietermaritzburg in 2009 she quickly noted a lack of beer variety in the area. Luckily, salvation was at hand at the university, where she was about to begin her Master's degree in microbiology. Her department was the proud owner of a 30-litre brewery donated by SAB for the nationwide Intervarsity Beer Brewing Challenge (page 48), and she wasted no time in figuring out how to use it.

BREWER
spotted on

Date

Signature

Megan Gemmell is a self-confessed control freak – not a bad thing for a brewer to be

SCHWARZBIER

Clockwork Brewhouse is one of the only breweries in the country brewing a Schwarzbier. This dark German-style lager is deep brown in colour, with roasted malt on the nose and just a hint of coffee. It's a malt-forward beer, with a touch of dark chocolate and a dry, bitter yet pleasing finish.

BREW TALK... BREWSTER
The name traditionally given to a female brewer.

'I could go and brew any time I wanted to,' she beams, recalling her surprise at how her fellow students weren't interested in producing their own beer. 'I think people tried it once, but didn't realise how long a brew day actually is, so I often had the equipment to myself. It really was fantastic!' Megan learnt by trial and error and in 2012 she was a part of the team representing UKZN at the intervarsity competition. She helped the team take first place in the lager category with her schwarzbier (a dark German lager).

Gradually, other students started to show interest and Megan realised she needed to get her own brewery up and running at home. 'It was a pretty labour-intensive system,' she says of the homebrew setup that she still brews test batches on today, but quickly admits that's just the way she likes it. 'I like to be able to control what's going on.' This desire for everything to be done just right is, in part, the inspiration for the brewery name. 'I've always been fascinated with clocks. My grandfather used to build clocks, my father has clocks in every room of the house. But of course it also speaks of my approach to brewing – the meticulous need to be organised, to have everything in its place.'

In 2013, Megan decided to take the plunge and invest in a larger brewery along with brewing buddies Dion van Huyssteen (Doctrine Brewing) and Travis Boast (Mo'Gravity). 'It was a big decision on my part,' she says. 'I was just a student and I basically had zero capital to put in.' She launched her brand, along with those of her fellow Pietermaritzburg brewers, at the 2014 SA on Tap Craft Beer Festival in Durban, and while the event was exhausting, you can tell Megan loved every moment. Does she plan to become a full-time brewster one day? Megan's not so sure she could easily leave microbiology behind having invested so many years of study into it... 'But if I could build a little lab in the brewery to look at the yeast side of things, then maybe I would,' adds the renowned yeastie with a glint in her eye.

BEER MENU

★

SCHWARZBIER (5.2%)

OCTOBERFEST (5.2%)

ENGLISH BITTER (4.5%)

THE PITTER [PORTER-BITTER HYBRID] (5.2%)

DOCTRINE
BREWING

Willowton, Pietermaritzburg; doctrinebrewing.co.za

'I hated beer,' announces Dion van Huyssteen, though the emphasis here is definitely on the past tense. He recalls the university years, when he would opt for a brandy and coke or a cider over a beer, but he later realised that it was just light lagers that he didn't care for.

In fact, it was a local and long-standing craft beer that gave Dion a thirst for ale – Pickled Pig Porter from the Nottingham Road Brewing Co. (page 240). A tour of the newly opened Shongweni Brewery (page 224) was next, followed by a teambuilding day at the 1000 Hills Chef School – also the site of the Porcupine Quill Brewing Co. (page 228). Drinking other people's beers wasn't enough, though, and Dion soon started dabbling in kit beers.

It wasn't his first brush with beer-making – as a child he'd helped his father to brew and fondly

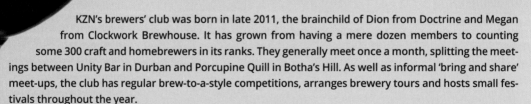

EAST COAST BREWERS
www.eastcoastbrewers.za.org

KZN's brewers' club was born in late 2011, the brainchild of Dion from Doctrine and Megan from Clockwork Brewhouse. It has grown from having a mere dozen members to counting some 300 craft and homebrewers in its ranks. They generally meet once a month, splitting the meetings between Unity Bar in Durban and Porcupine Quill in Botha's Hill. As well as informal 'bring and share' meet-ups, the club has regular brew-to-a-style competitions, arranges brewery tours and hosts small festivals throughout the year.

meetings that gave him the final shove towards becoming a craft brewer.

Today, Dion brews at the 'Willowton Tea Factory' (WTF) with Travis (Mo'Gravity, page 234) and Megan Gemmell of Clockwork Brewhouse (page 230). The three take turns to brew on their, let's say, unusual brewery, which has been put together on a budget, but is churning out some crowd-pleasing brews.

Dion doesn't tend to brew to BJCP guidelines, though he admits, 'I'm kind of religious about my beer' – which explains how he came by the name Doctrine. 'This is how I feel beer must be,' says Dion, the one-time hater of beer who has indeed been born again.

remembers the batches that he got to sample, those where fermentation had failed so he got to swig the sweet and alcohol-free malt juice. But when he rekindled the hobby as an adult, Dion really embraced it. 'I read obsessively,' he says, recalling how he devoured John Palmer's *How to Brew* before cracking open the tin for his first kit beer. And it wasn't just reading up on brewing techniques that Dion was obsessed with – he has to be the only homebrewer around who watched weather reports religiously before brewing his first kit beer. 'I realised that February was not the best time for fermenting, so I delayed the first brew for a couple of months,' Dion tells. 'I kept an eye on the weather forecasts and waited for a cold front, so I knew we'd have a week of cooler weather to ferment the beer in!'

He continued to 'literally brew by the weather' until he chose to go pro towards the end of 2012 – a decision that involved investing in equipment that would assist with temperature control during the fermentation process. Although he had been toying around with the idea for a while, it was success at that year's National Homebrew Championships that provided the confidence he needed and meeting fellow brewer Travis Boast at the East Coast Brewers

Dion van Huyssteen is known for his extreme and outlandish beers

MO'GRAVITY

Willowton, Pietermaritzburg; mogravity.co.za

★ OPEN BY APPOINTMENT ONLY ★

Some people's hobby is collecting stamps, some collect beer coasters, others collect beers themselves. Travis Boast, the brewer behind the Mo'Gravity brand, is a self-confessed collector of hobbies. After building an electric guitar, hand-crafting a knife (which pretty much turned out to be a prison shank), cultivating chillies, dabbling in landscape photography and trying his hand at poker, Travis was introduced to the world of homebrewing by a beer-loving friend. Two kit beers later and he was hooked, venturing into all-grain brewing with his signature style.

'I'm not a traditionalist in anything I do,' he explains, going on to describe his maverick approach to brewing and the fact that, until he decided to turn his hobby into a profession, he had never brewed the same beer twice. He doesn't always follow a recipe and sometimes 'brews by nose', chucking in an extra handful of hops if the boil doesn't smell quite right. But, of course, since he made the leap from homebrewer to professional, Travis has had to make a few concessions and has come up with a couple of beers that he'll repeat for his hop-hungry fans.

It's an interesting juxtaposition since Travis shares a brewery with Megan Gemmell of Clockwork Brewhouse (page 230), as well as Dion van Huyssteen from Doctrine Brewing (page 232). Travis's devil-may-care style couldn't be more contrary to Megan's approach to brewing – as methodical as her brand's name would suggest. But the team works well together, assisting each other with brews on their slightly unorthodox system, which 'really makes you feel like you've brewed beer', Travis laughs, referring to the hands-on nature of their brewhouse.

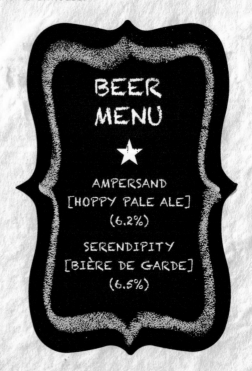

BEER MENU
★
AMPERSAND
[HOPPY PALE ALE]
(6.2%)

SERENDIPITY
[BIÈRE DE GARDE]
(6.5%)

The collaborative brewery idea was Travis's and he says he hounded the others, who he'd met at local brew club meetings, until they agreed to come on board. The result is a small brewery in the Willowton industrial area, northeast of Pietermaritzburg. Despite differences in brewing philosophy, it's clear that the trio have a lot of fun together. They rib each other and finish each other's sentences as they introduce their brewery (they call it the Willowton Tea Factory, of WTF for short) and display a penchant for bad puns (the walk-in fridge is called Chris, as in Christopher Walken...).

Travis, like so many of the brewers in South Africa, has a background in IT and he'd actually begun researching a potential IT start-up when he got embroiled in the world of beer. He used his business model for the brewery instead and Mo'Gravity – a name that refers to the fact that his beers are not going to be light in alcohol – launched in June 2014.

The beers are difficult to put into style parameters, but for those interested in something different, something experimental, those who like the idea of breaking the rules and throwing the BJCP style guidelines out of the window, then Travis almost certainly has something for you. He'll keep two flagship beers on the menu, but otherwise there'll always be something new brewing, and considering how all-absorbing beer seems to be, I get the feeling that Travis might just have collected his last hobby.

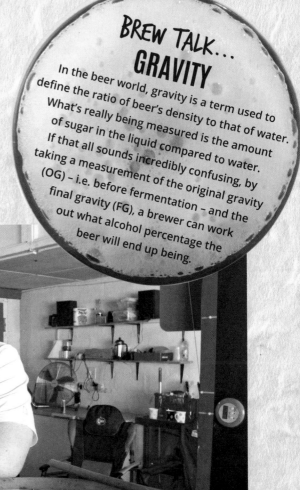

BREW TALK... GRAVITY

In the beer world, gravity is a term used to define the ratio of beer's density to that of water. What's really being measured is the amount of sugar in the liquid compared to water. If that all sounds incredibly confusing, by taking a measurement of the original gravity (OG) – i.e. before fermentation – and the final gravity (FG), a brewer can work out what alcohol percentage the beer will end up being.

Travis Boast admits that he has an unorthodox brewing style, sometimes doing away with a recipe and brewing 'by nose'

OLD MAIN
BREWERY

Dennis Shepstone Dr, Hilton; rdmitchells.co.za; 033 343 3267

★ OPEN MON-SAT 11AM-MIDNIGHT, SUN 11AM-4PM ★

Tasters of Old Main's beers can be sipped alongside the brewhouse

Old Main has been operating in its current guise since 2012, though the kettles were churning out pints of Foxx Lager as far back as 2006, when the brewhouse was set up in the Firkin Brewery in Durban. Owner Robbie Mitchells admits that the rooftop of a mall wasn't the best spot for a brewpub. 'People didn't seem to respect a brewery within a mall,' he says. So eventually Robbie moved the brewery to pretty Hilton, sitting in the Valley of a Thousand Hills, 90 km north-west of Durban.

Old Main's beers are of the easy-drinking nature – even the stout, which is imperial only in name – with recipes devised by Paul Sims, a former SAB brewer who has been pulled out of retirement to serve in the craft beer revolution. Paul generally supervises every brew, but his assistant brewer confidently takes the reins when required. Sandile Magwaza is relatively new to the craft beer scene, but he has a history with a different type of beer. 'I love brewing,' says Sandile. 'I grew up with my granny and

BEER MENU

★

FOXX LAGER (3.5%)

HONEY BADGER IMPERIAL
STOUT (3.5%)

1806 REAL ALE (3.5%)

OYSTER CATCHER IPA (3.5%)

Assistant brewer Sandile Magwaza takes great pleasure in seeing people enjoy his beers

'I told Paul that I wanted to work with him and he said I could come in and see what it was all about,' says Sandile. Six months later, Sandile was still there, giving up his days twice a week to volunteer at Old Main and learn the ins and outs of brewing. Today, his pride in his product is evident and he admits that his favourite thing about the job is seeing people enjoying his beer, whether it's in Old Main's restaurant and pub, or at one of South Africa's beer festivals, which the team started attending in 2014.

Since the brewery launched in 2012, production has almost tripled and the team are adding new fermenters to try to keep up with demand. They're finally going to be bottling their beer and with a few taps already scattered around KZN and Johannesburg, the brewery is beginning to make its mark on the South African beer scene.

she would brew *umqombothi* at home.' Although the traditionally brewed sorghum beer doesn't have a great deal in common with its clearer counterpart, the interest in fermentation was sparked and when Sandile met Paul and found out what he did for a living, he made it his mission to become a brewer.

Honey **Badger**
IMPERIAL STOUT
Small Batch Beer
FINEST NATURAL INGREDIENTS
PRESERVATIVE FREE

BEER
MENU

★

BOHEMIAN PILSNER
(4.5%)

NICE WEISS (5.5%)

VANILLA PORTER
(5.8%)

GERMAN FEST BEER
(4%)

LIONS RIVER
BREWERY

Riverside Farm, off the R103, Lions River; lionsriverbrewery.co.za; 083 775 8549

★ OPEN SAT–SUN 11AM–4PM ★

'You can't be a smart arse when it comes to brewing,' says Ronald McClelland, owner of Lions River Brewery. 'You never know everything. You're always learning.' He should know, for Ronald got a fair amount of practice in before deciding to go pro with his brewing. After a noteworthy start in homebrewing (his first ever brew was completed in the car park of a Joburg craft beer pub), he brewed every Friday for around two and a half years, racking up an impressive 100 brews on his 50-litre system.

'I was meticulous about recording everything that I did and would practise recipes over and over until they were perfected,' Ronald says. The result is a range of four well-polished beers that Ronald now produces on his 500-litre setup imported from Germany.

Attention to detail is a big deal for Ronald. 'I should have been a German,' he jokes, referring to his desire to have everything done just the right way. Glasses must be appropriate for the beer style, beers cannot be rushed (his take a minimum of 10 weeks) and he's even hired a horticulturalist to give just the right look to the beer garden that will accompany the brewery at his off-the-beaten-track smallholding on the Midlands Meander.

Lions River is about as remote as a brewpub can be, tucked away at the end of a dirt track leading off a network of gravel roads. So once people arrive, they're likely to want to stick around a while to see the setup, nibble on platters of meat and cheese sourced from the Meander, and sip the painstakingly practised beers that Ronald is pouring – in all the right glassware, of course.

The Lions River system was imported from Germany

NOTTINGHAM ROAD
BREWING CO.

R103, Nottingham Road; www.nottsbrewery.co.za; 033 266 6728

★ OPEN DAILY 8AM-4.30PM ★

BREWER
Spotted on
_____
Date
_____
Signature

Thokozani Sithole has been manning the Notties brew kettles since 2007

Some of South Africa's breweries have restaurants, some have pubs, but there are precious few where you can eat, drink and sleep without ever leaving the grounds. Nottingham Road Brewery is one of those few and it is very precious indeed. Founded in 1996, the brewery sits in the grounds of the Rawdons Hotel, along the popular Midlands Meander tourism route. The often misty weather marries perfectly with the British-style beers served in the quaint and cosy pub.

'It seemed like a place that needed to have draught beer,' says Peter Dean, son-in-law of the hotel's owner. From Australia, Peter moved to Nottingham Road in 1993 and, having seen the rise of microbrewed beer in his homeland, he suggested installing a brewery in the hotel. It started modestly, with a 30-litre home-brew setup in the basement. With Trevor Morgan, a retired SAB brewer as a mentor, Peter learnt to brew on a spectacularly small scale, grinding malt in a coffee roaster when he graduated from extract to all-grain. Once a test batch hit the taps of the hotel's bar, it was obvious that the brewery would take off and in 1996, with Trevor at the helm, one of South Africa's earliest and longest-standing microbreweries was born.

Brewer Thokozani Sithole has been at the kettles since 2007 after starting his booze-production career

BREWERS OF FINE ALE

BEER MENU

★

WHISTLING WEASEL
PALE ALE (4.5%)

PICKLED PIG PORTER (3.9%)

PYE-EYED POSSUM
PILSNER (4.6%)

TIDDLY TOAD LIGHT
LAGER (3%)

making wine and spirits. His wide grin is just as much a feature of the brewery as the omnipresent pictures of pigs – Notties' well-known logo. The 'Beware the Pig' motto harps back to the days of the pet pig with a penchant for pilfering food from diners' plates.

Nottingham Road was the first microbrewery in South Africa to put their beers into cans

Also immortalised on one of Notties' beer labels, the pig is now featured on cans as well as bottles, coasters and T-shirts. In 2013, Nottingham Road became the first South African microbrewery to start canning their beer, though the unfiltered, unpasteurised brew still has a recommended shelf life of just six to eight weeks.

Although Notties is pretty traditional, both in the feel of the on-site pub and the beer styles produced, they have started to experiment and in 2014 they released a new beer for the first time in decades. Look out for the Tipsy Tiger English IPA and other seasonal brews alongside the long-standing alliterative foursome, whose names were apparently thought up after a few too many tasters.

BARDWELL
BREWING COMPANY

R600, Champagne Valley; bardwellbrewery.com; 036 469 1393

★ OPEN BY APPOINTMENT ONLY ★

The brewer behind the Drakensberg's first micro-brewery has grand plans, but then when you have a name as magnificent as this brewer's, perhaps you naturally have plans to match. Bardwell Henry Patrick Hall has been brewing for five years and is determined that his beer will stand out from the ever-expanding crowd. 'I want it to be authentic,' he says. 'Truly authentic, so eventually I want to use my own hops, my own barley – everything grown right here.' A spring on the premises means that the brewing liquor is covered, but the other ingredients might be a little tougher to produce.

Bardy, as the genial brewer is known, has a background that will certainly help on his quest to become the owner of South Africa's first 'estate brewery' (one where all the ingredients are grown or sourced on-site). As well as working as an electrical engineer, he has been at the helm of a sugar cane farm, and indeed has already planted sugar cane in the unlikely location of the Drakensberg Mountains – something he hopes to use when bottle conditioning his beers. His hop and barley seeds were germinating when we met, though the climate conditions on the approach road to Cathedral Peak are not exactly ideal for either, so it's certainly not going to be an easy feat.

But Bardy certainly seems like he'll relish the challenge. In the meantime, he's playing around with recipes, experimenting with ingredients and no doubt wondering how he can harvest natural yeast to produce a truly authentic local brew.

BEER MENU
★

BERGUMBER (6%)

RUSTY GUN BITTER ALE (7.5%)

EBENIUS AURO ALE (6%)

THE TOTI
BREWING COMPANY

Unit 6, 11 Palmgate Cres, Southgate Industrial Park, Amanzimtoti; www.totibrewing.co.za; 061 000 0535

Toti's brewery sits in a somewhat unassuming position on an industrial estate just outside Amanzimtoti. But as your mother might have taught you, it's not what's on the outside, but what is within that counts. And once you step inside the brewery, you're instantly struck by its unique brewhouse.

Toti launched with an impressive range offering something for every type of beer lover

Sitting on a five-metre-high custom-built frame, this is probably South Africa's first gravity-fed craft brewery. If you've ever homebrewed on one of those three-tier systems fashioned from kegs, well this is that, but on a far grander scale. The best part of it is the irony of what brewer Jason Nel does for a day job. 'I work with industrial pumps,' he says sheepishly, casting a sideways glance at one of the only pump-free breweries in the country.

But Jason isn't the only brewer and Peter Hamilton Hoskins, the other half of the team, has a rather different outlook when it comes to building. 'I deal with pumps, Peter builds mobile phone masts,' explains Jason, 'so I guess in the end he won!' But it's turned out to be a boon to this start-up brewery, since avoiding pumps keeps things economical, cutting down on the electricity it takes to complete a brew.

Jason started brewing back in 2006. 'I decided I wanted to learn something,' he explains, 'and I thought to myself, "if I could make something for

Jason Nel started brewing in a rather unusual fashion, with makeshift equipment and improvised ingredients

myself, what would it be?'" The answer was simple, though the road to producing that first pint was not. Jason doesn't seem to realise what a bizarre and challenging path he took on the way to brewing his first beer. After googling 'how to make beer', he discovered that ingredients and equipment were thin on the ground. 'I couldn't find malt anywhere, so I ended up going to a pet shop and buying pigeon feed barley, malting it at home and roasting it in the oven,' he recalls, shaking his head. He then went on to realise that he was also missing a mill and crushed that first batch of pigeon feed malt with a fire extinguisher and a lot of elbow grease.

He changes the subject when asked how that first beer tasted, but Jason persevered, admitting that brewing quickly became an obsession. He and Peter met in 2013 'over a canister of CO_2' (something else that was in short supply and great demand with local homebrewers) and the pair decided to try and turn their hobby into a profession. The result is this quirky brewery that puts out a range of beers, including the wonderfully named 'hopstrosity', an American IPA. 'I love hops,' says Jason, simply, explaining the profile of a few of the Toti beers.

The beers will be available at liquor stores in the area and also on tap at the brewery's small bar, where you can gaze up at what must be South Africa's tallest microbrewery and contemplate the good: it's an incredibly efficient system that Jason likens to 'driving a train' – with the bad: hoisting 50 kg of malt to the top is a mission to say the least. And while Jason admits that the system works wonderfully, he speaks with regret that the lack of handrails make it tricky to do the one thing brewers like to do while they work – enjoy a glass of their own, chilled hoppy ale.

BEER MENU

★

TOTI BLACK (5.5%)

HOPSTROSITY IPA (6.8%)

HAMILTON HAMMER
AMBER ALE (5.8%)

TOTI GOLD PALE ALE (5.5%)

PULPIT PILSNER (5.5%)

WINKLE WEISS (5.1%)

THE TOTI BREWING COMPANY

BASSET
BREWERIES

R102 South Coast Rd, Pennington; 083 778 8988

★ OPEN DAILY 7.30AM–6PM ★

> 'MY GIRLFRIEND NATALIE – BEST GIRLFRIEND IN THE ENTIRE WORLD – SOLD HER SPORTS CAR TO SPONSOR THE BREWERY ...'

The darling little brewhouse was bought from a local farmer

Like a number of South African craft brewers, Andy Turner's love for beer blossomed while he was living overseas. But despite falling in love with European ales during a five-year stint in the UK, he hardly gave the foreign brews a second thought once he returned to South Africa. It took a second – and much shorter – trip to Europe to convince him that he was missing out at home. 'I went to Ireland for a friend's wedding and I fell in love with the Irish styles all over again,' Andy recollects. This time, he was smitten and he soon set about attempting to clone his favourite beer, Smithwick's Red Ale.

He certainly had the right equipment – and a particularly supportive partner. 'A local farmer had had a brewery commissioned and decided it was too much work, so he wanted to sell it,' Andy continues. 'My girlfriend Natalie – best girlfriend in the entire world – sold her sports car to sponsor the brewery and I was soon brewing on a 120-litre system.' Quite a capacity for a homebrewer just getting started. Over two weeks he dismantled the brewery and transported it in pieces, making repeat trips in his bakkie and reassembling it at his Pennington home. Three and a half years later, Andy finally admitted that the system was a little too large for homebrew-

KWAZULU-NATAL

246

ing and decided, since he had the equipment, he might as well look into setting up the South Coast's first craft brewery. By September 2013, the brewery was up and running in its new home alongside the Lynton Hall driving range.

It's a charming-looking brewery and the only one in the country that sits in a log cabin. 'The land is zoned as agricultural, so you can't build a permanent structure,' Andy explains. 'It also had to blend into the forest.' The end result is easily one of the prettiest brewery buildings in the country and the attached golf club makes it a great spot for families or groups of friends.

The brewery is named for Andy's beloved Basset hound and two of the beers take their monikers from the area. The third, though, is a particularly special brew. The beer that inspired Andy's love affair with ale is named for the woman that made the dream possible and every time Andy raises a glass of his Befreckled Red, he toasts the three loves of his life – beer, dogs and the best girlfriend in the world.

Andy Turner is in charge of the first brewery on KZN's South Coast

BEER MENU

★

UMDONI GOLD
(3.5%)

BEFRECKLED RED
(3.5%)

PENNINGTON PRIDE
[SMOKED PORTER]
(4.5%)

COMING SOON...

KASI BREWERY
Durban; kasibrewery.co.za
Mfundo Thango is behind this brewery, whose beers – primarily a lager – are aiming to target some of Durban's townships.

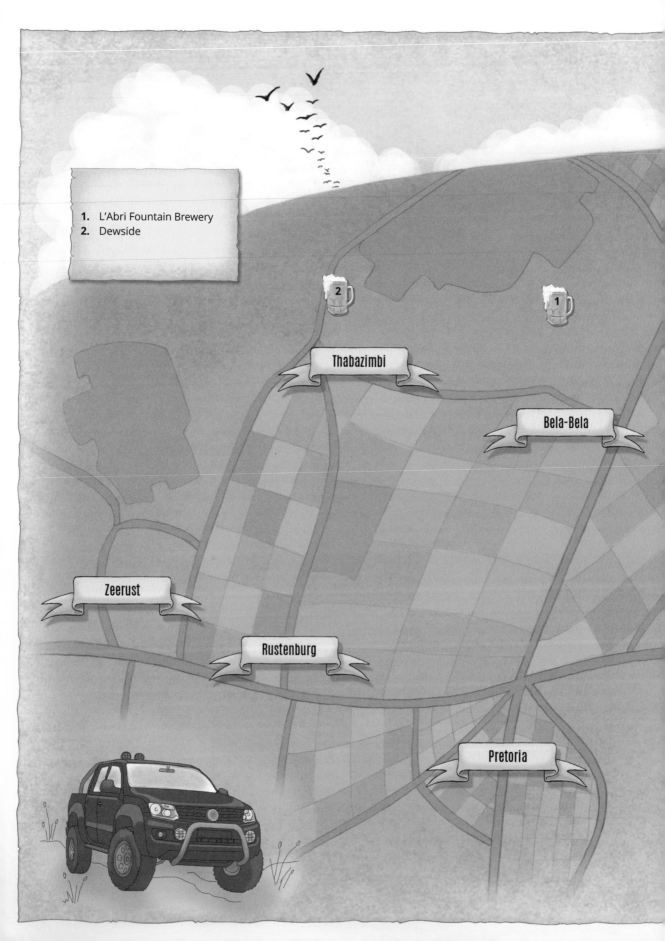

1. L'Abri Fountain Brewery
2. Dewside

2

1

Thabazimbi

Bela-Bela

Zeerust

Rustenburg

Pretoria

Mokopane

Groblersdal

LIMPOPO

Limpopo's first microbrewery actually opened its taps back in 2008, but it flew way under the radar until the craft beer movement in South Africa really started to gain momentum. The country's northernmost province is a great place to combine your beer tasting with a little game viewing as both of the up-and-running breweries are an easy hop from game farms or national parks. These breweries are in the southwest of the province and are a fairly short drive from Johannesburg or Pretoria. It makes a great weekend away, or you could tack on some of the breweries in the North West (pages 180–199) if you want to make a longer trip of it.

L'ABRI FOUNTAIN
BREWERY

Off the R516, 37 km west of Bela-Bela; www.labrifountainbrewery.co.za; 082 605 1492

★ OPEN TUE–SAT 8AM–6PM, SUN 8AM–1PM ★

'I sound like a guy who's complaining that he has too many girlfriends,' Andries Saunders laughs as he explains the problem he has with his tiny brewery. 'We keep running out of beer, we've got festival organisers pestering us to attend and we've never even advertised our brewery anywhere! In the past couple of years it's exploded and we just can't keep up.'

L'Abri Fountain is one of South Africa's smallest breweries. Andries brews just 45 litres at a time on

Andries Saunders is surprised at the success of his off-the-beaten-track nanobrewery

his family farm in the Waterberg. It's as pretty a setting as you could hope for, the rustic brewpub sitting far from anywhere on a gravel road surrounded by bushveld scenery, roaming game and abundant birdlife. The farm offers a host of outdoor activities such as horse riding, fishing and mountain biking and there's a range of self-catering accommodation available. Andries admits that this remote spot, which stands absolutely no chance of capturing any drive-by traffic, is an odd place to set up a brewpub, but then that wasn't really the plan.

The whole thing happened after a chance encounter at a neighbour's braai, where Andries met André de Beer, a well-known face on the South African beer scene. 'I turned up at this braai with my six-pack of Castle Lite and André invited me to try his homebrew,' he recalls fondly. 'I took one sip, turned to him and said, "you didn't brew this!"' Once Andries realised that André, now the owner of The Cockpit Brewhouse (page 166), did indeed brew the excellent English bitter in question, he threw himself into the hobby of homebrewing. 'I was the fastest convert he's ever had,' says Andries of a man who has inspired many people to brew their own beer. 'I went to brew with André one Saturday, during the

L'Abri Fountain is tucked away on a dirt road far from anything

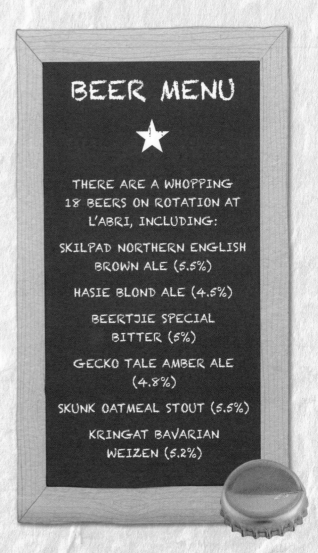

BEER MENU

★

THERE ARE A WHOPPING 18 BEERS ON ROTATION AT L'ABRI, INCLUDING:

SKILPAD NORTHERN ENGLISH BROWN ALE (5.5%)

HASIE BLOND ALE (4.5%)

BEERTJIE SPECIAL BITTER (5%)

GECKO TALE AMBER ALE (4.8%)

SKUNK OATMEAL STOUT (5.5%)

KRINGAT BAVARIAN WEIZEN (5.2%)

week I bought all the equipment and I brewed my first batch the following weekend.'

L'Abri Fountain opened to the public two years later, in 2008, and since then Andries, a proponent of brewing to BJCP guidelines (see box), has worked on recipes and narrowed down the beer menu to 18 lagers and ales. The quality of the beer is astonishing, especially when you see the fairly rudimentary setup. At the time of writing, Andries was in the process of upgrading his brewhouse in order to up the capacity. He wants to be able to keep up with demand, but Andries isn't interested in taking it too large. 'If you brew 1 000 litres at a time, you have to wait to finish it before you can try something new!' he says.

Andries now has a staple range and at any one time you'll find six brews on tap at the farm pub – the only place L'Abri's beers are available. A regular on the brew sheet is the Beertjie Special Bitter, a tribute to André de Beer that is based on the ale that inspired Andries to open a brewery after a single sip.

BJCP

The Beer Judge Certification Program (BJCP) is an American organisation that publishes guidelines on over 100 styles of beer, mead and cider. The guidelines include information on what a particular style should look like, smell like and taste like, and are a huge help to brewers wanting to improve their techniques and refine their beers. As the name suggests, the BJCP also runs exams for those wishing to become a certified beer judge. As well as an online, multiple-choice theory exam, there is a tasting exam to pass before you can become certified. If you're interested in taking the exam and judging in local and national competitions in South Africa, contact your local homebrewing club to find out about study groups and future exam dates. In the Western Cape, get in touch with the SouthYeasters (page 85), in Gauteng, contact the Wort Hogs (page 157) and in KZN, check out the East Coast Brewers (page 232). For style guidelines and study materials, go to www.bjcp.org

DEWSIDE

17 2nd Ave, Thabazimbi; dewside.co.za; 014 777 1434

Dewside is quickly gaining a local following in Thabazimbi

Much like L'Abri Fountain, Dewside's brew kettles are older than the average South African beer enthusiast would imagine. The brewery relaunched in February 2013, but, in fact, wort has been bubbling here for a few years.

The brewery is an attractive setup: a wood-panelled 200-litre system, laid out to make it easy for visitors to watch what's going on when the brewer is at work. The brewer in question is Rudolf Vorster, who runs things in the Dewside brewhouse while his wife Tanya takes care of the adjoining restaurant. It was Tanya's father, Pieter Coetzee, who actually started brewing back in 2010, but the concept was a little ahead of its time and never quite took off. The audience is perhaps a tough one: Dewside sits in Thabazimbi, an iron-mining town 200 km north of Pretoria, an area that hasn't had much – or really any – exposure to ales.

But since reopening as a stylish brewpub, Tanya and Rudolf have made great strides, developing new recipes and offering food and beer pairing on the menu. Tanya had fond memories of her Thabazimbi upbringing, and the couple made a decision to leave their corporate Johannesburg jobs and raise their children in the quiet, provincial town. They wondered how receptive the local market would be to a trio of ales in what is very much a lager-drinking corner of the country, but it turns out they didn't

need to lose any sleep over it. 'One of the things we really want to do is to help promote tourism in the town,' says Tanya, 'but at the moment we can't even keep up with the local market – they've been incredibly supportive and are loving the beer.'

The Vorsters really jumped in at the deep end when they decided to take over the brewery and restaurant, having never worked in the food and beverage industry before. The couple admits that the learning curve was steep and hellish, but the slow-paced lifestyle in Thabazimbi seems to have influenced their business style. 'We're taking it slow and we're trying to do it right,' says Tanya. 'We need to enjoy what we're doing... and not work too hard – we already did that when we lived and worked in the city.'

There are plans to add further beers to the menu, but that, like other aspects of the business, will come in time. Meanwhile, Rudolf, whose varsity background was in engineering and scientific fields, is studying for the Institute of Brewing and Distilling (IBD) diploma and experimenting with cider-making – a beverage that is likely to go down a treat in this hot and dusty bushveld town.

Rudolf Vorster spends some time cleaning the equipment between brew days

BEER MENU

★

TALKING DOG AMERICAN AMBER ALE (5.5%)

CRAZY DOG APA (4.5%)

SPOTTED DOG DARK ALE (6%)

'We need to enjoy what we're doing...and not work too hard,' says Tanya Vorster

DIRECTORY

MAIN FESTIVALS

January/February
Clarens Craft Beer Festival
March/April
SA on Tap (Johannesburg)
SouthYeasters Summer
Festival (Cape Town)
Wort Hogs Summer
Festival (Gauteng)
May/June
Jozi Craft Beer Fest
(Johannesburg)
Capital Craft (Pretoria)
Solstice Festival
(Broederstroom)
July/August
Hop 'n' Vine (Cape Town)
SA on Tap (Durban)
September/October
Bierfest (Cape Town,
Durban, Johannesburg)
November/December
Cape Town Festival
of Beer (Cape Town)

HOMEBREWING CLUBS

SouthYeasters
Homebrew Club
(Western Cape)
southyeasters.co.za

Wort Hog Brewers
(Gauteng and North West)
worthogbrewers.co.za
East Coast Brewers
(KwaZulu-Natal)
eastcoastbrewers.za.org
Port Elizabeth
Homebrewers
Association
(Eastern Cape)
facebook.com/PEHBA

HOMEBREW SUPPLY STORES

Western Cape
BeerLab
Ndabeni, Cape Town
beerlab.co.za
BeerGuevara
Woodstock, Cape Town
beerguevara.com
The Bootlegger
Garden Route
thebootlegger.co.za

Gauteng
Beer Kitchen
Paulshof, Johannesburg
beerkitchen.co.za

Brewcraft
Jet Park, Boksburg
brewcraft.co.za
Brewmart
Brooklyn, Pretoria
brewmart.co.za
National Food Products
Emmarentia, Johannesburg
thehomebrewshop.co.za
The Beer Keg
Kya Sands, Johannesburg
thebeerkeg.co.za
Toppie's Brewing Company
Mayberry Park, Alberton
tbco.co.za
Tradeger Brewing Concepts
Walkerville
tradeger.co.za

KwaZulu-Natal
Beer Bros
Hillcrest, Durban
beerbros.co.za

Eastern Cape
Brew and Braai
Port Elizabeth
brewandbraaipe.com

BREWING COURSES AND TRAINING

Western Cape
BeerLab
beerlab.co.za
BeerGuevara
beerguevara.com

Gauteng
Brewster's Craft
brewsterscraft.co.za
Global Beverage Solutions
gbsinfo.com
The Beer Keg
thebeerkeg.co.za

KwaZulu-Natal
Beer Bros
beerbros.co.za

ONLINE CRAFT BEER STORES

League of Beers
leagueofbeers.com
Bottle Shop
bottleshop.co.za
Gourmandium
gourmandium.com
The Liquor Shop
theliquorshop.co.za

THE SAFARI CONTINUES...

While South Africa is very much the hub of the African beer scene, mash tuns are stirring elsewhere on the continent. If you're venturing north, keep an eye out for these trailblazing breweries:

ETHIOPIA
Garden Bräu, Addis Ababa
beergardeninn.com
Based in the grounds of
a guesthouse, the duo of
beers here have a German
influence.

KENYA
Big Five Breweries, Nairobi
thebigfivebreweries.com
Kenya's first microbrewery
launched in 2009. It produces five permanent beers plus
a range of seasonal ales.
Sierra Premium Beer,
Nairobi
sierrapremium.com
There's a stout, a blonde
and a Vienna lager on offer
at the brasserie, which also
serves excellent steaks.

MAURITIUS
Flying Dodo Brewery,
Bagatelle
flyingdodo.com
You'll find a couple of permanent brews on tap, but
the brewers at this large
brewpub are constantly
experimenting, meaning
there'll always be some-
thing new to taste. The
glass mash tun/kettle is
particularly cool.

ZIMBABWE
Bespoke Brewers, Harare
bespokebrewers.com
Taste the six-pack of brews
at the Harare Beer Engine,
a long-running pub.

INDEX

Page numbers in **bold** indicate main entries.